Legacies of State Violence and Transitional Justice in Latin America

Legacies of State Violence and Transitional Justice in Latin America

A Janus-Faced Paradigm?

Edited by Nina Schneider
and Marcia Esparza

LEXINGTON BOOKS
Lanham • Boulder • New York • London

Published by Lexington Books
An imprint of The Rowman & Littlefield Publishing Group, Inc.
4501 Forbes Boulevard, Suite 200, Lanham, Maryland 20706
www.rowman.com

Unit A, Whitacre Mews, 26-34 Stannary Street, London SE11 4AB

British Library Cataloguing in Publication Information Available

Library of Congress Cataloging-in-Publication Data

Legacies of state violence and transitional justice in Latin America : a Janus-faced paradigm? / Edited by Nina Schneider and Marcia Esparza.
p. cm.
Includes bibliographical references and index.
ISBN 978-1-4985-1385-2 (cloth : alk. paper) – ISBN 978-1-4985-1386-9 (ebook)
1. Transitional justice–Latin America. 2. Violence (Law)–Latin America. 3. Crimes against humanity–Latin America. 4. Political violence–Latin America. I. Schneider, Nina 1980- editor. II. Esparza, Marcia, editor.
KG574.L44 2015
340'.115098–dc23
2015029159

∞™ The paper used in this publication meets the minimum requirements of American National Standard for Information Sciences Permanence of Paper for Printed Library Materials, ANSI/NISO Z39.48-1992.

Printed in the United States of America

For all those who resist and engage in efforts against oppression and state violence.

Contents

Acknowledgments ix

Introduction: Whose Transition? Whose Voices? Latin American Responses to Transitional Justice xi
Nina Schneider and Marcia Esparza

Part I: Argentina **1**

1 "What Do You Mean By Transitional Justice?": Local Perspectives on Human Rights Trials in Argentina 3
Rosario Figari Layús

Part II: Brazil **17**

2 Scopes and Limits to the Transitional Justice Discourse in Brazil 19
Edson Teles and Renan Quinalha

3 Transitional Justice from the Margins: Legal Mobilization and Memory Politics in Brazil 37
Cecília MacDowell Santos

Part III: El Salvador **73**

4 Toward Reconsidering the Root Causes of Violence: Free Trade, Mining, and Transitional Justice in Central America 75
Steve Dobransky

Part IV: Peru **89**

5 First Empowerment, Then Disillusion: The Ambivalent Legacy of the Transitional Justice Process in Local Peru 91
Laura Tejero Tabernero

6 How Transitional Is Justice?: Peru's Post-Conflict Revisited 109
José Pablo Baraybar, Jesús Peña, and Percy Rojas

Part V: Uruguay **133**

7 Uruguay and the Reconceptualization of Transitional Justice 135
Debbie Sharnak

Part VI: Latin America **155**

8 Concluding Reflections 157
Roberto Gargarella

Useful Online Resources 167

Index 171

About the Contributors 183

Acknowledgments

Most important, the editors wish to thank the contributors to this volume for their wonderful work and engagement, Rosario Figari Layús, Edson Teles, Renan Quinalha, Cecília MacDowell Santos, Steve Dobransky, Laura Tejero, Jose P. Baraybar, Jesús Peña Romero, Percy Rojas, Debbie Sharnak, and Roberto Gargarella; and Kristy Eldridge for her invaluable editing work. Special thanks go to Nora Morales de Cortiñas and Carlos Rosanski whose critical interventions convinced us of the necessity to edit this volume.

We also wish to thank our acquiring editor at Lexington/Rowman & Littlefield, Nicolette Amstutz, for her much appreciated help and guidance; Fal Vitiello for translating the chapter by Teles and Quinalha into English; Gabriella Citroni (University of Milano) and Paola Viteri for their greatly valued support; and José Otávio Nogueira Guimarães (National University of Brasília) and his team for providing information about the Latin American Network of Transitional Justice (Rede Latino-Americana de Justiça de Transição, RLAJT).

Furthermore, we would like to warmly thank Leigh A. Payne (University of Oxford), Raluca Grosescu (University of Exeter), and an anonymous reviewer for comments on early chapter drafts. We are especially grateful to Itai Shnei who commented on some of this book's chapters.

We are deeply grateful to the *Zukunftskolleg* at the University of Konstanz, in particular the EU FP7 Marie Curie ZIF Program (grant no. 291784), and the Office of Undergraduate Studies (OAR) at the John Jay College of the City University New York (CUNY) for their relentless support of this book project.

Last, we wish to send special thanks to the team of the Historical Memory Project in New York, for their continuing engagement documenting human rights abuses and resistance; Célia Lontra in Brasília for her hospitality and moral involvement; and Pierre-Yves for his kind support in allowing us to use his photograph for this book cover.

Introduction

Whose Transition? Whose Voices? Latin American Responses to Transitional Justice

Nina Schneider and Marcia Esparza

Since the demise of war, genocide, and dictatorships in Latin America, the field of transitional justice has greatly influenced interdisciplinary discussions of justice and democratization processes, and shaped international and national policies. A large body of academic and non-scholarly literature has embraced the paradigm, hailed its achievements and called for further transitional justice efforts.[1] Our experience at conferences and symposia, however, has been that many Latin Americans seeking to clarify a violent past—judges, human rights activists, and scholars alike—more often than not raise questions about the paradigm, from sharp criticisms to outright refusal. Asked about her opinion of the concept of transitional justice, Nora Morales de Cortiñas, a founding member of the Argentinean Association of the Madres de la Plaza de Mayo, replied: "Transitional justice?! What is this? Justice is justice—what do you mean by transitional?!" And yet, Argentinean scholars and scholars focusing on Argentinean's aftermath of dictatorship have repeatedly referred to Argentina as a global "role model" of transitional justice.[2]

This book aims to tease out the striking mismatch between global transitional justice discourses and Latin American historical experiences when confronting its violent past. Based on historical evidence rather than theoretical or normative assumptions, this book will tackle the complex ways in which the transitional justice paradigm in Latin America has resonated on the ground—or not. The purpose is to initiate a critical debate about normative discourses, such as transitional justice. We use the terms "response" or "resonance" in a broader and more active sense than usual, seeking to elucidate how the transitional justice paradigm as a whole has either been rejected, accepted, appropriated, or redefined by local organizations addressing state violence.

While government and non-government institutions, human rights practitioners, and scholars across the world have used and embraced the concept of transitional justice for nearly a quarter of a century, this book raises these important questions: How have different Latin American groups (state officials, human rights and victims groups, scholars, etc.) responded and contributed to the development of the transitional justice paradigm? Does empirical evidence from across Latin American confirm that the transitional justice paradigm has impacted positively on post-authoritarian societies?

From an interdisciplinary perspective, and exploring different countries, we will challenge the idea that the transitional justice field has been unanimously supported in the aftermath of the Cold War. Despite a rising body of critical scholarship, the notion that transitional justice has resonated in the region is an unproven assumption prevailing among Westernized scholars.[3] Instead, we critically analyze a spectrum of responses from Latin America. In fact, we know very little about how different groups advocating for truth, memory, and justice have reacted to the transitional justice paradigm (Olsen, Payne, and Reiter 2011, 564). The authors of this volume are field-experienced; they have worked closely with (or in a few instances) are survivors of or have witnessed the bloodshed that engulfed the region in the Cold War. Some have helped to exhume the bodies of forcibly disappeared persons, others have worked for truth commissions and international or national human rights institutions, or conducted dozens of interviews during their field work. They will show that there is a striking mismatch between what is rhetorically claimed and the de facto socioeconomic, political and civil human rights situation on the ground.

TRANSITIONAL JUSTICE AS A JANUS-FACED PARADIGM

We will posit that the transitional justice paradigm is Janus-faced. On the positive side, it can combat denial, contribute to accountability measures, and help mobilize grassroots groups ideologically and practically (Keck and Sikkink 1998; McEvoy 2007, 431; Shaw and Waldorf, 2010, 20). Ideologically, the concept can provide a strategic vocabulary (rights talk), and practically, it can offer support like funding, know-how, or legal training. Scholars like Risse, Ropp and Sikkink (1999), for instance, have studied how the link between local and international activists empowers civil society to put state elites under political pressure. At the same time, transitional justice may have a positive impact in providing national judges with a legal tool to pursue criminal investigations. It may also function as a catalyser for spreading a reading of international law that promotes retributive justice (Simmons 2009; Almquist and Espósito 2012, 12). On the negative side, it may ultimately weaken the agency of human rights protagonists, strengthen rather than combat impunity, deny responsibility in past human rights crimes (Leebaw 2008, 113, 118), and in the case of truth commissions, even help silence enduring postcolonial relations, tying sectors of Indigenous peasants to the army (Esparza 2014).[4]

Chapters in this volume assert a risk previously stressed by Vinjamuri and Snyder (2003): national political elites may adopt accountability mechanisms as a political cover for "less human rights-friendly policies." Most contributions in this volume demonstrate the manifold forms of mismatch between discourses and praxis. For instance, Jose P. Baraybar, Jesus Peña Romero, and Percy Rojas' chapter on Peru shows that not just state-level but even local politicians have misused reparation payments for their own political interests. Disillusion may be a matter of time, as Laura Tejero's chapter on Peru, "First Empowerment then Disillusion," argues in this book.

The existing literature on responses to transitional justice in Latin America seems to support the paradigm's two-faced consequences. Legal scholar Catalina Diaz (2008) has analyzed how various Colombian groups have attempted to appropriate transitional justice discourse with fundamentally opposed intentions. For example, the Uribe government, on the one hand, "demobilized" the paramilitary groups (*Autodefensas Unidas de Colombia*, AUC) and celebrated this as a "peace" and a transitional justice success. On the other hand, human rights advocates and NGOs argued that the demobilization process legitimized and further empowered paramilitary troops across the country—including those who had previously been involved in serious human rights crimes. Hence, the government seized the transitional justice rhetoric, proclaimed a Colombian "transition," and once again covered up past human rights crimes. At the same time, human rights groups from below, with the support of international groups, appropriated the legal terminology and language of "rights to truth, justice and reparation" to challenge the official narrative (Diaz 2008, 199–200). The case of Argentina also shows this Janus-faced nature. Kirchner's post-2003 Argentina is often taken as an example of the downsides of an official human rights agenda, when the government exploits the topic of past violence in an act of "ideological appropriation" (Collins 2012, 420). The political instrumentalization of justice discourses and practices has been a key critique leveled against transitional justice scholarship. Because the paradigm has brought both benefits and disadvantages to Latin America, it is difficult to outright reject it, and the authors of this volume have varying positions on this matter. The ultimate question that this volume seeks to raise is: How can the transitional justice paradigm be modified in order to prevent the kind of misapplication experienced in Latin America and elsewhere? Is there a way to fix it, or do we need an entirely new model?

This volume dovetails in a timely manner with studies from countries outside of Latin America that have demonstrated how local politicians have misused global transitional justice norms and practices to achieve their own political goals. This misapplication may result in unintended detriments to justice, as this volume will confirm. Lars Waldorf (Shaw, Waldorf, and Hazan 2010, 10, 12), for instance, has argued that the Gacaca courts in post-genocide Rwanda turned into a means of state coercion and victor's justice. In sum, the transitional justice vocabulary can potentially be abused to legitimize governmental power of any political shade—be it right-wing like in Colombia or left-wing like in Argentina.

Transitional Justice: A Post-Cold War Paradigm on the Rise

The importance of transitional justice has increased markedly since the early 1990s. Pierre Hazan (2010, 8–9), both a scholar and experienced political advisor for the United Nations and ministries of foreign relations for various countries, maintains that transitional justice established a new model of democracy and introduced a novel vocabulary that was unknown during the Cold War. In 2004, the United Nations established a guideline that explicitly declared transitional justice initiatives as its mission (Annan 2004, 1). According to Brooks (2003) and Oomen (2005, 890–91), funding for transitional justice programs run under the label "rule of law" has skyrocketed. Today, dozens of specialized university departments, websites, and journals have been founded, and hundreds of conferences have been convened (Olsen, Payne, and Reiter 2010, 2–5; Forsyth 2011a, 554).

Transitional justice has been identified as a field that is heterogeneous, interdisciplinary, practice-driven—a concept continuously evolving without an authoritative definition (Bell 2009). Scholars criticize it as undertheorized and based on ill-defined concepts (Hazan 2010, 30; Clark and Palmer 2012, 2; Buckley-Zistel, Koloma Beck, Braun, and Mieth 2014, 1). Initially the paradigm was related to countries associated with political transitions. One of the most-cited definitions of transitional justice was provided by Ruti Teitel (2003, 69): "justice associated with periods of political change, characterized by legal responses to confront the wrongdoings of repressive predecessor regimes. . .]." Teitel provided a rather narrow legal concept that was still related to a repressive regime in the past. Today it seems that scholars increasingly extend the concept to long-established democracies like the United States or Canada (Leebaw 2008, 111; Heine 2011), an extension that again testifies to the paradigm's growing prominence. More recent definitions like that offered by the United Nations (Annan 2004, 1) define transitional justice as a "range of . . . mechanisms" aiming at "accountability," "justice" and "reconciliation." The arguably most important private advocate of the transitional justice concept, the New York based non-governmental organization International Center or Transitional Justice (ICTJ), similarly defines it as "the set of judicial and non-judicial measures that have been implemented . . . to redress the legacies of massive human rights abuses."[5] More strictly related to transitional justice mechanisms, these newer definitions reflect the broader use of the term now also applied to formally democratic regimes. Cathy Collins (2010) has meanwhile proceeded to talk about "post-transitional justice." In this volume, we will consider transitional justice a paradigm, because it is both a *discursive* pattern and a set of socially embodied *practices* (truth commissions, reparations, amnesties, lustration, memory initiatives, and prosecutions) that guide and shape thought and action *in* and *about* post-conflict societies.

Numerous scholars have examined the origins of transitional justice (Teitel 2003; Elster 2004; Leebaw 2008, 96–103; Hazan 2010, 29–62; Olsen, Payne, and Reiter 2010, 1–5; Forsythe 2011a; Balasco 2013), and Debbie Sharnak's chapter in this volume will trace the paradigm's genealogy in more detail. Teitel (2003) traces transitional justice's roots to the post-1945 period; however, she stresses that at the time accountability mechanisms today associated with transitional justice (punishment, lustration, reparations) were still exceptions. In the post-Cold War period, transitional justice became a norm to measure regime change.

Two aspects are noteworthy about the historical development of the concept and play a role for the arguments in this book: First, the rise from an idea into a powerful paradigm in a short period of time, given insufficient time to be fully developed and critically evaluated. Second, a characteristic noted by Clark and Palmer (2012, 1): the diverse origins of the field may account for its "energy and vibrancy," on one hand, and its many unanswered questions, on the other. These pending questions are not just theoretical but also political and ethical in nature, as the chapters in this volume will show.

MAIN CRITICISMS AND NEW DIRECTIONS

While the transitional justice concept has developed and gained in importance, studies that critically revisit the field's underlying assumptions seem to be on the rise (Leebaw 2008; Lundy and McGovern 2008; Fletcher, Weinstein, and Rowen 2009; Shaw, Waldorf, and Hazan 2010; Palmer, Clark, and Granville 2012). A central assumption of the transitional justice paradigm is that societies "move forward" (e.g., by reforms, projects, prosecutions) and succeed in leaving the experience of gruesome state violence behind (Castillejo-Cuellar 2013, 17).[6] Numerous scholars have objected to the elusive and teleological model of transition and the normalization of an exceptional take on justice (Teitel 2003, 85; McGregor 2008, 47; Clark and Palmer 2012, 8; Quinalha 2013, 220–35). Paul Seils (2012, 265) claims that even those who have been working in the field of transitional justice have noted that the term "transitional" is "fundamentally unsatisfactory . . . and even more so when translated into Spanish."

The transitional justice concept has been faulted for failing to study the larger history of structural violence, and most importantly, the problem of social inequality and economic exploitation that authors in this volume take issue with, as well as continuing violence and human rights crimes (Torpey 2003, 8–9; Lundy and Mark McGovern 2008, 273). This can partly be explained by the fact that transitional justice studies are rooted in legal studies and only recently moved to encompass disciplines, including, history and anthropology (Hinton 2010; Castillejo-Cuellar 2013). Other scholars like Quinalha (2013) and Grocescu (2015) relate this to the field's link to transitology studies.[7]

This volume will show that in Latin America certain forms of structural violence persist significantly, shaping people's and communities' everyday lives. In fact, we argue that there are stubborn structural continuities leaving underlying political and socioeconomic schemes of repression nearly untouched—rather than a real *transition*. Latin America, with its entrenched political and socioeconomic inequalities, is a particularly vivid illustration of the gap between the rich and the poor in the context of a rapacious globalization.[8] In this volume, Steve Dobransky, Laura Tejero, and José Baraybar's team will show how the transitional justice paradigm failed to address the root causes of state repression in Latin America.

The criticism of the notion of "transition" as inadequate to tackle structural problems of violence has often been related to critics' discontent with the paradigm's "narrow justice concept." Besides calling for extending the concept's temporal frame, scholars have demanded to broaden its thematic scope (Mani 2002, 19; McEvoy 2007, 411, 414; Cavallaro and Abuja 2008, 59; Lundy and McGovern 2008, 273). Kieran McEvoy (2007, 411–21) has argued for scholars and practitioners to recognize the "limitations of legalism." These limits include its exclusive focus on the state at the expense of civil society or an idealistic view of law as a neutral instrument beyond the political. Legal scholars themselves have acknowledged that judicial answers tend to dominate the field (Engstrom 2012, 213) and have argued that prosecutions alone are insufficient (Garretón 2012, 100–101; Roberto Gargarella in this volume).

Another problem is what Pierre Hazan (2010, 29) coins the "hubris of transitional justice"; the paradigm's exaggerated claims, including reconciliation to heal individuals, let alone societies. Conflict-ridden societies, in particular survivors, have noticed this mismatch between proclaimed faith-based transitional justice goals and realities on the ground (Hazan 2010, 37).

Marjorie D. Jobson (2012, 488–89), the national director of the South African Khulumani support group, regards the field's claims as "exaggerated, leaving the expectations of victims largely unfulfilled." According to Jobson, these overstated prospects include the idea of "moving on" from the past and departing from the experience of violence, to rehabilitate victims and re-establish their relation to the state, to guarantee the rule of law, and to curb human rights violations. Most recently, scholars have therefore demanded to lower transitional justice expectations (Duthie 2010, 254; Olsen, Payne, and Reiter 2010, 131).

NEW CONCEPTIONS OF LOCALITY

There is also a rising body of studies refuting a state-focused view calling for greater attention to civil society ownership and local participation in post-conflict initiatives (Backer 2003, 297; McEvoy 2007, 421–28, 434; Arriaza and Roht-Arriaza 2008, 145, 166; McGregor 2008, 282; Boesenacker and Vinjamuri 2011, 345–46; Lambourne 2012, 260). Scholars of this branch of research have used different concepts invoking the idea of "the local"; for example, "locality," "participation," "from below," and "legitimacy." As "the local" has played such a crucial role in the recent critical transitional justice scholarship, it is worth addressing some of its main traits. Rosalind Shaw, Lars Waldorf, and Pierre Hazan (2010, 4–7) use the category of locality to revisit posited "truths" by examining how transitional justice mechanisms crisscross with survivors' practices, views, and main concerns. When discussing who precisely represents the local, the authors rightly express the criticism that all too often the local is defined as the national state, national elites or domestic NGOs, thus ignoring the survivors' views and demands. Shaw, Waldorf, and Hazan (2010, 6–7) thus opt to define the local as "remote" and "marginal"—a kind of "counterview." Similarly, McEvoy and McGregor invoke the term "from below" as a form of "resistance" or opposition to justice initiatives that are conceived of as insufficient.

Mapping the term locality is important, because it is closely related to the significance we give to certain groups in academic and political discourses. Weinstein, Fletcher, Vinck, and Pham (2010) relate the definition of the term locality to the important question of "whose priorities take priority." McEvoy and McGregor (2008, 3) use the category of "from below" to highlight the issue that regular locals have often been key actors, while other actors (international or official ones) have been highlighted as protagonists. Cecília Santos in this volume makes a similar claim when she discusses the crucial role of civil-society groups in Brazil's struggle for accountability measures. While most scholars arguing toward a local approach prioritize the survivors' view, the question of "whose priorities take priority" gets even more complicated because survivors themselves are a heterogeneous group, and because public opinion and local survivors' opinions vary (Shaw, Waldorf, and Hazan 2010, 24; Engstrom 2012, 212). While it is true that civil society has increasingly supplemented, challenged, or sabotaged top-down and alien mechanisms (McEvoy 2012, 311), civil society remains a complex category comprising groups with diverse interests (Boesenacker and Vinjamuri 2011).[9]

More recently, scholars have further complicated the local, conceiving of it as a dynamic, contested and relational category, one that is no longer a fixed "place in which history happens," but a space that is continually constituted and reconfigured (Nieftagodien 2010, 43, 47). In practice, however, the local tends to be associated with the under-researched remote periphery and thus with a level below the state (Nieftagodien 2010, 56–57). The chapters of this volume understand the local in this sense, as the marginal periphery. They focus on those groups that have directly or tacitly been silenced by mainstream transitional justice discourses: victims and survivors, local groups beyond the state level. The fact that all contributors to this volume are field-experienced practitioners (and some even survivors) is of vital importance here. Juxtaposing their field knowledge with transitional justice scholarship will allow us to identify aspects that require revision and develop future directions.

Our volume dialogues with a number of single-case, bottom-up studies that have shown that local non-state viewpoints contrast sharply with the predominantly state-focused transitional justice literature (Theidon 2006; Shaw 2007; Subotić 2009; Drexler 2010; Hovil and Okello 2011, 340; Kent 2011; Riano-Alcalá and Baines 2011). The disparity between historical evidence and discourse has not just been perceived by locals on the ground, as numerous contributions in this volume demonstrate. Debbie Sharnak's chapter on Uruguay shows that even the transitional justice community noted this mismatch, because scholars and practitioners selected different countries as role models over the time. While initially Uruguay was regarded as an exemplary case for the success of transitional justice, it was later discarded, because the country had failed to punish its perpetrators—even with the population's consent issued through referenda.[10] ICTJ representatives had to correct its course, as Uruguay's historical experience no longer matched the "model."

Transitional justice processes are multifaceted, particularly the global-local entanglements in negotiating justice (Theidon 2000). As various scholars (Fletcher, Weinstein, and Rowen 2009, 164; Olsen, Payne, and Reiter 2010, 77; Merwe 2012, 487; Atencio 2014; Foresythe 2011b, 90) have argued, transitional justice histories are complex, dynamic processes where diverse interest groups move into different directions leading to both intended and unintended consequences (Duthie 2010, 252–53; Laban 2010, 9).

Hugo van Merwe (2012, 487), for instance, has pointedly remarked: "The fight for justice is . . . not a one-off battle determined by a decision to amnesty or prosecute offenders" but "a protracted struggle involving various institutions and shifting political alliances." More recently, scholars have recognized that transitional justice mechanisms' resonance with local cultures are understudied (Hinton 2010, 11; Boesenecker and Vinjamuri 2011, 348). Alexander Hinton Laban (2010, 1, 9) proposes to speak of "negotiated" justice, because during these processes some voices are strengthened while others are silenced. Boesenacker and Vinjamuri (2011, 345–47) have argued that local actors have by far always conformed to but frequently contested international justice norms and strategies—a finding that is backed by this volume.

There are many reasons why studing the local history is important. Local historical experience can serve as a *corrective* to empirically unconfirmed ideas, ideas that sustain problematic transitional justice discourses and practices. Moreover, there is a gaping hole with regard to local views on the paradigm. As Olsen, Payne and Reiter (2011, 564; 2010, 160) and Boesenacker and Vinjamuri (2011, 347–48) have noted, we lack studies on civil society support for mechanisms and systematic cross-national research of attitudes about transitional justice. Besides contributing to knowledge, a positive local response to transitional justice mechanisms would help to improve such policies' efficiency and would increase their legitimacy. The local is thus of pragmatic interest. Lastly, studying the local reinforces the ideal of epistemic pluralism (to offer various perspectives on a subject) and egalitarianism, and is thus of ethical importance.

WHY LATIN AMERICA?

Knowing and understanding Latin American local views is a particularly rich source for studying the varied resonances of transitional justice and the Janus-faced nature of the paradigm. Latin America has played a pivotal role in the development of the transitional justice paradigm. Olsen, Payne, and Reiter (2011, 558–59) have argued that "Latin America has become the undisputed global leader in transitional justice and a model for efforts around the world."[11] The ICTJ, for example, has its regional focus on Latin America and Africa (Olsen, Payne, and Reiter 2010, 91).

Argentina, for example, is rightly regarded as the inventor of truth commissions and of having inspired dozens of following truth commissions (Sikkink and Walling 2006, 305–6, 308),[12] while Guatemala and El Salvador pioneered gender-specific investigations.[13] In quantitative terms, 38 percent of the world's truth commissions happened in Latin America, Africa accounting for 36 percent (Sikkink and Walling 2006, 309). Sikkink and Walling (2006, 306) argue that Argentina's so-called Junta trials in the mid-1980s pioneered what they call a "cascade . . . of transitional justice trials." Burt (2012, 145) agrees that the Junta trials in Argentina were landmark cases in the global movement toward punishment, and reminds us that the Peruvian trial against Fujimori marked a similar watershed for both the continent and the global human rights community. While Sikkink and Walling (2007, 428) identified Latin America as the world leader of both trials and truth commissions, Olsen, Payne and Reiter (2010, 106) only confirmed its leading position regarding truth commissions and amnesties. Latin America also leads efforts concerning domestic trials, even though scholars disagree over details. Whereas Sikkink and Walling (2007, 434) have argued that Argentina had most domestic trials worldwide, Collins (2012, 400) has maintained that Chile did.[14] Sikkink and Payne suggests that Argentina had more trial verdicts than Chile, but Chile had more trials.[15]

Latin America has also played an important role in inventing new forms of redress and protest. Argentina established new forms of lustration processes; the informal *impugnación*, when civilians protest against official promotions and staff suggestions (Olsen, Payne, and Reiter 2011, 559). Rosario Figari Layús, in this volume, addresses the *juicios de la verdad* (truth-finding trials), a new kind of specialized trials that emerged in the late 1990s in various Argentinean cities. These hearings provided victims' families and survivors with the opportunity to denounce past repression. Argentina has also famously invented the unofficial naming and shaming practice called *esclachos*, a creative form of protest in the absence of formal punishment (Kaiser 2002). Similar social practices were adopted in Chile (funas) and post-2012 Brazil (escraches) (Atencio 2014).

THE APPROACH OF THIS BOOK

In-depth studies on the resonance of the transitional justice paradigm in Latin America are wanting. In part, this may be rooted in the lack of an appropriate methodology to gauge the paradigm locally. Fletcher, Weinstein, and Rowen (2009, 170) pointedly ask: "Is there an accurate method of assessing local attitudes towards justice and if so, who should do the assessment?" Previous studies have often been database-driven. Databases have the benefit of providing "good indication of probabilities" (Foresythe 2011a, 558) and are convenient for donors. But unlike qualitative studies, high-aggregate quantitative studies are inadequate for fleshing out the details, the dynamics, and to advance our comprehension for differing situations. They fall short of elucidating the understudied conflicted processes of translating international justice norms into local systems. Shaw, Waldorf and Hazan (2010, 22) have suggested repeated surveys to avoid narrow "snapshot" results and analyze a broader and more meaningful reception. Palmer, Clark, and Granville (2012, 7) adopt an in-depth ethnographic approach and emphasize the importance of context sensitivity. Olsen, Payne and Reiter (2010, 131) have also underlined the difficulty of measuring success when varying goals and imprecise definitions coexist; for example, such malleable terms like "justice" or "truth." While in their own study they focus on improvements in democracy and human rights indicators, they argue that "[p]erceptions of justice, fairness, or rule of law may provide a more valuable measure of success . . . though we do not yet have effective ways to measure those types of successes" (Olsen, Payne and Reiter 2010, 161).

This volume's overall research approach involves the study of empirical evidence: It seeks to examine how the people transitional justice proclaims to help relate to the paradigm. Adopting a source-based perspective, it asks what kind of evidence is available about the reception of the paradigm in selected Latin American countries. This collection of qualitative case studies focuses on remote and marginalized communities and survivors. Yet, the editors' goal is not to *speak for* local sufferers of violence, claiming to speak in their names. Instead the editors' seek *to listen to* and *amplify* local voices that are often silenced in transitional justice discourses.

While previous studies have either focused on ahistorical theoretical debates or criticized transitional justice mechanisms in a specific region, this volume builds upon those recent critical transitional justice studies that have demanded more research on the complex process of translation at the local-global boundary. Rather than blindly promoting a Janus-faced paradigm invoking the benevolent language of "justice" and "human rights," this volume suggests revising the global transitional justice discourse. Similar to Boesenacker and Vinjamuri (2011, 349) the editors hope and expect that studying the local will trigger "future changes at the level of practices and expectation at the international level."

This collection of cross-national empirical studies shows that diverse Latin American groups have responded to transitional justice in a variety of ways. While the complex question of Latin American responses to the paradigm requires further research, the episodes here share several concerns: First, the role of civil-society organizations (often run by survivors) has been downplayed in the field's literature and practice. While most authors cover this aspect, it is explored in depth in Cecília Santos' chapter on Brazil. Second, as mentioned previously, too much is expected from transitional justice, leading to deception toward the population it promised to support—the survivors, families of victims, and human rights activists. Third and most importantly, the transitional justice paradigm failed to tackle root causes of violence (poverty, social inequality, and economic exploitation), as shown by the chapters of Steve Dobransky and Jose P. Baraybar, Jesus Peña Romero, and Percy Rojas. Certainly, Latin America is a very diverse region and we cannot generalize. Yet, it seems that in many cases local, national, and global power relations have by and large remained unchanged despite processes of democratization, except maybe for the case of Argentina. The problem remains that powerful actors like states or local politicians can easily abuse the paradigm. If the transitional justice paradigm lends itself to silencing response to continuing structures of violence, the question must be raised whether it may be time to let go of the adjective "transitional." These common concerns may serve as a starting point for future studies on Latin American responses to the paradigm. Impending studies can, first, refine methods to measure resonance; second, locate or produce sources about the paradigm's varying reception; and, third, analyze how the paradigm has been resignified in different Latin American countries. Lastly, they can explore competing responses at the local level in depth.

This volume offers contributions on Argentina, Brazil, El Salvador, Peru, and Uruguay. In the first chapter, Rosario Figari Layús argues that the current prosecutions in Argentina cannot be considered as a mechanism of transitional justice, because rather than being temporary and extraordinary mechanisms, Argentine trials have been conducted in regular and national institutions of criminal law. The second and third chapters focus on Brazil, which has received scant attention in international transitional justice scholarship. Edson Teles and Renan Quinalha analyze the entry of the transitional justice discourse in Brazil at a time when the country was no longer in a state of exception. They argue that the discourse had ambiguous effects; while human rights movements adopted the concept of demanding official memory and justice initiatives, the notion of an "exceptional political moment"—one of the paradigm's core assumptions ("transition")—simultaneously set limits to these efforts. Cecília Santos' chapter on Brazil focuses on local and transnational legal actions by families of the disappeared and survivors. Legal mobilization, she stresses, played a key role in the families' struggles for justice both during and after the regime and justice struggles have a longer history than the transitional justice discourse supposes. Politics of transitional justice in Brazil were complex, dynamic, and shaped by various actors, including an active civil society and a responsive state.

Chapter four by Steve Dobransky studies the case of Central America, mainly El Salvador. He criticizes the transitional justice paradigm for turning a blind eye on the most fundamental components of justice, which coincide with the root causes of violence—mass poverty and inequality. The narrow political focus of transitional justice operates with a very limited notion of justice and democracy. While transitional justice has been promising justice, democracy and reconciliation, it failed to provide average citizens with the most basic needs—food to survive, physical integrity, and an environment free from toxins.

Chapters five and six explore the case of Peru. Drawing on her ethnographic fieldwork on victims' organizations across the country, Laura Tejero Tabernero shows that the role of transitional justice was ambivalent in Peru and changed over time. While the framework was at first helpful for victims in their pursuit of claiming rights, they have meanwhile become disillusioned. Meaningful forms of justice and reparation remain wanting and historically rooted political and socioeconomic inequalities persist. Many of those who first welcomed the rhetoric and policies of transitional justice now reject it or even show resistance.

In chapter six, José P. Baraybar, Jesús Peña Romero, and Percy Rojas elucidate the Peruvian context from the perspective of the Peruvian Team of Forensic Anthropology, a non-governmental organization. Dovetailing with Tabernero's chapter, the authors' main critique is that the transitional justice paradigm failed to tackle the root causes of violence: poverty and unequal citizenship. They, too, question whether a transition has at all occurred in Peru, and advocate a more comprehensive approach that includes social and economic rights.

Chapter seven takes us to the still comparatively rarely discussed case of Uruguay. Drawing on both her field experience as a former member of the Research Unit at the International Center for Transitional Justice (ICTJ) and her scholarly research, Debbie Sharnak explores the global-local dialogue about transitional justice and its changes over time. While initially Uruguay served as a role model for the international community, its politics of impunity were later discounted as a failure. Yet, because of Uruguay's renewed transitional justice efforts, on one hand, and the field's evolvement, on the other, it has recently caught more attention. While transitional justice initiatives can "offer opportunities to open space for discussion and further grappling with traumatic periods," her research reveals that Uruguayans themselves remain reluctant to describe their struggle against impunity as transitional justice.

In the final chapter, Argentine lawyer and sociologist Roberto Gargarella provides concluding remarks on the book's chapters and the diverse, protracted and contradictory impact of transitional justice in Latin America. Any evaluation, he argues, "cannot but be complex, balanced and nuanced, rather than simple, categorical and unqualified." Focusing on the role and limits of law to transitional justice efforts, he maintains that legal reforms have not been accompanied by structural socioeconomic and political reforms, changes that law cannot deliver and an expectation that is simply too high. Gargarella finds it important to discuss the tensions between the self-congratulatory transitional justice discourse and Latin America's historical experience, but he also calls for cautiousness. While the book's overall focus on victims and human rights activists may help to elucidate the paradigm's shortcomings, he advocates that the sophisticated problems that follow from periods of massive rights abuses "are fundamentally collective [and] should be understood, examined, deliberated and decided collectively."

NOTES

1. The University of Wisconsin's Transitional Justice Database project compiled a bibliography (starting in 1970), which as of February 2014 contained 2,497 entries of scholarly work related to the subject of transitional justice. Available at: https://sites.google.com/site/transitionaljusticedatabase/ (accessed February 5, 2014).

2. See Rosario Figari Layús in this volume. Authors referring to Argentina's leading role in the field of transitional justice include among others Teitel (2000; 2003) and Sikkink (2011).

3. While some scholars use the adjective "Western," we prefer the term "Westernized" to point out that a large body of the transitional justice literature was either published by journals and presses in North America or Europe, or discussed at universities, research centers, and official and non-official human rights organizations in the Global North.

4. See also Esparza (2015), *Silenced Communities: Legacies of and Resistance to Militarization and Militarism in Santo Tomás Chichicastenango, Guatemala.* Forthcoming, New York: Berghahn.

5. International Center for Transitional Justice, "What Is Transitional Justice?" Available at: https://www.ictj.org/about/transitional-justice (accessed March 5, 2015).

6. For an excellent critique of transitional justice's politics of time see Bevernage (2012).

7. A more pragmatic explanation for the paradigm's short-term approach would be that transitional justice mechanisms need to satisfy their donors who want fast, measurable results (for a critique of donor pressure's impact on the field, see de Greiff (2011, 103–5).

8. MercoPress News Agency, "Gap between rich and poor in Latinamerica is largest in the world, says UN" (March 27, 2010). Available at: http://en.mercopress.com/2010/03/27/gap-between-rich-and-poor-in-latinamerica-is-largest-in-the-world-says-un (accessed November 1, 2014).

9. We conceive of civil society as diverse entities of social identity and joint interest that are in principle independent of the state (though they may receive officials funding) that may form an intermediary sphere of governance between the individual and the state. This definition draws on Schmitter and Karl (1991, 79–80).

10. For more literature discussing the Uruguayan referendum, see for example Fried and Lessa (2011) and Lessa (2013).

11. Similar claims have, however, also been made for Africa's pioneering role. Carla de Yazca and William Schabas (2011, 570) have emphasized Africa's "pioneering role in developing truth commissions" and argued that the South African Truth and Reconciliation Commission, in particular, had a worldwide influence (especially in Peru). The authors also note that the African model was unique in its capacity of incorporating local practices and customs and adapting transitional justice programs.

12. Uganda instated the first "truth commission" in 1974 followed by Bolivia in 1982, but neither produced a final report like Argentina's CONADEP (Sikkink and Walling 2006, 308).

13. Guatemala and Peru first incorporated an ethnic dimension into truth-seeking processes, paying specific attention to indigenous populations.

14. Collins refers to a total fifty imprisonments in 2009.

15. The editors would like to thank Leigh Payne for this insightful information.

BIBLIOGRAPHY

Almquvist, Jessica, and Carlos Espósito, eds. 2012. *The Role of Courts in Transitional Justice: Voices from Latin America and Spain*. New York and London: Routledge.

Annan, Kofi. 2004. *Report of the Secretary-General on the Rule of Law and Transitional Justice in Conflict and Post-conflict Societies*, UN Doc. S/2004/616 (August 24, 2004).

Arriaza, Laura, and Naomi Roht-Arriaza. 2008. "Social Repair at the Local Level: The Case of Guatemala." In *Transitional Justice from Below: Grassroots Activism and the Struggle for Change*, eds. Kieran McEvoy and Lorna McGregor, 143–66. Portland, Or: Hart.

Atencio, Rebecca J. 2014. *Memory's Turn: Reckoning with Dictatorship in Brazil*. Madison: Wisconsin University Press.

Backer, David. 2003. "Civil Society and Transitional Justice: Possibilities, Patterns and Prospects." *Journal of Human Rights* 2 (3): 297–313.

Balasco, Lauren Marie. 2013. "The Transitions of Transitional Justice: Mapping the Waves From Promise to Practice." *Journal of Human Rights* 12 (2): 198–216.

Bell, Christine. 2009. "Transitional Justice, Interdisciplinarity and the State of the 'Field' or 'non-Field'." *International Journal of Transitional Justice* 3: 5–27.

Bevernage, Berber. 2012. *History, Memory, and State-Sponsored Violence: Time and Justice*. New York and London: Routledge.

Boesenecker, Aaron P., and Vinjamuri, Leslie. 2011. "Lost in Translation? Civil Society, Faith-Based Organizations and the Negotiation of International Norms." *International Journal of Transitional Justice* 5: 345–65.

Brooks, Rosa Ehrenreich. 2003. "The New Imperialism: Violence, Norms, and the 'Rule of Law.'" *Michigan Law Review* 101: 2275–340.

Buckley-Zistel, Susanne, Koloma Beck, Teresa, Braun, Christian, and Mieth, Friederike. 2014. *Transitional Justice Theories*. Abingdon and New York: Routledge.

Burt, Jo-Marie. 2012. "Accountability After Atrocity in Peru: The Trial of Former President Alberto Fujimori in Comparative Perspective." In *Critical Perspectives in Transitional Justice*, eds. Nicola Palmer, Phil Clark, and Danielle Granville, 119–45. Cambridge, Antwerp, Portland: Intersentia.

Carothers, Thomas. 2002. "The End of the Transition Paradigm." *Journal of Democracy* 13 (1): 5–21.

Castillejo-Cuellar, Alejandro. 2013. "On the Question of Historical Injuries: Transitional Justice, Anthropology and the Vicissitudes of Listening." *Anthropology Today*, 29 (1): 17–20.

Cavallero, James L., and Sebestián Albuja. 2008. "The Lost Agenda: Economic Crimes and Truth Commissions in Latin America and Beyond." In *Transitional Justice from Below: Grassroots Activism and the Struggle for Change*, eds. Kieran McEvoy, and Lorna McGregor, 121–42. Portland, OR: Hart.

Clark, Phil and Nicola Palmer. 2012. "Introduction: Challenging Transitional Justice." In *Critical Perspectives in Transitional Justice*, eds. Nicola Palmer, Phil Clark, and Danielle Granville, 1–16. Cambridge, Antwerp, Portland: Intersentia.

Collins, Cath. 2010. *Post-Transitional Justice: Human Rights Trials in Chile and El Salvador*. University Park, PA: Pennsylvania State University Press.

———. 2012. "The End of Impunity? 'Late Justice' and Post-Transitional Prosecutions in Latin America." In *Critical Perspectives in Transitional Justice*, eds. Nicola Palmer, Phil Clark, and Danielle Granville, 399–424. Cambridge, Antwerp, Portland: Intersentia.

Das, Veena, and Arthur Kleinman. 2001. "Introduction." In *Remaking a World: Violence, Social Suffering, and Recovery*, eds. Veena Das, Arthur Kleinman, Margaret Lock, Mamphela Ramphele, and Pamela Reynolds, 1–30. Berkeley: University of California Press.

Diaz, Catalina. 2008. "Challenging Impunity from Below: The Contested Ownership of Transitional Justice in Colombia." In *Transitional Justice from Below: Grassroots Activism and the Struggle for Change*, Kieran McEvoy, and Lorna McGregor, 189-216. Portland, OR: Hart.

Drexler, Elizabeth F. 2010. "The Failure of International Justice in East Timor and Indonesia." In *Transitional Justice: Global Mechanisms and Local Realities After Genocide and Mass Violence*, ed. Laban Hinton, 49–66. Newark: Rutgers University Press.

Duthie, Roger. 2010. "Afterword: The Consequences of Transitional Justice in Particular Contexts." In *Transitional Justice: Global Mechanisms and Local Realities After Genocide and Mass Violence*, ed. Laban Hinton, 249–56. Newark: Rutgers University Press.

Elster, Jon. 2004. *Closing the Books: Transitional Justice in Historical Perspective*. Cambridge: Cambridge University Press.

Engstom, Par. 2012. "Commentary on Accountability, Human Rights and the Rule of Law." In *Critical perspectives in transitional Justice*, eds. Nicola Palmer, Phil Clark, and Danielle Granville, 211–15. Cambridge, Antwerp, Portland: Intersentia.

Esparza, Marcia. 2014. "Impossible Memory and Post-Colonial Silences: A Critical View of the Historical Clarification Commission (CEH in Spanish) in Guatemala." In *Indigenous Peoples' Access to Justice, Including Truth and Reconciliation Processes*, eds. Chief Wilton Littlechild and Elsa Stamatopoulos, 170–81. New York City: Columbia University Press/ Institute for the Study of Human Rights.

Falk, Richard. 2000. *Human Rights Horizons: The Pursuit of Justice in a Globalizing World*. London: Routledge.

Fletcher, Laurel E., Harvey M. Weinstein, and Jamie Rowen. 2009. "Context, Timing and the Dynamics of Transitional Justice: A Historical Perspective." *Human Rights Quarterly* 31: 163–220.

Forsythe, David P. 2011a. "Forum: Transitional Justice: The Quest for Theory to Inform Policy." *International Studies Review* 13: 554–78.

———. 2011b. "Human Rights and Mass Atrocities: Revisiting Transitional Justice." *International Studies Review* 13: 85–95.

Fried, Gabriela, and Francesca Lessa, eds. 2011. *Luchas contra la impunidad: Uruguay 1985–2011*. Montevideo: Trilce.

Garretón, Roberto. 2012. "Chilean Transitional Justice and the Legacy of the De Facto Regime." In *The Role of Courts in Transitional Justice: Voices from Latin America and Spain*, eds. Jessica Almquvist and Carlos Espósito, 81–102. New York and London: Routledge.

Gibson, James L. 2004. "Overcoming Apartheid: Can Truth Reconcile a Divided Nation?" *Politikon* 31 (2): 129–215.

Greiff, Pablo de. 2011. "Some Thoughts on the Development and Present State of Transitional Justice." *Zeitschrift für Menschenrechte/Journal for Human Rights* 2: 100–26.

Grocescu, Raluca. 2015. "The Use of Transitology in the Field of Transitional Justice: A Critique of the Literature on the 'Third Wave' of Democratisation."

Gugelberger, Georg M. 1991. "Voices of the Voiceless in Testimonial Literature." *Latin American Perspectives* 18 (3): 1–128, and *Latin American Perspectives* 18 (4): 1–118.

Hazan, Pierre. 2010. *Judging War, Judging History: Behind Truth and Reconciliation*. Stanford: Stanford University Press.

Heine, Jorge. 2011. "Politics as Usual? US Torture Practices 2001–2008 and Transitional Justice'." *International Studies Review* 13: 570–77.

Hinton, Alexander Laban. 2010. "Introduction: Toward an Anthropology of Transitional Justice." In *Transitional Justice: Global Mechanisms and Local Realities After Genocide and Mass Violence*, ed. Laban Hinton, 1–22. Newark: Rutgers University Press.

Hovil, Lucy, and Moses Chrispus Okello. 2011. "Editorial Note." *The Journal of Transitional Justice* 5: 333–44.

Huntington, Samuel P. 1991. *The Third Wave: Democratization in the Late Twentieth Century*. Norman, OK: University of Oklahoma Press.

Jobson, Marjorie D. 2012. "Commentary on Transitional Justice After Transition." In *Critical Perspectives in Transitional Justice*, eds. Palmer, Nicola, Phil Clark, and Granville, Danielle, 485–91. Cambridge, Antwerp, Portland: Intersentia.

Kaiser, Susanna. 2002. "Escraches: Demonstrations, Communication and Political Memory in Post-Dictatorial Argentina." *Media, Culture and Society* 24: 499–516.

Keck, Margaret E., and Kathryn Sikkink. 1998. *Activists beyond Borders: Advocacy Networks in International Politics*. Ithaca, NY: Cornell University Press.

Kent, Lia. 2011. "Local Memory Practices in East Timor: Disrupting Transitional Justice Narratives." *International Journal of Transitional Justice* 5: 434–55.

Lambourne, Wendy. 2012. "Outreach, Inreach and Civil Society Participation in Transitional Justice." In *Critical Perspectives in Transitional Justice*, eds. Palmer, Nicola, Phil Clark, and Granville, Danielle, 235–61. Cambridge, Antwerp, Portland: Intersentia.

Leebaw, Bronwyn Anne. 2008. "The Irreconcilable Goals of Transitional Justice." *Human Rights Quarterly* 30 (1): 95–118.

Lessa, Francesca. 2013. *Memory and Transitional Justice in Argentina and Uruguay: Against Impunity*. London: Palgrave.
Lundy, Patricia, and Mark McGovern. 2008. "Whose Justice? Rethinking Transitional Justice from the Bottom Up." *Journal of Law and Society* 35 (2): 265–92.
Mani, Rama. 2002. *Beyond Retribution: Seeking Justice in the Shadows of War*. Cambridge: Polity Press.
McEvoy, Kieran. 2007. "Beyond Legalism: Towards a Thicker Understanding of Transitional Justice." *Journal of Law and Society* 34 (4): 411–40.
———. 2012. "Commentary on Locality and Legitimacy." In *Critical Perspectives in Transitional* Justice, eds. Nicola Palmer, Phil Clark, and Granville, Danielle, 311–17. Cambridge, Antwerp, Portland: Intersentia.
McEvoy, Kieran, and Lorna McGregor. 2008. eds. *Transitional Justice from Below: Grassroots Activism and the Struggle for Change*. Portland, OR: Hart.
McGregor, Lorna. 2008. "International Law as a 'Tiered Process': Transitional Justice at the Local, National and International Level." In *Transitional Justice from Below: Grassroots Activism and the Struggle for Change*, eds. Kieran McEvoy and Lorna McGregor, 47–74. Portland, OR: Hart.
Merry, Sally Engle. 2006. *Human Rights and Gender Violence: Translating International Law into Local Justice*. Chicago: University of Chicago Press.
Merwe, Hugo van der. 2012. "Prosecutions, Pardons and Amnesty: The Trajectory of Transitional Accountability in South Africa ." In *Critical Perspectives in Transitional Justice*, eds. Nicola Palmer, Phil Clark, and Danielle Granville, 311–17. Cambridge, Antwerp, Portland: Intersentia.
Nieftagodien, Noor. 2010. "The Place of 'The Local' in History Workshop's Local History." *African Studies* 69 (1): 41–61.
Oettler, Anika. 2008. "Staatliche Initiativen zur Ahndung von Massengewalt: Perspektiven einer transnationalen Geschichte und Gegenwart." *Peripherie* 109/110 (28): 83–109.
Olsen, Tricia D., Leigh A. Payne, and Andrew G. Reiter. 2010. *Transitional Justice in Balance: Comparing Processes, Weighing Efficacy*. Washington, DC: United States Institute of Peace.
———. 2011. "Transitional Justice in Latin America." *International Studies Review* 13: 558–64.
———. 2012. "An Exploratory Analysis of Civil Society and Transitional Justice." In *Civil Society, Conflict and Violence*, eds. Regina A. List and Wolfgang Dörner, 62–84. London and New York: Bloomsbury.
Oomen, B. 2005. "Donor Driven Justice and Its Discontents: The Case of Rwanda." *Development and Change* 36: 887–910.
Palmer, Nicola, Phil Clark, and Danielle Granville. 2012. eds. *Critical Perspectives in Transitional Justice*. Cambridge, Antwerp, Portland: Intersentia.
Payne, Leigh A. 2008. *Unsettling Accounts: Neither Truth nor Reconciliation in Confessions of State Violence*. Durham and London: Duke University Press.
Quinalha, Renan H. 2013. *Justiça de tranisção: Contornos de um conceito*. São Paulo: Dobra.
Rajagopal, Balakrishnan. 2008. "Invoking the Rule of *Law in Post-Conflict Rebuilding*: A Critical Examination." *William and Mary Law Review* 49: 1347–74.
Riano-Alcalá, Pilar, and Eric Baines. 2011. "The Archive in the Witness: Documentation in Settings of Chronic Insecurity." *International Journal of Transitional* Justice 5 (3): 412–33.
Risse, Thomas, Stephen C. Ropp, and Kathryn Sikkink. 1999. *The Power of Human Rights: International Norms and Domestic Change*. New York: Cambridge University Press.
Schiff Berman, P. 2006. "Review Essay: Seeing Beyond the Limits of International Law." *Texas Law Review* 84: 1265–1306.
Schmitter, Philippe C., and Terry Lynn Karl. 1991. "What Democracy Is . . . and Is Not." *Journal of Democracy* 2 (3): 79–80.
Seils, Paul. 2012. "Restoring Civic Confidence Through Transitional Justice." In *The Role of Courts in Transitional Justice: Voices from Latin America and Spain*, eds. Jessica Almqvist and Carlos Espósito, 264–81. New York and London: Routledge.

Shaw, Rosalind. 2007. "Memory Frictions: Localizing Truth and Reconciliation in Sierra Leone." *International Journal of Transitional Justice* 1 (2): 183–207.

Shaw, Rosalind, Lars Waldorf, and Pierre Hazan. 2010. eds. *Localizing Transitional Justice: Interventions and Priorities After Mass Violence*. Stanford: Stanford University Press.

Simmons, Beth A. 2009. *Mobilizing for Human Rights: International Law in Domestic Politics*. Cambridge: Cambridge University Press.

Sikkink, Kathryn. 2011. *The Justice Cascade: How Human Rights Prosecutions Are Changing World Politics*. New York: Norton.

Sikkink, Kathryn, and Carrie Booth Walling. 2006. "Argentina's Contribution to Global Trends in Transitional Justice." In *Transitional Justice in the Twenty-First Century: Beyond Truth versus Justice*, eds. Naomi Roht-Arriaza and Javier Mariezcurrena, 301–25. Cambridge: Cambridge University Press.

———. 2007. "The Impact of Human Rights Trials in Latin America." *Journal of Peace Research* 44: 427–45.

Subotić, Jelena. 2009. *Hijacked Justice: Dealing with the Past in the Balkans*. Ithaca: Cornell University Press.

Teitel, Ruti. 2000. *Transitional Justice*. New York: Oxford University.

———. 2003. "Transitional Justice Genealogy." *Harvard Human Rights Journal* 16: 69–94.

———. 2010. "Preface." In *Localizing Transitional Justice: Interventions and Priorities After Mass Violence*, eds. Rosalind Shaw, Lars Waldorf, and Pierre Hazan, pp. vii–viii. Stanford: Stanford University Press.

Theidon, Kimberley. 2000. "Editorial Note: Special Issue: Whose Justice? Global and Local Approaches." *International Journal of Transitional Justice* 3 (3): 295–300.

———. 2006. "Justice in Transition: The Micropolitics of Reconciliation in Postwar Peru." *Journal of Conflict Resolution* 50 (3): 433–57.

Thoms, Oskar N. T., James Ron, and Roland Paris. 2010. "State-level Effects of Transitional Justice: What Do We Know." *International Journal of Transitional Justice* 4 (3): 329–45.

Torpey, John. 2001. "Introduction: Politics and the Past." In *Politics and the Past: On Repairing Historical Injustices*, ed. Torpey, John, 1-36. Lanham: Rowman and Littlefield Publishers.

Vinjamuri, Leslie, and Jack Snyder. 2004. "Advocacy and Scholarship in the Study of International War Crime Tribunals and Transitional Justice." *Annual Review of Political Science* 7: 345–62.

Venema, Derk. 2012. "Transitions as States of Exception: Towards a More General Theory of Transitional Justice." In *Critical Perspectives in Transitional Justice*, eds. Nicola Palmer, Phil Clark, and Danielle Granville, 73–89. Cambridge, Antwerp, Portland: Intersentia.

Weinstein, Harvey M., Laurel E. Fletcher, Patrick Vinck, and Phuong N. Pham. 2010. "Stay the Hand of Justice: Whose Priorities Take Priority?" In *Localizing Transitional Justice: Justice Interventions and Local Priorities After Mass Violence*, eds. Rosalind Shaw and Lars Waldorf, with Pierre Hazan, 27–48. Stanford: Stanford University Press.

Ycaza, Carla de, and William Schabas. 2011. "Transitional Justice and the African Experience." *International Studies Review* 13: 564–70.

Part I

Argentina

Chapter One

"What Do You Mean By Transitional Justice?"

Local Perspectives on Human Rights Trials in Argentina

Rosario Figari Layús

By examining the implementation of human rights trials in Argentina beginning in 2006 to prosecute those responsible for human rights violations during the Dictatorship (1976–1983), this chapter will address and challenge two assumptions frequently found in transitional justice literature. First: Even though many scholars have tried to classify these trials in Argentina as transitional justice, the labeling of them as such is a critical point. Transitional justice mechanisms are initially regarded as temporary and extraordinary measures, whereas the Argentine trials are being conducted in regular and national institutions of criminal law. As I will show, in Argentina the current prosecutions should not be considered a mechanism of transitional justice. Most of the local actors I interviewed did not use the concept of transitional justice in referring to the trials. In most of the cases, either they did not even know the term or they did not see any applicability to the Argentinean case.

My second point is that according to the transitional justice paradigm, it is assumed that the implementation of certain measures and the lack of others is the result of a choice. As I will assert in this chapter, some scholars have described the implementation of trials as a matter of "preference" (Forsberg 2001). This viewpoint represents prosecutions as a special mechanism, which may be implemented or not. However, the implementation of certain measures and the lack of others is not merely the result of a "choice" or " free decision." Rather, it reveals the larger power relations and socio-political conditions underlying a given society.

I will present my critique in four sections. The first section provides a brief description of the modus operandi of the military dictatorship during the repression and introduces the justice initiatives established right after the return to a civilian government. The second section discusses the local perceptions of transitional justice, which range from unfamiliarity with the concept to severe criticism. Having analyzed local perspectives on the criminal prosecutions and their distance from the transitional justice terminology, in the third section I address some critical assumptions underlying this paradigm. The main one is the need for justification of criminal trials in cases of human rights violations in order to initiate their implementation. Finally, the article presents some brief preliminary conclusions on criminal trials in Argentina and the difficulties of viewing them through a transitional justice lens.

This article is based on seventy interviews carried out during 2011 and 2012 with key protagonists of the Argentinean trials: victims, witnesses, lawyers, members of the judicial system who participated in the trials, academics, and activists in the field of human rights. The multiregional fieldwork took place in six cities in the country (Buenos Aires, La Plata, Rosario, Córdoba, Tucumán, and Santiago del Estero).[1] For reasons of confidentiality, the interviewees have been anonymized by removing their names.

REPRESSION AND THE PATH TO HUMAN RIGHTS TRIALS IN ARGENTINA

In order to understand Argentinean justice policies it is crucial to summarize the features of the socio-political violence which took place in Argentina in the late 1970s and 1980s. Even though the military coup took place in March of 1976, repressive activities began years before. The death of president Juan Domingo Peron in July 1974 heralded a period of great escalation of violence. Under the presidency of his wife and Vice President Isabel Perón, attacks on the left became more violent and directed at targets far beyond the guerrilla forces. The activities of para-police groups such as the *Alianza Anticomunista Argentina* (Argentine Anti-Communist Alliance, Triple A), which had started in 1973, intensified and reached their peak in 1974 and 1975 (Van Drunen 2010). These death squads had a well-known base of operations in the Ministry of Social Welfare of the Perònist government, managed by José López Rega, and included members of the security forces (Feierstein 2006). The Triple A abducted, tortured and killed more than 1,000 activists and left their bodies on the roads to instill terror in society. Numerous opponents, e.g., intellectuals and journalists, went into exile after seeing their names on the death lists of the Triple A (Van Drunen 2010, 17; Robben 2005, 136–38; Gillespie 1982, 154). The political situation worsened when in January 1975 the involvement of the army in matters of internal security was extended in the operation against the rural guerrilla forces of the ERP (Ejército Revolucionario del Pueblo) in the northern province of Tucumán under the military name of "Operation Independence."[2] Many of the repressive practices that would be carried out during the military Dictatorship of 1976–1983 were applied for the first time in Tucumán (Robben 2005, 148–51; Feierstein 2006, 150). The involvement of the armed forces in internal security was taken a step further in October 1975, when the army became part of an internal security council led by Isabel Perón. In this same period, newspapers reported daily on acts of political violence, real and supposed armed confrontations between guerrillas and security forces, political assassinations and bombings (Novaro and Palermo 2003, 80). Social protests, especially from the workers' movement, further marked the period (Gillespie 1982, 203–4). In this context of economic crisis, social protest, political repression and guerrilla activity, an alliance began to emerge between powerful economic groups and the armed forces with the purpose of reorganizing the country in favor of their economical and political interests.

The coup d'état in 1976 institutionalized a system of repression justified by an alleged "struggle against subversion." Within this dictatorial framework, the modality of violence included a double system supported by State power, in which a facade of legality was combined with the clandestine or para-legal activities of "task forces" (Feierstein 2006).[3] The levels of repression that characterized this military regime, however, were unforeseeable. Abductions, torture, assassinations and even disappearances had already taken place in 1974–1975. But after 1976, the repression acquired a systematic and widespread, though clandestine, character. Arbitrary and illegal arrests, torture and the forced disappearance of people became commonplace. In most of the cases, prisoners were held in secret detention and torture centers, though some were also illegally detained in regular prisons (Comisión Nacional sobre la Desaparición de Personas, Conadep 1984). During so-called "death flights," political opponents were drugged and thrown alive into the sea from airplanes. Others were killed during summary executions and buried in mass graves, where their bodies still remain undiscovered (Conadep 1984; Verbitsky 2004).

When Argentina returned to civilian rule, the commanders-in-chief of the first three Argentine Juntas of 1976–1983 were put on trial and some of them sentenced to life imprisonment (1984–1985). However, hopes that all perpetrators would be sued were dashed by the adoption of amnesty laws that foreclosed any successful prosecution of ex-military leaders for human rights crimes. The "Full Stop" and "Due Obedience" laws were passed in 1986 and 1987, respectively, and pardons were granted by former president Carlos Menem in 1989 and 1990.[4] Even though prosecutions were impossible, human rights groups continued to gather evidence about perpetrators as well on the whereabouts of the disappeared with the goal of knowing the truth and demanding justice. In 2003, the Argentinean parliament finally revoked the amnesty laws (a decision confirmed by the Supreme Court in 2005), giving rise to a new period of trials for human rights violations—the ones that are currently taking place across the country. Along with the intense work of human rights organizations, the government of former president Néstor Kirchner (2003–2007) and Cristina Fernández de Kirchner (2007–2011, 2011–2015) initiated a new justice policy focusing on the criminal prosecution of human rights violations during the military Dictatorship.[5] Between January 2004 and September 2014, 114 verdicts were issued by different federal courts in almost all of the twenty-three Argentine provinces (Prosecution Unit 2014). During this period, more than 500 former members of the security forces (military and police) and some civilians (among them a Catholic priest, a doctor, and a judge) were tried (Special Coordination Unit of the Public Prosecutor 2014). After many years of impunity, the introduction of human rights trials in 2003 marked a significant change in State policy regarding the crimes of the past and their perpetrators.

DEVELOPMENT OF HUMAN RIGHTS TRIALS: CHALLENGES AND ADVANCES

The human rights trials in Argentina are oral and public, and are conducted like any other criminal prosecution. Oral and public proceedings are instituted only in cases of criminal offenses. These proceedings are divided into two stages: an investigation stage and a stage consisting of an oral and public trial before a three-judge court. Each stage has its own judges and prosecutors. At the first stage—the investigation stage—documentary evidence is collected, witnesses are interrogated, expert reports are prepared, and the prosecutor and judge make formal charges against the accused. Later, witnesses, the victims and the accused are interrogated. The defense and the prosecution make their closing arguments and the court proceeds to read the judgment—the acquittal or conviction of the accused.

The dynamics and political difficulties of the trials reflect social and political struggles in the country.[6] Many interviewees perceive the current trials as the result of a decades-long struggle on behalf of human right movements which finally found some resonance in the governments of Nestor and Cristina Kirchner.

An interviewee and survivor of the clandestine center known as “El Olimpo” in the city of Buenos Aires, who participated in the trials as claimant, explained the political role of the Kirchner government as follows:

> I think it’s dialectic. The human rights organizations have already been struggling since the military Dictatorship. The [human rights] organizations were

> always [there]. What I believe is that when Menem passed the pardons, the human rights organizations were there, but he did not care. When Alfonsín passed the Due Obedience and Full Stop laws, there were the same human rights organizations that there are no. . . . [But he] passed the impunity laws anyway. I think it is a political decision to say, "Whom do I hear at the time of making such an important political decision?" The human rights organizations were always here. "Who do they listen to? To those who want impunity? . . . Or those who are struggling for truth and justice?" I think there is a political decision of who to listen to.[7]

Many interviewees understand the launching of trials as a "political decision," but that does not mean that the conducting of those trials afterward is political or "victor's justice," as many detractors of the trials contend.[8] Once started, the trials follow the normal course and typical procedural steps of any regular trial in Argentina. One of the elements that actually makes this kind of decision a political one is the previous implementation of amnesty laws. Those laws were the first political decision, since they disrupted the normal legal course that these cases should have taken in any criminal justice system in which a violation of the law was at issue. Amnesty laws and pardons belong to a special category of laws. These are not laws which prohibit a certain conduct like torturing or killing but, on the contrary, they create a legal—and political—exception of those prohibitions for, initially, a specific group of people: the perpetrators. In this sense, when asking some interviewees if they consider the conduction of trials "right," one of them, a son of disappeared parents of the city of La Plata who is a claimant in the current trials, answered: "It is not a question of right or wrong. It [a trial] is what usually occurs when someone did something wrong."[9] From this perspective, criminal trials are perceived as that "should happen" when a crime is committed in a society with a functioning criminal justice system. These kinds of affirmations challenge one of the underlying assumptions of transitional justice scholarship, which conceives prosecutions as one instrument among others, whose implementation needs to be justified depending on their positive or negative effects. In Argentina, that "political decision" for the reopening of trials was a decision in favor of normalization of justice—in contrast to the exceptionality that amnesty laws involved in a regular justice system. The fact that trials are being conducted under the ordinary laws, procedures and institutions of the judicial system provides them and their resulting sentences with legitimization. A claimant survivor of the city of Buenos Aires refers to the high credibility of the trials and their judgments:

> When there is an acquittal or a sentence to 25 years or life imprisonment (in the current trials), it is being shown that when there is a penalty it is because the crime was proven conclusively. And no one can question that evidence. . . . It is not a show. . . . The judges have to find the evidence . . . it is not just

> another formality. Things [crimes] have to be proven. And these things are being proved. [10]

A judicial process involves carrying out investigations that otherwise would not have taken place in order to prove the crimes being prosecuted. Due to a widespread acceptance of the judicial methodology and State character of judicial institutions, criminal trials confer heightened legitimacy to the facts and crimes as contained in the judicial record.

CRITICAL DISTANCE TO THE TRANSITIONAL JUSTICE RHETORIC

When discussing the pros and cons of the trials, the interviewees mentioned different aspects regarding the relevance of the judicial processes as well as those factors that they perceived as meaningful obstacles (such as the slowness of the judicial system, the threats and assaults to victims and witnesses, the decreasing public attendance at the trials and the poor media coverage). If at all, they only referred sporadically to the transitional justice terminology. When I directly asked the interviewees what were their perceptions of the trials as a transitional justice mechanism, most of them did not even know what the concept of transitional justice meant. This was especially the case of victims of human rights violations participating in the trials, the majority of whom argued they had never heard of it. They do not identify different types of justice. In most of the cases, when I referred to the concept, they asked me "What do you mean by transitional justice?" The relevant question for them is whether there is "justice" or not in the ordinary criminal justice system. The lack of knowledge about this transitional justice terminology showed some nuances according to different factors, such as the local context of the interviewees and their level of participation in social and human rights organizations. The unfamiliarity with the transitional justice concepts was thus even higher in those cases in which the interviewees lived in rural areas, especially in northern provinces of the country, or if they had little or no participation in social and human rights organizations.

However, the ones who more often recognized the term "transitional justice" were academics, judges and lawyers. Remarkably, most of them related the concept of "transitional justice" to distant and negative experiences, especially regarding the Truth and Reconciliation Commission (TRC) in the South African process in the 1990s. None of them referred to the local prosecutions as a transitional justice policy. When I asked about the transitional justice concept and its absence in Argentina, a social scientist in Buenos Aires explained to me: "Do not get confused. Transitional justice is what happened in South Africa or Colombia, where there were reduced sentences, but not here."[11] The paradigm was thus being associated with a lack of ordinary prosecutions, a failure to enforce the ordinary criminal code, and reduced sentences—in short, a synonym of impunity.

Transitional justice is also linked to other questionable notions such as "reconciliation," which is a very discredited concept in Argentina since it is also understood as lack of justice. A federal judge of the current prosecutions in the city of La Plata described it as follows:

> Transitional justice, beyond the good intentions of those who implement it, is very similar to the laws in favor of reconciliation processes. . . . I link this to the South African process and . . . their reconciliation law. . . . Victims, according to my experience, find themselves limited in their possibilities to make a decision. And this means accepting proposals ending up in impunity. In South Africa to reconciliate with those who for decades, massacred, tortured, murdered and raped the population has had a huge social cost . . . , the cost of impunity, which will transmit from generation to generation.[12]

All the interviewees reject transitional justice because they understand it as impunity as opposed to the justice exerted by regular tribunals. The same interviewee stressed:

> Any other proposal [different to the regular justice system], in the name of . . . all these proposals are made on behalf of peacekeeping, etc. . . . [any other proposal] leads to impunity. At the end of the analysis you wonder . . . but then won't we do anything against this man who tortured?"[13] Interviewees perceived those distant experiences of transitional justice as negative cases and many even felt pity for those societies involved in transitional justice policies. A lawyer of the province of Santiago del Estero compares the local experience with the South Africans' and regrets: "Poor Africans, they suffered the Apartheid and after that they did not have any justice. Poor Mandela, he will die without seeing a single trial."[14]

Thus, the concept of transitional justice, when known by the local actors participating in the current trials, is not perceived as a familiar, beneficial or fair phenomenon. There is no identification of the current justice policy with those kinds of processes abroad which are always identified with impunity.

It is also interesting that the concept of transitional justice is neither applied to amnesty laws nor to justice policies in Argentina. None of the interviewees described the amnesty laws or the National Commission on the Disappearance of Persons (Conadep) as transitional justice measures, while international scholarship refers to them as "typical instruments of transitional justice." Locals describe the current trials as "trials for crimes against humanity" (in Spanish "juicios por crímenes de lesa humanidad") and the amnesty laws as the "impunity laws" but never as transitional justice policies. Even the Conadep commission has not even been identified by locals actors as a classical "truth commission," as it is usually described in most of the transitional justice scholarship (see for example Hayner 2002).

Only international scholars (e.g., Kritz 1995; Teitel 2000; 2003; Sikkink 2011) or local authors publishing in international outlets (e.g., Parenti and Pellegrino 2009; Balardini, Collins, and Burt 2013) have used the term "transitional justice" to describe the Argentinean reckoning with its military past. As Arthur explains, the field of transitional justice and its conceptual boundaries emerged in the late 1980s at an international level to describe local modalities to deal with the crimes of the State, where authoritarian regimes had been replaced by more democratic ones (2009). Even though more than two decades have gone by since then, the use of transitional justice terminology remains a foreign concept for local practitioners and academics in Argentina. Indeed, this terminology has barely been used in the local scholarship or official documents and NGOs' reports regarding the current criminal process of the previous amnesty laws. Official documents, for instance, like the report of the Special Coordination Unit of the Public Prosecutor and the annual reports of the NGO Center for Legal and Social Studies (Centro de Estudios Legales y Sociales—CELS),[15] also litigating in the trials, do not utilize transitional justice rhetoric.

Having analyzed the absence of the transitional justice paradigm in the local perceptions and understanding of the justice policies, I will now address and question some underlying assumptions of the transitional justice concept. Criminal prosecutions are standard procedure in any regular justice system. Thus, the question needs to be raised: why the need to justify the implementation of ordinary justice instruments, and present them as extraordinary ad hoc policies?

THE TRANSITIONAL JUSTICE PARADIGM: WHAT NEED FOR A JUSTIFICATION OF TRIALS?

According to the transitional justice paradigm, accountability is pursued by a variety of mechanisms, such as: holding trials in domestic or international courts, and also granting amnesties and reduced sentences; vetting and purging wrongdoers from public or security posts; creating truth commissions; providing reparation to victims; and offering public apologies (Kritz 1995; Teitel 2000; Posner and Vermeule 2003). Within this framework, criminal trials also become a matter of a "preference" among many other options (see for example Ratner and Abrams 1997; Forsberg 2001; Olsen, Payne, and Reiter 2010; Sikkink 2011). According to Forsberg, there is no ideal procedure to deal with the crimes of the past because "different cases require different measures . . . only a few have offered guidelines regarding the factors relevant to the choice of strategy" to deal with the past (Forsberg

2001, 66, 67). Similarly, Ratner and Abrams state that "there are different ways to uphold the principle of accountability" (1997, 22, 23). This focus, which I call the "choice perspective," tends to present trials of State agents and the rights to justice, proclaimed in many international treaties, as a matter of contingency, or as the result of factors such as culture and religion and not as regular mechanism of the rule of law (Benedict 1996, 222; Forsberg 2001, 61). Criminal prosecutions in the frame of the transitional justice model are conceived as an extraordinary mechanism which can be adopted or not depending on the evaluation of different factors. In this framework, several international organizations provide advice to post-conflict societies, offering them a package of transitional justice standardized mechanisms (truth commissions, monuments building, workshops, amnesties, trials, etc.) which, according to them, would be the proper ones for those countries. This standardization of "options," usually proposed by foreign agencies, involves different challenges and risks. One of them is the exclusion of local realities and traditions, needs, and interests (Figari Layús 2014).

On the other hand, all these standardized "optional" mechanisms underlying the transitional justice discourse assume that the implementation of any of them must be properly justified and explained. The justification of the strategy to deal with the crimes of the past depends on their success, i.e., whether they have a positive or negative impact on different aspects (Forsberg 2001, 68). This could even be understandable in the case of mechanisms which, in fact, are actually extraordinary and specific in a post-conflict society (such as truth commissions or reparations programs). However, trials are not specific and extraordinary mechanisms in a society with a system of criminal justice. Thus, why justify a mechanism that already belongs to the regular functioning of the country's judiciary such as criminal trials? Is it not the absence of ordinary prosecutions that should be justified? Since the question seems to be excluded from the transitional justice literature, there exist some debates on the success and effects of prosecutions between those scholars who argue in favor of the positive impact of trials and those who question their scope and impact.[16]

In this regard, the so-called "Legal Paradigm" considers the use of law as the most appropriate tool to provide reparation to victims. Many scholars and activists conceive trials and the right to justice as being the centerpiece of social repair to victims' rights and needs (Baristain 2009, 33; Edelman 2010, 107; Lagos 2010, 116) and to promote the rule of law after mass atrocities (Orentlicher 1991; Sriram 2005; Sikkink 2011). According to them, trials dealing with human rights violations may contribute to rebuilding communities after mass violence and atrocities through their pursuit of goals, such as: 1) to discover and publicize the truth of past atrocities; 2) to punish perpetrators, thereby preventing future human rights violations; 3) to respond to victims' needs or wishes; 4) to promote the rule of law in emerging democracies; and 5) to promote reconciliation (see De Greiff 2008; Van Boven 2005; Orentlicher 1991 for a representative sample of these views). From a quantitative perspective, one of the main works on the institutional consequences of domestic trials is the series of studies by Kathryn Sikkink analyzing the development of a "justice cascade," a much-cited term that describes the increase of criminal accountability for human rights violations worldwide (Sikkink 2011; Sikkink and Booth Walling 2007; Lutz and Sikkink 2001). Similarly, Olsen, Payne and Reiter (2010) analyzed the impact of prosecutions but also of amnesties and truth commissions. In their quantitative analysis, these authors disagree with Sikkink's work by arguing that trials only improve human rights indexes if combined with amnesties. The question must be raised: why is it necessary to justify prosecutions in cases of human rights violations? Secondly, is it really possible to measure their impact? According to Forsberg (2001, 68), one of the main problems of a justice policy is "the lack of agreement about the standards of success."

This question of the "desirability" of human rights trials depending on their effects, e.g., whether they have positive or negative impact, puts the actual implementation of judicial processes at stake. These arguments stress the need to justify why prosecutions should take place or not. That is the case, for instance, in the work of Sikkink who analyzed the impact of domestic trials by evaluating (in different countries) whether the growing frequency of trials is associated with positive developments in democracy and human rights (Sikkink 2011).

Yet though these scholars make some well-intentioned efforts to describe the benefits of human rights trials, it raises the question: why do these kinds of criminal trials require justification? Does anybody question the "desirability" or "success" of ordinary criminal trials to deal with ordinary crime? The question arises when the people on trial are those who still have power. Only in the prosecution of powerful actors such as former state agents does it become a matter of discussion. This "desirability" issue tends to reinforce a legal asymmetry in the implementation of criminal law: the question is usually raised to people who belong to marginalized sectors of society but is used sparingly against State officials, entrepreneurs and powerful groups in society. However, it is interesting that there are all these debates regarding the "desirability" of trials, which makes invisible the other "face of the coin," i.e., the "desirability" of impunity and its consequences, since the lack of the former leads automatically to the latter.

CONCLUSION

Justice in the courts is one of the most prominent and desired mechanisms to obtain accountability for human rights violations, but it is also one of the most difficult to obtain. Political constraints and asymmetrical power relations in favor of the perpetrators are some of the main obstacles. Prosecutions of human rights violations are often considered one of the essential instruments of transitional justice. Many scholars, especially at an international level, have tried to classify the current post-dictatorship trials in Argentina as transitional justice policies. However, labeling them such is a critically misleading identification. As this article has shown, the Argentinean trials are being conducted in regular and national institutions of criminal law, and they are not considered a mechanism of transitional justice in the national context. Most of the victims interviewed did not even know what transitional justice meant. Even the few interviewees who knew the concept—mainly scholars and lawyers—always linked it to distant and negative regimes like Colombia and South Africa, countries that in their view lacked *any* justice. The interviewees understand transitional justice as synonym of impunity. Although the term "transitional justice" is employed by international scholarship to describe Argentina's justice policies, it is not recognized or used by local activists, policy makers or scholars. Thus, the concept has not been adopted by Argentineans. It remains—for those who know of it at all—a distant and foreign category employed at an international level to describe other countries' failed experiences. Transitional justice is linked to concepts of impunity, which contrast with the understanding of the regular criminal prosecutions in Argentina. The interviewees associate the concept of justice with regular criminal prosecutions.

Some scholars have described the implementation of trials as a matter of a "preference" or "free decision." This approach presents prosecutions as a special mechanism that may be implemented depending on their positive or negative effects. In the transitional justice framework, trials can be negotiated with perpetrators leading to reduced sentences, small numbers of perpetrators on trials, temporary tribunals, etc. The result of these kinds of soft trials has been their very limited scope and impact at a social level, and specifically for the reparation and acknowledgment of victims.

By contrast, trials in Argentina are not the result of negotiation with the perpetrators. And the fact that they are being conducted under the ordinary laws and institutions of the judicial system shows a meaningful difference from the trials framed by transitional justice discourse. In the eyes of the victims, the use of the ordinary legal framework to deal with the crimes of former power holders gives these processes legitimacy. Thus, the inclusion of prosecutions in the frame of the regular criminal justice system and not under the modality of transitional justice is an important step toward the construction of a norm when it comes to dealing with human rights violations. Perhaps only then, human rights violations will also stop being the rule and become, if they exist all, an exception.

NOTES

This article is a product of the research project No. 240984: "Narrative of Terror and Disappearance," located at the University of Konstanz and funded by the European Research Council (ERC).

1. These cities correspond to five different provinces of Argentina: the provinces of Buenos Aires, Santa Fe, Córdoba, Tucumán, and Santiago del Estero.

2. In February 1975, the government of Isabel Perón gave its official approval to army involvement, as key members of her government signed the Decree Law No. 261, which authorized the armed forces to "annihilate" the rural guerrilla insurgency in the northwest province of Tucumán.

3. A series of laws framed the repressive activities. Among others, the historian Gabriela Águila describes Law No 21264, which punished with up to ten years of prison those who "publicly, and by any means, promote collective violence and/or cause a breach of peace," Law No 21460 which established that the Armed Forces would investigate subversive crimes, Law No 21461 which constituted special court-martials for subversive activities, etc. (Aguila 2006, 176).

4. Impunity, as a political phenomenon, assumes different forms. Impunity may be de jure or de facto. De jure impunity arises directly or indirectly from laws or regulations, especially amnesty or presidential pardons. By contrast, *de facto impunity* is the result of factual implementation mechanisms or social and political constraints which impede criminal prosecution and punishment (Ambos 1999, 34). The amnesty laws did not extend to the following three offenses: kidnapping of children, theft, and sexual abuse (CELS 2012, 34). Thus, it was possible to carry out trials against the suspects of such crimes. However, only criminal trials took place in the case of child appropriation. Cases of theft and sexual crimes were not reported and prosecuted.

5. There have been some controversies regarding the human rights' center politics of both Kirchners' governments, especially from some opposition political groups. They have questioned the Kirchners' human rights' policy, arguing that they used it politically to obtain greater political support , especially from human rights organizations (Majul 2010).

6. In Argentina there was a combination of amnesty and prosecution. There was not a uniform movement from justice (trial of the "Juntas Militares" in 1984–85) to impunity (amnesty laws in 1986–7 and pardons in 1989–91) and again to justice (annulment of the amnesty laws 2003 and 2005), but a simultaneous coexistence and tension of legal and de facto impunity, minimal accountability and implementation of some reparations laws that expressed the contradictions of the different political interests in a society.

7. Interview conducted in the City of Buenos Aires, March 2011. This and all otherwise specified translations were made by the author.

8. Among those who oppose the trials and describe them as a form of "revenge" are mainly right-wing groups and conservative political parties who justify the military repression in the 1970s (Diario Norte 2010, Telam 2015).

9. Interview conducted in the City of La Plata, September 2012.

10. Interview conducted in the City of Buenos Aires, March 2011.

11. Interview conducted in the City of Buenos Aires, February 2011.

12. Interview conducted in the City of La Plata, March 2011.

13. Ibidem.

14. Interview conducted in City of Santiago del Estero, April 2011.

15. The Center for Legal and Social Studies (CELS) is one of the Argentina's leading human rights organizations. Since its creation in 1979, in the midst of the country's military Dictatorship, CELS has strived to eradicate the nation's systemic human rights violations by investigating, documenting, denouncing, and litigating in favor of fundamental rights and accountability. With Argentina's return to democracy in 1983, CELS also began working to strengthen the state's capacity to protect human rights, weighing in on the design and implementation of public policies while maintaining its critical necessary distance.

16. In general terms, several scholars stress that trials are not as effective as other justice mechanisms. For example, the focus of trials on individual criminals responsible for ordering

or carrying out acts of mass violence would not address all the responsibilities involved: particularly, perhaps, the aspect of systematicity and/or State instigation or complicity (Jaspers 1979; Arendt 1990; 2003; Hayner 2002). In this stream of thinking, the so-called "justice vs. peace dilemma" suggests that the conduction of trials would destabilize democracy and block peace attempts (Huntington 1991). Similarly, some scholars argue that justice has to be sacrificed in order to get some truth about the past (Hayner 2001). At this point, both assumptions seem to be out of date, not recognizing a paradigm shift in Latin America and more characteristic of the early 1990s.

SELECTED BIBLIOGRAPHY

Aguila, Gabriela, "Dictatorship, Society, and Genocide in Argentina: Repression in Rosario, 1976–1983." *Journal of Genocide Research*, vol. 8, no. 2 (2006):169–80.

Ambos, Kai, Impunidad y Derecho Penal Internacional, Buenos Aires, AD – HOC SRL, 1999.

Arendt, Hannah, Totalitarianism. Part Three of the Origins of Totalitarianism. New York: Harvest Book, 1985.

Arthur, Paige, "How 'Transitions' Reshaped Human Rights: A Conceptual History of Transitional Justice." Human Rights Quarterly, vol. 31, no. 2 (2009): 321–67.

Balardini, Lorena, Caths Collins, and Jo-Marie Burt, "Mapping Perpetrator Prosecutions in Latin America." *Journal of Transitional Justice*, vol. 7, no. 1 (2013): 8–28.

Benedict, Ruth, The Chrysanthemum and the Sword. Rutland, Charles E. Tuttle, 1996.

CELS - Centro de Estudios Legales y Sociales, Informe 2012 sobre la situación de los derechos humanos en Argentina. Buenos Aires: Siglo Ventiuno Editores S. A., 2012.

Crawford, Adam, and Anthea Hucklesby, "Introduction. Compliance and legitimacy in criminal justice." In Legitimacy and Compliance in Criminal Justice, edited by Adam Crawford and Anthea Hucklesby, New York: Routledge, 2013: 1–7.

De Greiff, Pablo, "Justice and Reparations." In The Handbook of Reparation, edited by Pablo de Greiff. New York: Oxford University Press, 2008: 451–77.

Diario Norte, "Los juicios por delitos de lesa humanidad no buscan justicia, sino venganza." December 13, 2010, accessed April 17, 2015, http://www.diarionorte.com/article/53306/los-juicios-por-delitos-de-lesa-humanidad-no-buscan-justicia-sino-venganza.

Edelman, Lucila, "Testigos." In Sur, Dictadura y Después . . . Elaboración psicosocial y clínica de los traumas colectivos, edited by Kordon, Diana, Edelman, Lucila, Lagos Dario and Kersner, Daniel, Buenos Aires: EATPI. Psicolibro Ediciones, 2010: 107–13.

Feierstein, Daniel, "Political Violence in Argentina and Its Genocidal Characteristics." *Journal of Genocide Research*, vol. 8, no. 2 (2006): 149–68.

Figari Layús, Rosario, "Implementing Transitional Justice: Insights from Latin America." In *Moving Beyond: Towards Transitional Justice in the Bangsamoro Peace Process*, edited by ForumZFD Civil Peace Service, 2014: 16–20.

Fletcher, Laurel and Harvey Weinstein, "Violence and Social Repair: Rethinking the Contribution of Justice to Reconciliation." *Human Rights Quarterly*, vol. 24, no. 3, (2002): 573–639.

Gloppen, Siri, Roberto Gargarella, and Elin Skaar, "Introduction: The accountability function of the courts in new democracies." In *Democratization and the Judiciary*, London: Frank Cass Publishers, 2004: 1–6.

Hayner, Priscilla, *Unspeakable Truths: Facing the Challenge of Truth Commissions*, New York: Routledge, 2002.

Huntington, Samuel, *The Third Wave: Democratization in the Late Twentieth Century*. University of Oklahoma Press, 1991.

Kritz, Neil J. (ed.), *Transitional Justice: How Emerging Democracies Reckon with Former Regimes* Vol. 1. Washington DC: United States Institute of Peace Press, 1995.

Lagos, Mariana, "Juicio a Represores. Testimonios y Testigos. Algumas implicancias psicológicas y psicosociales." In *Sur, Dictadura y Después . . . Elaboración psicosocial y clínica de los traumas colectivos*, edited by Kordon, Diana, Edelman, Lucila, Lagos Dario and Kersner, Daniel, Buenos Aires: EATPI. Psicolibro Ediciones, 2010: 114–25.

Majul, Luis, "Son los Kirchner los dueños de los derechos humanos?," La Nación, December 16, 2014, accessed December 16, 2014, http://www.lanacion.com.ar/1247001-son-los-kirchner-los-duenos-de-los-derechos-humanos.

Neier, Aryeh, "What Should Be Done About the Guilty?," *New York Review of Books*, vol. 37, no. 1. February 1. 1990.

Nikken, Pedro, "El concepto de Derechos Humanos." Estudios de Derechios Humanos vol. 1 (1994): 15–35.

Novaro, Marcos and Palermo, Vicente, La dictadura militar [1976–1983]: del golpe de estado a la restauración democrática, Buenos Aires: Paidós, 2003.

Olsen, Tricia, Leigh Payne, and Andrew G. Reiter, *Transitional Justice in Balance: Comparing Processes, Weighing Efficacy*. Washington DC: United States Institute of Peace Press, 2010.

Orentlicher, Diane, "Settling Accounts: The Duty to Prosecute Human Rights Violations of a Prior Regime." Vol. 100 *Yale Law Journal* (1991): 25–37.

Parenti, Pablo, and Lisandro Pellegrino, "Argentina." In *Justicia de Transición Informes de América Latina, Alemania, Italia y España*, edited by Kai Ambos, Ezequiel Malarino and Gisela Elsner. Berlin: Konrad Adenauer Foundaiton, 2009: 133–52.

Posner, Eric, and Adrian Vermeule, "Transitional Justice as Ordinary Justice." Public Law and Legal Theory: Working Paper 40, University of Chicago (2003): 3–50.

Ratner, Steven and Jason Abrams, *Accountability for Human Rights Atrocities in International Law: Beyond the Nuremberg Legacy*. Oxford: Clarendon Press, 1997.

Robben, Antonius, *Political Violence and Trauma in Argentina*. Philadelphia: University of Pensylvania Press, 2005.

Sikkink, Kathryn, *The Justice Cascade: How Human Rights Prosecutions Are Changing World Politics*. New York: W. W. Norton, 2011.

Special Coordination Unit of the Public Prosecutor, Informe sobre el estado de las causas por violaciones a los derechos humanos cometidas durante el terrorismo de Estado. Actualización al 18 de julio del 2014. Buenos Aires, 2014.

Sriram, Chandra Lekha, *Globalizing Justice for Mass Atrocities: A Revolution in Accountability*. New York: Routledge, 2005.

Teitel, Ruth, *Transitional Justice*. New York: Oxford University Press, 2000.

———, "Transitional Justice Genealogy." *Harvard Human Rights Journal*, vol. 16 (2003): 69–94.

Telam, "Carrió cuestionó los juicios de lesa humanidad y dijo que ser presidenta impulsaría la revisión de las cosas juzgadas," April 11, 2015, accessed April 17, 2015, http://www.telam.com.ar/notas/201504/101159-carrio-cuestiono-los-juicios-de-lesa-humanidad-y-dijo-que-ser-presidenta-impulsaria-la-revision-de-las-cosas-juzgadas-irritas.html.

Van Boven, Theo, "Basic Principles and Guidelines on the Right to a Remedy and Reparation for Victims of Gross Violations of International Human Rights Law and Serious Violations of International Humanitarian Law." UN Doc. E/CN.4/2005 L, 2005.

Van Drunen, Saskia, *Struggling with the Past: The Human Rights Movement and the Politics of Memory in Post-Dictatorship Argentina (1983–2006)*. Amsterdam: Rozenberg Publishers. Preface, 2010: 15-19.

Verbitsky, Horacio, El vuelo: una forma cristiana de muerte, confesiones de un oficial de la armada. Buenos Aires: Ed. Sudamericana, 2004.

Part II

Brazil

Chapter Two

Scopes and Limits to the Transitional Justice Discourse in Brazil

Edson Teles and Renan Quinalha

Depending on the kind of transition, and especially on the continuing political power of the members of the previous regime, either justice measures can be taken or impunity be guaranteed. Adopting this tension as a reference point, the so-called transitional justice concept emerged, located at the frontier between political and legal sciences.[1] The term "transitional justice" is a discursive framework that deals with political responses to a violent historical past in which justice and social transformations are confined to an exceptional period. In this transitional moment a nation is no longer under the aegis of an authoritarian regime, yet democratic institutions are not strong enough either. After moments of state violence there is the need to adopt a series of measures aimed at strengthening democratic relations. It is a moment of urgent negotiations. In these historical and contingent periods, so-called "political transitions," the new governments are supposed to adapt the ideals of justice, to investigate human rights violations, and to reform political institutions. With the double objective of dealing with the victims' claims for justice and truth and, at the same time of avoiding the risk of destabilization of the old regime, a specific kind of discourse was elaborated able to authorize governmental practices to manage this exceptional period. This goal of these transitional politics' would be to ensure the legitimacy of the new regime, including the recognition of commitments made during the negotiations that allowed the new democracy to emerge.

The researcher Ruti Teitel has based her definition of the transitional justice concept on three historical moments: the first is the post-WWII and Nuremberg Trials period, when trials were structured in an exceptional way and were international in character; second, the transition after authoritarian regimes in Latin America, Africa, Asia and Eastern Europe, when negotiations and attempts to promote justice were marked by local and national solutions, always in the form of negotiations between the old and the new political actors; and a third period, whose main characteristic is that the exception became standardized and institutionalized.[2] Exception becomes a rule accepted by international law and by new, democratic governments, exactly by taking into account the limits imposed by the transition negotiations.[3]

With few variations, the transitional justice discourse includes four central ideas. The first one deals with the right to reparation, be it financial or symbolic, individual or collective. The second one, the right to memory, includes investigation commissions and homages to the victims, or measures such as the building of memorial sites. The third measure of transitional justice, the right to truth, comprises access to information about the repressive organs or files located or produced by truth commissions. A fourth measure includes the right to justice, and consists of the investigation of facts and the enforcement of legal responsibility of those responsible for human rights' violations. These are the four general lines of the concept according to its traditional understanding, which, despite being disputed, does comprise a minimal consensus that has been commonly accepted among researchers and public officials. With that in mind, it is now interesting to examine some of the criticism that has been leveled against the field's literature.

CRITICISM OF THE TRADITIONAL DEFINITION OF "TRANSITIONAL JUSTICE"

A major point of criticism relates to the inaccuracy of the terms "transition" and "justice"—which are imprecise in themselves and even worse when combined. Transitions usually have suffered interferences from former dictators. The new democratic leaders could only initiate the process of power transference and institutional reform, once they had entered a pact with the old regime. In these periods of political contingence, old authoritarian forces kept a certain control over the economy, maintained political power, and continued to control the armed forces. In the social imaginary, they represented a permanent threat, because people feared the possibility of a new coup, and a destabilization of the new, more democratic regime. According to this perspective, the choice for consolidating democracy trumps the victims' demands for their right to truth and justice.

The concept's most remarkable limitations include: the way the relation between rights and politics is conceived of; the dominance of the State and of legalism; the linearity of the concept of both transition and democratization; the selectivity of some human rights' violations and exclusion of others; and lastly, the normativity and universality of the concept and its indiscriminate application in very different conflict settings. Let us take a closer look at each of these shortcomings: The most traditional definition of transitional justice assumes, uncritically and without "hard evidence," that in transitional moments rights are more influenced by politics than in times of stability. However, critics have argued that in reality politics inform rights in any context. The transitional justice field's privileging of legalism and of the state have also been questioned. The fact that such a traditional conception implies a certain notion of progress and an idea of state performance as a kind of logical and coherent action have likewise been criticized.[4] The difficulty in accurately pointing out the initial and final moments of the transitional process, which could delimitate the peculiar moment of (transitional) justice, gives further weight to that criticism. Yet another problem is the concept of democratization—and also that of transition—generically adopted. They are usually conceived of as linear, and thus, incapable of grasping form of historical continuity. McEvoy points out the remarkable dominance of legalism shown in traditional analyses by arguing that "transitional justice has become over-dominated by a narrow, legalistic lens."[5]

Another point of criticism is that transitional justice mechanisms are too selective and exclusive, since they are limited to human rights violations in the realm of civil and political rights. From this point of view, this minimalist conservatism silences and even hides other kinds of social and economic suffering imposed by authoritarian regimes.[6] We might add the silencing of sexuality or gender differences, including violence directed at the gay, lesbian, bisexual and transgender population that is usually ignored or trivialized by the current transitional justice approaches.[7]

Here it is worth mentioning the words of Hugo Merwe, who states that "official transitional mechanisms are generally narrow in scope, focusing on particular forms of abuse, designated time frames, and specific categories of perpetrators. The field is also usually defined as criminal, either in terms of international law or according to the law of the affected state . . . . This focus effectively sidelines the more common economic or social kinds of abuses."[8] Therefore this author affirms that transitional justice is a conservative term, and one that usually only befalls victims and perpetrators of physical violence. Going further, he argues that "transitional justice mechanisms have been seriously criticized as a form of ideological obfuscation of underlying social injustices."[9]

Further critics have pointed to the problematic standardization and universality, whether implied or explicit, imbued in the transitional justice rhetoric.[10] Transitional measures, these critics claim, are often presented as democratization formulas, created after models that could be used in very different realities. In more recent reflections, the model of combining preexistent mechanisms has been problematized, but only to a limited degree. The traditional vision ultimately reduces the possibilities of what could be a rich and complex experience to a kind of "toolkit."[11] That way universal elements would be available for mobilization in preconceived combinations by the different actors in their local realities. The problem is that the mediation of rules between the universal and the particular are not properly worked out, which leads to an enormous casuistry, and an arbitrary judgment of each case. The indiscriminate use of a model in highly specific contexts, involving actors with conflicting interests, disrespects the specific content and historical character of each post-violence setting.

Still a bigger problem is the assumption that the models would work anywhere, despite the fact that the political regime changes occur in very different historical contexts; from the pioneering international post-war trials to South-American dictatorships, from post-apartheid South Africa and to the downfall of Eastern Europe regimes, from the Yugoslavian wars and armed conflicts in Colombia to the recent mobilizations in various countries in the Middle East. A universal model cannot be equally applicable or effective in such diverse contexts.

One could argue that the models have been applied to countries which have gone through transitions or conflicts in different periods of their history. For instance: to modulate the same concept of transitional justice for Brazil, which has gone through an agreed and negotiated redemocratization decades ago; for Germany, that emerged from Nazism more than half a century ago; and for the very recent experiences of political change in the Arabic countries, inevitably overstretches the concept. Above all, doing so would obstruct the understanding of those situations, obviously all very different from each other from any analytical angle. This very palpable overstretching risks applying standardizing assumptions from one context to another and underestimating the particularities of these different processes.

Some authors acknowledge that transitional justice politics in the form of models have brought some benefits, in spite of the limitations they set for the concept. Despite their reservations toward the traditional view of transitional justice (and its variations), these analysts distance themselves from the concept as based on specific mechanisms and on standardized expectations, and instead request to effectively test these hypotheses. They propose the elaboration of an "empirically founded theory on transitional justice."[12] This approach is suggested by the historian Elster for whom a standardizing theory of transitional justice would necessarily collide with the peculiar temporal and spatial experiences. To him, "the context-dependence of the phenomena [is] an insuperable obstacle to generalizations."[13] To Elster's mind, however, the difficulty of establishing a law and a general theory on the matter does not impede the attempt to "to identify recurring patterns of behavior." It must be said that such a perspective does not necessarily imply the universalization of particular patterns, generally observed in an indiscriminate fashion.[14]

That way, in order to understand why transitional justice patterns have taken distinct forms in different transitions, Elster considers that "the analysis of transitional justice is part of the empirical study of justice."[15]

Further criticism is directed at the concept of "transitional justice from above," in contrast to those models that try to emphasize civil society participation.[16] McGregor and McEvoy, for instance, reject the view "from above," and propose analyzing "transitional justice 'on the ground' in the communities or organizations which have been directly affected by violent conflict."[17] The main objective, thus, would be to break away from the "looking down" approach. That approach tries to reach what is "below the gaze of transitional justice's formal institutions" attributing to the term *from below* "a 'resistant' or 'mobilizing' character to the actions of community, civil society and other non-state actors in their opposition to powerful hegemonic political, social or economic forces."[18] Those criticisms intend to recover the relevance of civil society mobilization in the transitional processes, diminishing the concept's standardizing dimension as well as its emphasis on state institutions.

Regarding the Brazilian case, among the limitations of the transitional justice concept, it is interesting to note the hegemonic narrative that privileges the state over the disappeared persons families' social movements, rendering the victims' fight invisible or less important (for exceptions see Santos 2009 and Atencio 2014). Besides, there is a noticeable difficulty in the reparation politics in incorporating a broader look on the various forms of human rights violations and on the amplification of victims' categories. In the light of the limits of the traditional understanding of transitional justice, it is interesting to analyze how this discourse has been imported to Brazil and how it has impacted upon memory and justice initiatives organized by state and local level politicians.

TRANSITION THE BRAZILIAN WAY

Concerning both the discourse and the political mechanisms related to transitional justice, two features have become increasingly relevant, lending a central ambiguity to the subject: victims' rights stand out and appear as an imperative to be considered in the transition process; and yet, at the same time, forces that promoted violence in the previous regime remain present. These two contradictory realities require a method to ease the tension and hostility, in order to facilitate the negotiation into a new democracy. Under the surface of this kind of pacifist discourse lies the structure of a constant state of exception, which juggles demands for justice with political blockades. This paradoxical situation can be translated into the motto: in order to make justice, it is necessary to limit it first. That way, the democratic order is violated when criminal law is not applied, allowing restricted or emergency-only access to victims, due to the specific conditions of transition negotiations. It is also an exception to the rule of law because the same forces that have held important roles in the repressive structure of the previous regime are still accepted in the democratic game.

Brazil is a good example of an ongoing state of exception during the transition process, and this would fundamentally flaw its new "democracy" (Teles and Safatle 2010). The official pro-regime party (ARENA) created a new political group with a democratic varnish, so as to be a part of the transition, and to this day that group has been represented in the various governments constituted in Brasília. Worse than that is the fact that not a single perpetrator has ever been convicted or jailed, nor has the military institution ever been reformed in an effective and substantial manner.

On the other hand, the victims have had access to reparations, albeit with few measures of recognition of their suffering (memorials, publications, discourses, health treatments, etc.). Brazil's democratic governments have constantly used the transitional justice discourse while at the same time denying access to justice or making it difficult. While some state bodies have been sponsoring initiatives to strengthen human rights, other official organs have been blocking these initiatives and successfully defended impunity for the torturers of the dictatorship. Since the democratic State failed to carry out the sentence proffered by national courts in a suit filed by the surviving families of opposition members killed in the Araguaia River region, human rights movements were forced to resort to the Interamerican Human Rights System.[19]

While nationally the government has been defending access to memory and truth, the opposite behavior was adopted in front of the Organization of American States (OAS): here the state adopted measures against the victims' families, in an attempt to avoid the conviction of the Brazilian state by the OAS. Some monuments or memorials were created and financial compensation laws were edited; however, investigations into the dead and disappeared have not been adequately made. The families of dead and disappeared persons and politically persecuted people could neither use the national justice system nor invoke international treaties. They were prevented from both filing suits and having access to the information on the organs of repression kept among the military files which continue being withheld. Even now under civil and democratic command, the armed forces still claim that they lack documents on the repressive acts during the dictatorship. Allegedly they were destroyed at the end of the authoritarian regime. Even the National Truth Commission (2012–2014) was denied access to these documents. Thus the Armed Forces blatantly boycotted the commission, although the commission was itself an institution created by the state, mandated to investigate past human rights violations.[20]

In 2010, the judiciary justified impunity for public agents involved in crimes against humanity during the dictatorship, when it rejected an appeal filed by the Brazilian Lawyers Association (OAB)—an organ very similar to the American Bar Association.[21] By contrast, the Government Agency for Law Enforcement and Prosecution of Crimes (Ministério Público Federal) created a working group called "Transitional Justice," which has judged several criminal suits aiming to hold public agents responsible for crimes committed during the dictatorship.[22] This shows the ambiguous use of the transitional justice concept in Brazil.

Brazilian democracy was constituted during a transition grounded on a consensus that was obtained by agreements between old political oligarchies and new actors that appeared during the process (Skidmore 1988). Starting as early as 1974, with the so-called "slow, gradual and safe" redemocratization, transition dragged on until the promulgation of 1988 Constitution, taking up fourteen years—a record time when compared to other transitional processes. The long time needed for Brazil's democratization shows how old actors exerted control to ensure that the new regime would not make a clear break with the dictatorship. The logic of the process was to ensure a stable government, and to keep the conflicts at bay by using a discourse based on the notion of "pacification" and "reconciliation." This new kind of consensual government would have the exceptional state paradigm as its core underlying structure.[23]

Three historic moments of the transition illustrate this logic: the 1979 amnesty law; the election of the first non-military president via a so-called electoral college rather than direct elections; and the 1988 Constitution. These moments are symbolic for Brazilian democracy and share at least two common characteristics. On one hand, they emerged as solutions negotiated in private rooms within the Congress building, and silenced actions from the social movements. The other characteristic is that they promise ways out of political dilemmas through the institution of exception states. Legal order is suspended in favor of the "overcoming" of circumstances that might create instability in the political process.

In 1979, the amnesty campaign led to a rising popular pressure that resulted in a social movement that began to use the human rights discourse. However, the military government of General Figueiredo imposed an ambiguous law, which would become the starting point of the agreed impunity. Democracy would be born under the sign of an exception state, since instead of following the country's law and the international treaties accepted and signed by Brazilian State, the government preferred to overlook the rights and bet on the non-punishment of criminals as part of a consensual agreement that actually excluded ample segments of society from this "arrangement."

Near the end of the dictatorship, Brazilian society came together in the largest popular movement in the country's history, known as "Direct [elections] Now." In rallies and marches, millions of people demanded democratic change from a violent regime to one that governed under the rule of law. Once again private interests and indirect elections prevailed. Finally José Sarney was sworn in as president, the former leader of the pro-regime party at the time of the passing of Amnesty Law (due to the unexpected death of the elected President Tancredo Neves). The first civilian government in decades had its beginning marked by the exception to the democratic rule. With a varnish of legitimacy given by a multi-party Congress, the silencing of the political battle through indirect elections was validated.

Various social movements mobilized for the Constituent Assembly, elected in 1986. These social actions bore fruit in the form of a set of constitutional rights which at the time were considered as progressive, in particular in the fields of labor, native populations, and women and children's rights. However, in some aspects the new Constitution resembled the one imposed by the dictatorship in 1969, especially where land ownership, media, and civilian-military relationship were concerned.

THE SOCIAL CONSTRUCTION OF TRANSITIONAL JUSTICE

Justice became a more central question in Brazil in the beginning of the 1980s, still under the military regime and right after the passing of the Amnesty Law (the transitional justice vocabulary will be later discussed). An important document in the fight for justice and for democracy was the report of the dead and disappeared persons, organized by the victims' families' commission and by the Brazilian pro-amnesty committees. It reads:

> We reiterate our willingness to keep up our struggle for a broad, general and unrestricted amnesty, which implies the dismantling of the repressive apparatus; the end of the body of laws that oppresses Brazilian society; and the accountability of all the persons involved in the crimes committed by the political repression apparatus. (Amnesty 1984, 15)

Although these demands have been approved by the II National Amnesty Convention at the end of 1979 (when the military regime was still in full force), they already entailed propositions for the return to democracy. At the center of the political struggle stood a reform of the repressive apparatus and the punishment of those responsible for human rights crimes. This happened almost two decades prior to the advent of the transitional justice discourse, the kind of knowledge that would finally define a set of justice policies in times of transition. Yet at the time, as we have seen, social movements in Brazil were already struggling for the changes needed at that moment in pursuit of what they understood as democracy. The "exceptional" condition in 1979 was the fact that Brazilians were still living under a dictatorship, unlike the transitional justice discourse adopted during the 1990s that was based on the discursive idea of a specific kind of democratic exception during the so-called "transitional phase."

The idea of an exceptional moment can also be found in the goals of the project "Brasil: Nunca Mais"—"Brazil: Never Again"—(BNM), published in 1985 and produced by human rights movements and churches, especially the Catholic Church, which states:

> From its inception in August, 1979, until its conclusion in March, 1985, the research project "Brazil: Never Again" has no objective other than fulfilling the promise made in its title: that the violence, the ignominy, the oppression that took place in Brazil's recent past shall never happen again. (Archdiocese 1985, 26)

However, the project uses a different discourse and adds a kind of new information. Despite the difficulties of full access to justice, the report begins to analyze the return to democracy also by problematizing the experiences of other post-authoritarian or post-totalitarian countries. As *Brazil: Never Again* states, "it is not the intention of this project to provide evidence to be used for some kind of Brazilian Nuremberg [trial]" (Archdiocese 1985, 26). Among the documents' central propositions we can observe questions based on epistemic assumptions that conceive of the transition as an exceptional period, presenting ideas around reconciliation, truth, and institutional reform:

> It [the project] is not driven by any kind of sentiment of *revenge*. In their search for Justice, the Brazilian people have never been moved by feelings of *revenge*. . . . It is the evangelical precept that guides the knowledge that *truth* is a prerequisite for liberation. It is a happy coincidence that the release of the research findings occurs at a moment of national hope, of our *overcoming authoritarianism*, of a *reform on the country's laws*. A moment when there is the possibility of summoning a Constituent Assembly that may build *democratic institutions*. (Archdiocese 1985, 26. *Emphasis added*)

In our view it is difficult to determine to what extent the texts by the Brazilian Commissions and the *Brazil: Never Again* project are marked by significant differences. However, the texts put emphases on slightly different aspects. While the texts from the victims' families' commission make an emphatic demand for penal justice actions ("accountability for all the persons involved"), the BNM project, by contrast, focuses on "overcoming authoritarianism," and on building "democratic institutions" without "feelings of revenge." This was how the production of knowledge about the transitional periods in Brazil began.

In the beginning of the 1990s, a clandestine mass grave was found at the so-called Perus Cemetery in São Paulo. It was here that agents of the repressive organs got rid of the bodies of those first tortured and then murdered in police or a military torture facilities. A Parliamentary Commission of Inquiry (or CPI) was set up by the São Paulo Town Council tasked to investigate the history of that terrible place which had been used to hide the systematic violence of the military regime. Although the CPI took place at a state institution (the municipal legislative assembly), victim movements had a strong presence in this commission as noticed in the CPI report's opening: "[W]e knew there would be resistance from those who after the end of the dictatorship continued hiding behind the Amnesty Law, without having their crimes ever denounced much less judged" (Caligiuri 1992, 7). The notion of transition as a kind of temporary moment and a limit to the recent past is addressed here in an explicit way:

> Both institutional violence and impunity have not yet been eliminated from our society. Thus at this moment of *transition* to democracy, *social instruments* unfortunately remain *fragile* that could prevent the unacceptable occurrences of the past [violence] to repeat themselves. (Caligiuri 1992, 7; *Emphasis added*)

The allusion in the text—the "fragile social tools" in this moment of democratic transition—clearly indicates that the early 1990s were still considered a moment of exception, even after the ratification of a new Brazilian Constitution (1988) and the first direct elections for a civilian president (1989). The CPI of the Perus Mass Grave was the first moment of confluence between specific agents of the state and the human rights movements. Their cooperation was restricted to the country's largest municipality (São Paulo) and made possible by the mayor Luiza Erundina (1988–1992), a member of the left wing party, the Brazilian Labor Party (PT).

After that CPI the victims' families started assembling the "Dossier of the Political Dead and Disappeared after 1964," updating the number and biographies of the dictatorship's fatal victims. Conscious of their role in the Brazilian context, the dossier illustrates a "stubbornness" characteristic of the "popular social movements," for they "refuse the established standards and seek to somehow build other modes of subjectivities" (Commission 1996, 25). The rapprochement between the state and the social movements is noticed by the families' entities who acknowledge the joint work on one hand, but still assume a remarkably different relation to the government's logic, on the other hand. Despite starting political initiatives to address the dictatorship's crimes, the state's logic simultaneously blocked the search for truth and criminal liability. This was the moment when an official transitional justice discourse gained strength and progressively developed into the dominant framework.

THE STATE AS PROTAGONIST

In December 1995 and as the result of the victim families' pressure on the government, President Fernando Henrique Cardoso sanctioned the Law 9.140, which first officially acknowledged the state's responsibility for the dead and disappeared persons killed for political reasons. This law also granted financial reparations to the families of the dead and disappeared, but it failed to provide any accountability for the crimes and the whereabouts of the missing corpses.[24] While in theory the state took the responsibility for its agents' actions, it failed, however, to pursue the individual and actual liabilities for those violations. Simultaneously, the government's pacifist and conciliatory discourse grew stronger, contributing to an interpretation of the historical moment as a still unresolved conflict between two radically opposed sides. In article 2, the law states: "the application of this law's dispositions and all of its effects shall be oriented by the principle of reconciliation and national pacification."

In 2002, the Amnesty Commission was created, first through a provisional executive order and later with Congress' approval. The compensation payments for the politically persecuted during the regime were increased.[25] Although this was an important step toward the recognition of grave human rights violations, the law was restricted to financial reparations, and failed to allude to the victims' dignity or to offer any kind social and symbolic reparation. It did not even use the words "victims" or "persecuted."[26]

The Amnesty Commission was the first state institution to adopt and spread the transitional justice discourse in Brazil. In 2007, after Tarso Genro was sworn in as Minister of Justice, that discourse was gradually adopted as the national predominant discourse. The Commission's 2007 report made use of this new discourse and justified it with the institution's aim to foster a new human rights education:

> The Amnesty Commission broadened its activities adopting the concept and principles of Transitional Justice (the right to truth, to memory, to justice and to reparation payments), which led to initiatives like the treatment and preservation of documents, especially its iconographic and audiovisual materials, which started to be considered priorities due to their relevance for the strengthening of human rights and citizenship in Brazil. (Commission 2007, 9)

Thus in 2007, the scope of the Amnesty Commission broadened beyond financial reparations, thus moving beyond its initial legal mandate focused on compensation payments. The Amnesty Commission turned into a privileged space of state action addressing the dictatorship's crimes and legacy. According to its 2010 report: "it plays a significant role for politics of memory and for democracy-oriented education" (Commission 2010a, 4). In one of its official announcement the commission states; "amnesty, the peace commission!" In its proceedings and instruments, the institution began to establish a discourse presented as true knowledge about "Brazilian transitional model" (Commission 2010a, 4).

The rhetoric of a transitional process allowed the institution to establish itself as a body that strengthened democracy and allowed access to mechanisms in pursuit of justice. This discourse prevailed in spite of the fact that the country had not yet convicted a single perpetrator for his crimes during the dictatorship; and that military files on the repressive apparatus had never been entirely opened; let alone the deaths and torture sessions been satisfactorily clarified, or at least the location of the disappeared persons' corpses been disclosed. In its institutional journal called the "Amnesty Review" (Revista Anistia Política e Justiça de Transição), the Amnesty Commission has used the discourse of transitional justice in its struggle for accountability measures for former torturers. Here it is stated that "this process does not only *give back normality to* the legal system—which has its civil branch strongly anchored on the principle that those who do harm should pay compensations—but also, and especially, enables a form of *moral reconciliation* between the state and its citizens" (Commission 2009, 17, *emphases added*).[27] If, according to the Amnesty Commission (a state institution) the country has recovered its legal "normality," from the human rights movements' point of view, by contrast, that is impossible without prior investigation of the serious violations that took place during the dictatorship.

Hence, important advancements made in the period of transition and described through a discursive framework of transitional justice coexist with the longstanding impunity and with the boycott from other state organs to search for truth. Human rights movements and other state institutions have demanded justice with propositions that are very similar to the ones that have meanwhile been integrated in the transitional justice discourse. On the other hand, segments of the democratic state have pointed to the conditions of exception and transition in order to reproduce a historical interpretation of the "two sides" of the conflict, a narrative that was dominant during the dictatorship. The underlying idea of this line of action defended by the democratic government is that of a permanent threat of political destabilization, which helps to justify the politics of the supposedly possible (or feasible), based on a logic of securing the country's governability and built upon a rhetoric of peace and reconciliation.

USE OR ABUSE OF TRANSITIONAL JUSTICE?

In Brazil, we note an official, longstanding use of the transitional justice discourse that has specific characteristics. This discourse's main feature is a kind of ambiguity that we have been trying to identify in this chapter. It is a discourse that silences the voice of the victims' movements, whose demands keep being constantly blocked. We are not claiming here that the state is a monolithic entity characterized by homogeneous political actions. Nevertheless, it is necessary to acknowledge that the heterogeneity and the sometimes contradictory treatment that different state organs have given this issue have resulted bottom-line in maintaining impunity, despite the various pressures towards criminal prosecutions. While some state organs that are more peripheral in the decision-making structure adopt a discourse in favor of transitional justice measures, promoting specific advancements, the officially adopted politics that succeeded have safeguarded impunity and kept supposed "agreements," thus justifying the lack of punishment with reference to a specific kind of Brazilian transition.

The ambiguous character of the transitional justice discourse in Brazil has become evident mainly through the generous use of a certain kind of rhetoric (justice, truth, and reparation) used to justify legal mechanisms that, however, turned out to be clearly restrictive and harmful to victims' rights. An example of such a manipulative gamble with ambiguity is the limitation of the reparation payments of the law 9.140 of 1995, which granted victim families death certificates of their dead and disappeared loved ones, yet without filling the blanks referring to essential data such as the date, place, and cause of death, or the location of their relatives' mortal remains. The same manoeuver of using a transitional justice discourse while, at the same time, blocking full-hearted democratic procedures, also occurred with a later reparation law that guaranteed compensation payments to the surviving victims via the Amnesty Commission. According to this additional law, the reparation amount paid to each survivor would be decided by calculating the salary loss of each victim; a blue-collar worker, for instance, would thus receive far less than a higher-paid professional.[28]

The discourse about the court proceedings of Brazilian State and the OAS, when Brazil sent representatives from the Defense Ministry instead of the Human Rights Secretary to coordinate the country's delegation during the trial of the Araguaia case. It was as though Brazil still lived on the verge of some imminent armed conflict. In 2010, the Brazilian Supreme Court confirmed the 1979 Amnesty Law and defended impunity, by referring to the maintenance of a "political pact" that would safeguard the spirit of national reconciliation.

In our view there is no indication that we are currently living a moment of historical instability, that our democratic institutions are threatened, or that we are facing an immediate danger of another military coup. The term "reconciliation" invokes a rhetoric that alludes to the violent conflict that happened *during* the dictatorship. Today, the use of this word is yet another way to block to the possibility of State actions in favor of justice initiatives. The term protects the state from both the criminal and political responsibility for the grave human rights violations that occurred during the military regime.

The question must be raised: why do we keep using the transitional justice discourse when we no longer live in a period of historical exception, of uncertainty whether democracy or dictatorship will prevail? Why is the transitional justice rhetoric and associated terms such as reconciliation and pardon still being used?

Although four or five decades have passed since those crimes were committed, the victims' movements continue to be strong and new actors have emerged, for example, groups have been organizing public shaming events in front of the houses of notorious torturers. With some victims or direct relatives of victims still alive, public pressure will certainly continue and struggle for criminal prosecutions, and the actions contemplated in the transitional justice discourse will help to mobilize for the causes of the human rights' movements. In fact, the deeper we go into a rule of law culture, the more paths are open to these demands. However, the more time passes the smaller are the chances that testimonies are still alive and that they can pass their stories on. On the positive side, transitional justice discourse may have contributed to demands for an effective guarantee of victims' rights and for defending the non-repetition of human rights violations. The idea of "exception" has also helped to legitimate actions like the creation of the truth commissions (the national one and local ones have been created all over the nation).[29]

On the other hand, however, the exceptional character of memory politics in Brazil has also allowed for the government to control the political processes related to the demands of the victims of the dictatorship. One such means of control, for instance, is the 1979 Amnesty Law, which is interpreted as an act of impunity for those involved in state crimes during the dictatorship. In the year it was created, in 1979, Brazil still lived under the military regime, with a recently dissolved Congress; with "bionic" senators—indicated by generals without democratic election procedures—and with bombs exploding at newsstands that dared to sell the newspapers of the opposition. Although the law has sanctioned impunity and was ratified in this repressive context, in 2010 the Supreme Court confirmed the validity of the law freeing torturers from prosecutions. It maintained an interpretation of non-punishment of those responsible for torture and murder based on the argument that the 1979 law had been the product of great national agreement. This emblematic case shows that what is still left of the dictatorship is not only a legacy, but now appears as the product of a process that has been thought through by the rule of law and was sanctioned by the highest organ of the country's legal system, the Brazilian Supreme Court, imbued with the duty to preserve the democratic Constitution of 1988.

If we consider other aspects of the dictatorial legacy, we can see how dictatorial structures have remained intact and been reproduced by the current democratic system. Torture, a practice institutionalized during the dictatorship, is largely utilized in the current penitentiary system, in juvenile delinquents detention centers, and in poorer urban neighborhoods. Police violence has increased systemically, and also broadened its targets: today not only political militants are oppressed, but mainly young people from the poorer districts and younger black people.

We are not seeking to establish some kind of indistinguishability between democracy and dictatorship. To the contrary, under the varnish of a democratic discourse we find attitudes whose cleverness lies in combining authoritarian means with a democratic surface. Those are no longer authoritarian vestiges, but choices made in the present, which sanction state violence under the cover of democratic legitimacy. Our analysis reveals that there is something exceptional about Brazilian politics—the activation of emergency measures that override legislation that is democratically authorized (for example, the Amnesty Law or the absence of military files).

Transitional justice discourse, in the Brazilian context, can be utilized as a rhetorical strategy to hide and legitimate processes of impunity and to block demands for justice, truth and compensation made by victims. The discourse and theory of a certain transitional justice mobilizes a kind of knowledge that certainly has real power effects. It is these power effects that we have tried to spotlight in this essay.

NOTES

1. A deeper conceptual analysis of this theme can be found in Quinalha (2013).
2. The observation on the exceptional character of these historical moments, as well as the possibility of putting together in the same discourse the victims' demands and the legal blocks in the new regimes led researcher Ruti Teitel to use the definition "justice in times of transition" for an event that took place in 1992. The first time the terms appeared was in Neil Kritz, "Transitional Justice: How Emerging Democracies Reckon with Former Regimes," in 1995.
3. Kathia Martin-Chenut, "The Penal Exception System in Face of International Human Rights' Law" (2009), article in which the author analyzes the legitimating of exceptional measures in international law.
4. This critique is well developed in the article by Cecília MacDowell dos Santos in this compilation.
5. Mcevoy, Kieran. "Letting Go of Legalism: Developing a 'Thicker' Version of Transitional Justice," p. 16.
6. See the chapter by Steve Dobransky in this book.
7. Cf. "Dictatorships and Homosexualities: Repression, Resistance and the Search for Truth" (Quinalha and Green 2014).
8. Merwe, Hugo Van Der. "Delivering Justice During Transition," p. 117. Similarly oriented criticism can be found in the text: Cavallaro, James and Albuja, Sebastián. "The Lost

Agenda: Economic Crimes and Truth Commissions in Latin America and Beyond." In "Transitional Justice from Below: Grassroots Activism and the Struggle for Change," McEvoy, Kieran; McGregor, Lorna (Ed.). p. 121–41.

9. Merwe, Hugo Van Der. "Delivering Justice During Transition," p. 117. Similarly oriented criticism can be found in the text: Cavallaro, James and Albuja, Sebastián. "The Lost Agenda: Economic Crimes and Truth Commissions in Latin America and Beyond." In "Transitional Justice from Below: Grassroots Activism and the Struggle for Change," McEvoy, Kieran and McGregor, Lorna (Ed.). p. 121–41.

10. Also idealism is mentioned in critiques: "Transitional Justice Mechanisms Are Usually Presented in Very Idealistic Terms, Without Clearly Defined Goals." Merwe, Hugo Van Der. "Delivering Justice During Transition," p. 121.

11. "Contrary to the vision of transitional justice as a toolkit containing the predefined components conceived of as 'pillars,' should we not as practitioners be advocating instead for reflection on the subject of justice understood more broadly and ensure that diverse voices are able to join in the debate?'" Okello, Moses Chrispus. "Elevating Transitional Local Justice or Crystallizing Global Governance," p. 284.

12. Olsen, Tricia, Leigh Payne, and Andrew Reiter. "Transitional Justice in Balance," p. 16.

13. Elster, Jon, "Closing the Books," 2004, 7.

14. Elster, Jon. "Closing the Books," 2004, 77.

15. Elster, Jon. "Closing the books," 2004:79, 80.

16. McEvoy, Kieran and McGregor, Lorna. "*Transitional Justice from Below*," 2008: 5.

17. McEvoy and McGregor, "Transitional Justice from Below," 2008: 2–4.

18. McEvoy and McGregor. "Transitional Justice from Below," 2008: 5. Instead, it is about offering a perspective that, in many cases, proves to be privileged for the observation and understanding of aspects normally underappreciated by the traditional approach (2008, 3).

19. On December 2010, during the trial of Brazilian State in the Inter-American Court of Human Rights, an organ of the Organization of American States (OAS), Brazil was condemned to investigate the circumstances of the murder and torture of militants with the Araguaia Guerilla (1972–1975), to locate the bodies of the disappeared persons and to punish the responsible for those crimes. As of June 2015, the sentence had not yet been carried out.

20. Cf. O Globo newspaper of August 22, 2014, "Years of Lead: Commander Imposes Silence to the Army," available at http://oglobo.globo.com?brasil/anos-de-chumbo-comandante-impoe-silencio-ao-exercito-13690198.

21. In the Brazil's case, in 2008, the main legal action was proposed by the Federal Council of Brazil Lawyers—an organization similar to the American Bar Association—questioning the adequate interpretation of 1979 Amnesty Law by the Supreme Federal Court (Claim of Breach of Fundamental Precept no.153), which dismissed it as groundless on April 29, 2010.

22. Further information on the Federal Public Prosecutor's Office work group is available at http://2ccr.pgr.mpf.mp.br/coordenacao/grupos-de-trabalho/justica-de-transicao-material-dvd/acoes-penais.

23. About Brazilian transition, in a comparative study to South-African transition, see the book "Democracy and the Exception State" (Teles 2015).

24. Law 9.140/95, available at http://www.planalto.gov.br/ccivil_03/leis/L9140compilada.htm, accessed on May, 2013.

25. Law 10.559/02, available at http://www.planalto.gov.br/ccivil_03/leis/2002/l10559.htm, accessed on May, 2013.

26. Cf. article by Glenda Mezarobba, "The Process of Reckoning and the Logic of Discretion."

27. A highlight was the creation, in 2009, of the publication "Political Amnesty and Transitional Justice Magazine," by the Amnesty Commission.

28. Further information on the law that established the Amnesty Commission, see the article by Glenda Mezarobba, "The Process of Reckoning and the Logic of Discretion." With the Law 10.559, once again, "the precariousness of the national effort toward reparation and the permanence of the past in the present is made evident, as paradoxical as it may seem, by the mobilization of the memory of forgetfulness that the Amnesty Law proposed and the subsequent legislation hurried to reinforce" (Mezarobba 2010, 115).

29. During the process of the National Truth Commission creation, and as its work unfolded, many social segments have created their own commissions to investigate the violations that occurred during the military dictatorship. That was the case with various universities, workers' groups, native peoples defense organizations and other commissions created in municipal and some regional units of the State. This net structure created an important support mobilization, and also one of popular pressure on the Commission itself.

SELECTED BIBLIOGRAPHY

Anistia, Comitê Brasileiro pela. 1984. "Dossiê dos mortos e desaparecidos." Porto Alegre: Assembleia Legislativa.

Arquidiocese de São Paulo. 1985. "Brasil: Nunca Mais." Petrópolis, Vozes.

Atencio, Rebecca J. 2014. Memory's Turn: Reckoning with Dictatorship in Brazil. Madison: The University of Wisconsin Press.

Caligiuri filho, Júlio César e outros. 1992. "Onde estão? Relatório da Comissão Parlamentar de Inquérito que investigou a vala clandestina no Cemitério Dom Bosco, em Perus, e os desaparecidos políticos." São Paulo, Câmara Municipal de São Paulo.

Cavallaro, James, and Sebastián Albuja. 2008. "The Lost Agenda: Economic Crimes and Truth Commissions in Latin America and Beyond." In *Transitional Justice from Below: Grassroots Activism and the Struggle for Change,* eds. McEvoy, Kieran, and McGregor, Lorena, 121–41. Oxford; Portland: Hart.

Comissão de Anistia do Ministério da Justiça. 2007. "Relatório da Comissão de Anistia 2007." Brasília: Ministério da Justiça.

———. 2009. "Revista Anistia Política e Justiça de Transição." Número 1, jan-jun 2009. Brasília: Ministério da Justiça.

———. 2010a. "Relatório Anual da Comissão de Anistia 2010." Brasília: Ministério da Justiça.

———. 2010b. "Relatório Anual da Comissão de Anistia 2009." Brasília: Ministério da Justiça.

Comissão de Familiares de Mortos e Desaparecidos Políticos e Instituto de Estudos da Violência do Estado. Dossiê dos mortos e desaparecidos políticos a partir de 1964. Prefácio D. Paulo Evaristo Arns. São Paulo: Imesp, 1996.

———. Dossiê ditadura: mortos e desaparecidos no Brasil. São Paulo: Imesp, 2009.

Elster, Jon. 2004. "Closing the Books: Transitional Justice in Historical Perspective." Nova York: Cambridge University Press.

Foucault, Michel. 2008. "A ordem do discurso." Tradução de Laura F. de A. Sampaio. São Paulo: Loyola.

Hayner, Priscilla B. 2002. *Unspeakable Truths: Facing the Challenge of Truths Commissions.* New York: Routledge.

Kritz, Neil. 1995. "Transitional Justice: How Emerging Democracies Reckon with Former Regimes." v. I, II e III. Washington DC: United States Institute of Peace.

Lefranc, Sandrine. 2002. "Politiques du Pardon." Paris: Presses Universitaires de France.

Linz, Juan, and Alfred Stepan. 1999. "A transição e consolidação da democracia: a experiência do sul da Europa e da América do Sul." São Paulo: Paz e Terra.

Mainwaring, Scott, Guillermo O'Donnell, and J. Samuel. Valenzuela. 1992. *Issues in Democratic Consolidation: The New South American Democracies in Comparative Perspective.* Notre Dame: University of Notre Dame Press.

Martin-Chenut, Kathia. 2009. "O sistema penal de exceção em face do direito internacional dos direitos humanos." In *Desarquivando a ditadura: memória e justiça no Brasil,* eds. Teles, Edson, Santos, Cecília Macdowell, Teles, Janaína de Almeida, 225–49. São Paulo: Hucitec.

Mcevoy, K. 2008. "Letting Go of Legalism: Developing a 'Thicker' Version of Transitional Justice." In *Transitional Justice from Below: Grassroots Activism and the Struggle for Change*, McEvoy, K.; McGregor, L. (Eds). 15–45. Oxford; Portland: Hart.

Mcevoy, K., and L. Mcgregor. 2008. "Transitional Justice from Below: An Agenda for Research, Policy and Praxis." In *Transitional Justice from Below: Grassroots Actvism and the Struggle for Change*. Mcevoy, K., and Mcgregor, L. (Eds.). Oxford; Portland: Hart, 2008.

Méndez, J. 1997. "Defense of Transitional Justice." In *Transitional Justice and the Rule of Law in New Democracies,* ed. McAdams, A. J. Notre Dame: University Notre Dame Press.

Méndez, J.; Covelli, G. T. R. 2008. "Parecer técnico sobre a natureza dos crimes de lesa-humanidade, a imprescritibilidade de alguns delitos e a proibição de anistias. Solicitado pelo Ministério Público Federal, Procuradoria da República em São Paulo." Nova York: International Center for Transitional Justice, set. 2008.

Merwe, H. 2009. "Delivering Justice During Transition: Research Challenges." In *Assessing the Impact of Transitional Justice,* eds. Merwe, H.; Baxter, V.; Chapman, A. R. 115–42. Washington, D.C.: United States Institute of Peace, 2009.

Mezarobba, G. 2010. "O processo de acerto de contas e alógica do arbítrio." In *O que resta da ditadura: a exceção brasileira*. Teles, Edson e Safatle, Vladimir (orgs.), 109–22. São Paulo: Boitempo.

Moisés, J. A.; J. A. G. Albuquerque. (Org.). 1989. "Dilemas da consolidação da democracia." Rio de Janeiro: Paz e Terra.

O'Donnell, G. 1986. Contrapontos: autoritarismo e democratização. São Paulo: Vértice, Editora Revista dos Tribunais.

O'Donnell, G.; Schmitter, P.C. 1988. "Transições do regime autoritário: primeiras conclusões." São Paulo: Vértice, Editora Revista dos Tribunais.

O'Donnell, G.; Schmitter, P. C.; Whitehead, L. 1988. Transições do regime autoritário: América Latina. São Paulo: Vértice, Editora Revista dos Tribunais.

Okello, M. C. 2010. "Elevating Transitional Local Justice or Crystalizing Global Governance." In *Localizing Transitional Justice: Interventions and Priorities After Mass Violence,* eds. Shaw, R.; Waldorf, L.; Hazan, P., 275–84. Stanford: Stanford University Press.

Olsen, T.; Payne, L.; Reiter, A. 2010. "Transitional Justice in Balance: Comparing Processes, Weighing Efficacy." Washington DC: United States Institute of Peace.

Przeworski, A. 1991. "Democracy and market: political and economic reforms in Eastern Europe and Latin American." Cambridge: Cambridge University Press.

Quinalha, Renan Honório. 2013. "Justiça de transição: contornos do conceito." São Paulo: Expressão Popular.

———. e Green, James N (orgs.). 2014. "Ditadura e homossexualidades. Repressão, resistência e a busca da verdade." São Carlos/SP: EdUFSCar.

Santos, Cecília MacDowell. 2009. "A Justiça ao Serviço da Memória: Mobilização Jurídica Transnacional, Direitos Humanos e Memória da Ditadura." In Desarquivando a Ditadura: Memória e Justiça no Brasil, vol. II, eds. Cecília MacDowell Santos, Edson Teles, and Janaína de Almeida Teles, 472–95. São Paulo: Hucitec Press.

Skidmore, T. 1988. "Brasil: de Castelo a Tancredo (1964–1985)." Rio de Janeiro: Paz e Terra.

Teitel, R. 2000. *Transitional Justice*. Nova York: Oxford University.

Teles, E., Macdowell, Cecília e Teles, Janaína. 2009. "Desarquivando a ditadura. Memória e Justiça no Brasil."São Paulo: Hucitec.

———. e Safatle, Vladimir (orgs.). 2010. "O que resta da ditadura: a exceção brasileira." São Paulo: Boitempo.

———. Democracia e estado de exceção. A elaboração da memória política no Brasil e na África do Sul. 2015. São Paulo: Fap-Unifesp.

Chapter Three

Transitional Justice from the Margins

Legal Mobilization and Memory Politics in Brazil

Cecília MacDowell Santos

Since the beginning of the twenty-first century, a new transitional justice paradigm has been normalized and globalized (Teitel 2003; McEvoy 2008). This paradigm includes the establishment of normative mechanisms such as reparation, civil and criminal accountability, truth commissions, sites of memory, lustration, and so on. It is particularly remarkable to observe the global rise in legitimacy of the norm on individual (not simply state) civil and criminal accountability, a phenomenon that Lutz and Sikkink (2001) dub a "justice cascade." New studies on transitional justice have emerged to examine how this global paradigm has been constituted, absorbed, and translated into norms at the international, national, and local scales. But it remains to be further examined how transitional justice policies are contested in different countries; what narratives are produced by transitional justice policies at different locales; what becomes visible and invisible in these narratives; who becomes a concrete (not simply abstract) subject of the rights to memory, truth and justice; and who is acknowledged as a political subject of history, memory, and justice.

One of the main recent trends in the literature on transitional justice in Latin America has examined three types of questions: first, it asks what *type, model and/or phase* of transitional justice mechanisms have been adopted within the region (Olsen, Payne, and Reiter 2010; Payne, Abrão, and Torelly 2011); second, what *factors* explain the differences between the models and phases (Olsen, Payne, and Reiter 2010; Payne, Abrão, and Torelly 2011; Reátegui 2011; Brito, González-Enríquez, and Aguilar 2001); and third, what are their *impacts* on human rights and democracy (Lutz and Sikkink 2001; Roht-Ariaza and Mariezcurrena 2006; Olsen, Payne, and Reiter 2010; Sikkink 2012). This literature has emphasized the role of states, transnational human rights advocates and international organizations as the main motors of transitional justice politics. Notwithstanding its contributions to studies of transitional justice, this literature tends to assume that state action is linear and progressive and that the state is a homogenous actor. Moreover, it does not pay sufficient attention to the local cultural, social and political processes, as well as practices of civil society actors, such as groups of families of the disappeared and human rights non-governmental organizations (NGOs), that might shape the politics of transitional justice from inside and outside of the state.

A second recent trend in studies of transitional justice in Latin America focuses on *domestic political processes* and *civil society actors*, including, for example, comparative and single country studies of civil society mobilization practices (Collins 2006; 2008; 2010; Burt, Fried, and Lessa 2013). Paying particular attention to the role of domestic legal action and courts, Collins (2006) formulates the concept of "post-transitional justice" to refer to a new phase in the politics of memory and justice, characterized by the legal actions for justice (civil and criminal accountability) initiated by nonstate actors, as opposed to the previous phase of "transitional justice" controlled by states and characterized by the lack of civil and/or criminal accountability of perpetrators of human rights violations. Collins' analysis of social mobilization practices by domestic and nonstate actors is an important contribution to studies of transitional justice in Latin America. However, the concept of "post-transitional justice" does not move away from a linear, static-phase perspective on transitional justice, which tends to overlook the continuities in the practices and power dynamics both within state sectors and between the state and civil society actors. Moreover, this concept does not shed light on a critical understanding of the politics of representation involved in transitional justice politics. In fact, very few studies of transitional justice in Latin America examine the question of how some types of knowledge and practices become visible and are placed at the center of politics while others may be marginalized or hidden in accounts of transitional justice (for exceptions, see Maeso 2010; Atencio 2014).

The Brazilian case is often overlooked in the scholarship on transitional justice in Latin America produced outside of Brazil. When examined, it is usually depicted from the perspective of the state and without sufficient attention to the conflicts over the policies established by the state (for exceptions, see Santos 2010; Schneider 2011; Atencio 2014). Even the scholarly books and articles published on the politics of memory, truth, and justice in Brazil pay little attention to the mobilizations by civil society actors (for exceptions, see Teles 2005; 2010; Santos 2009). This chapter aims to fill this gap. It focuses on Brazil and proposes a local and transnational legal mobilization approach (McCann 2006) to transitional justice politics on the ground and from the margins. In the footsteps of the "sociology of absences" formulated by Boaventura de Sousa Santos (2014) as a critical analysis of the production by hegemonic thinking of certain types of knowledge and practices as nonexistent, this chapter seeks to uncover the legal mobilization practices by nonstate actors that are often represented at the margins, and are hidden or undermined in official accounts and in most scholarly works on transitional justice in and about Brazil. The uncovering of the "margins" is also inspired by the critical perspectives of feminists of color such as bell hooks (1984) and Audre Lorde (1984) in their calls for placing the experiences of black women at the center of feminist studies. At the same time, the "margins" are viewed as sites of production of multiple types of knowledge and practices, therefore they represent a plurality of engagements with memory politics. Furthermore, the memories produced in the "margins" or "peripheries" should not be conceived of as completely separate from the hegemonic memory produced at the "center," nor should the margins and the center be linked by a principle of causality (Kobalec 2014). Legal mobilization practices by families of the disappeared do not determine or cause the transitional justice policies established by the Brazilian state, and vice-versa. They might interact and shape each other at particular historical moments, but one is not the result of the other.

Drawing on cases of local and transnational legal actions initiated by families of the disappeared and by former political prisoners since the 1970s, this chapter argues that legal mobilization has been an important part of these actors' struggles for memory, truth, and justice, *during and after* the military regime, which lasted from 1964 to 1985. Most of these legal actions have had the goal of civil accountability. The claims and types of legal actions have certainly been shaped by the changing "political and legal opportunity structures" and socio-historical contexts in which they are embedded, as illustrated by the trajectory of the Araguaia Guerrilla case, which I examine in detail elsewhere (Santos 2010).[1] While the recent adoption of the "transitional justice" vocabulary and of the global norm of civil and criminal accountability by some sectors of the Brazilian state has been shaped by the discourses of and pressures from regional interstate organizations and international NGOs, it is certain that these pressures from above have been continuously provoked by local and transnational legal actions carried out by families of the disappeared, former political prisoners, and their allies. Yet, the official and scholarly publications on "transitional justice" in Brazil often make the political role played by these civil society actors invisible or marginal, or undermine the agency of these actors in their struggles for the rights to memory, truth, and justice.

This chapter is divided into three parts, in addition to this introduction and the conclusion. In what follows, I start with an overview of the new studies on transitional justice in Latin America, to which this chapter aims to contribute. This will be followed by an examination of how legal mobilization by nonstate actors is portrayed as marginal in the accounts of transitional justice politics in Brazil. I will then present some of the emblematic legal actions initiated by families of the disappeared and former political prisoners from the 1970s until the 2000s.

NEW STUDIES ON (POST-)TRANSITIONAL JUSTICE IN LATIN AMERICA

Contrary to assertions by scholars of "transitions" in the 1980s, new empirical studies on transitional justice in Latin America have challenged the argument that criminal and civil accountability in cases of serious violations of human rights committed in the recent past by authoritarian states damage democracy, peace, and reconciliation (Brito, González-Enríquez, and Aguilar 2001; Lutz and Sikkink 2001; Roht-Ariaza and Mariezcurrena 2006; Olsen, Payne, and Reiter 2010; Sikkink 2012). This literature examines what factors and actors (domestic and international) contribute to the emergence of transitional justice mechanisms in different regions, as well as the impacts such measures have on democracy and human rights.

Although it is not possible to identify a uniform pattern of transitional justice policy in Latin America, one trend in this literature indicates that both domestic and internal factors (e.g., the political will of governments, the level of civil society mobilization, and the power of the military), as well as external factors (e.g., pressures from international governmental and nongovernmental organizations) contribute to the emergence and the kinds of effects of transitional justice policies. This literature calls attention to the need to go beyond country case studies and qualitative analyses of individual cases. They combine both qualitative and quantitative methods, compiling a large sample of countries and databases, including statistical and historical analyses of the factors and models of transitional justice from a national and comparative perspective at regional and global scales (Olsen, Payne, and Reiter 2010; Sikkink 2012).

This type of comparative and large-scale quantitative and qualitative research is much needed. However, it tends to overlook the dynamics of local social, cultural, and political processes and the practices of actors that either contribute to or challenge the establishment of certain transitional justice policies on the ground. By mapping national and international *factors* without paying close attention to social, cultural, and political actors and *processes* on the ground, this type of analysis tends to center on the policies established by the state and assumes a linear, static-phase perspective on (transitional) politics.

Criticizing the state-centered and international normative approach to transitional justice, McEvoy and McGregor (2008) propose an alternative approach that they call "transitional justice from below." Contrary to "transitional justice from above," which focuses on states and international norms, "transitional justice from below" is an approach that highlights the need to study different scales of justice (local, national, and international) and calls for close attention to the practices of various actors beyond the state or international governmental organizations, such as victims' groups and organizations, non-governmental organizations, community and grassroots groups, and so on.

In her study on the emergence and effects of the global justice norm (i.e., individual criminal accountability), Sikkink (2012) considers both domestic and international factors and pays attention to historical political processes at multiple levels of analysis. Refuting the argument of "contagion" present in the literature on diffusion of norms, she argues that the "agency" and "choice" of individual activists involved in the promotion and diffusion of the justice norm were crucial for the global rise in legitimacy of this norm. Sikkink (2012) explains that this was made possible thanks to the work of human rights activists, especially from Argentina, who operated domestically and internationally to promote their ideals and the justice norm. Missing in this groundbreaking study is an in-depth analysis of collective action, such as mobilizations by former political prisoners, families of the disappeared and their allies, and how legal, social and cultural mobilization might shape the political and legal culture of different sectors of the state.

Indeed, as noted by Burt, Fried, and Lessa (2013), to better understand the politics of transitional justice in different countries in Latin America it is necessary to further examine the local historical processes and the mobilization waged by civil society actors, as illustrated in the case of Uruguay. Collins' (2006; 2008; 2010) comparative study of what she dubs "post-transitional justice," based on the cases of Chile and El Salvador, also calls for a grounded analysis of transitional justice, based on a social movement and political opportunity structure perspective on the use of courts. Observing the repealing of amnesty laws during the 1990s and a new wave of legal actions, Collins (2008, 22) characterizes this new wave as a "post-transitional justice" phase, "usually driven by nonstate actors, including individual claimants, lawyers, and human rights organizations." In contrast, she notes, the previous phase of "transitional justice" that marked the 1980s was characterized by transitional settlements and self-amnesty laws usually established by the state alone (Collins 2008, 22).

Collins (2010, 44) does not assume that "accountability actors"—actors promoting civil or criminal legal actions against perpetrators—only appear after "transition." These actors may emerge from existing human rights movements or may be new, joining pro-accountability actors during or after the establishment of "transitional justice" outcomes such as truth commissions. Likewise, Collins (2010, 44) does not assume that nonstate actors use the strategy of legal action only after the "transitional justice" period. "Transition is not necessarily the first time some of these groups and individuals have acted in broader human rights mobilization, or attempted to use legal strategies and international links to achieve certain goals. But the specific goal of accountability—civil or criminal legal actions against perpetrators—may be new" (Collins 2010, 44). Regarding the underlying factors shaping the impacts of "post-transitional justice," Collins (2006; 2008; 2010) argues that domestic factors, such as local legal action and the culture of the national courts, are more influential in shaping the development of "post-transitional justice" outcomes than the outside pressures coming from international institutions and transnational advocacy networks.

Collins' grounded perspective on the use of courts for the promotion of civil and/or criminal liability of perpetrators of human rights violations in Latin America is a major contribution to studies of memory and justice politics. The historical and political processes taking place in specific locales are carefully examined. This perspective is important for understanding the legal and political cultures of multiple social actors. Collins' comparative approach also helps to avoid generalizations from one case study. However, the concept of "post-transitional justice" does not help us to understand the continuities in the practices of both nonstate and state actors. Similarly to the studies on "transitional justice from above," this concept continues to frame the struggles for the rights to memory, truth, and justice from a developmental, linear, and static-phase perspective. Rather than replacing the term "transitional justice" with "post-transitional justice," it is necessary to pay attention to transitional justice as a historical and political process marked by both continuities and discontinuities.

In the case of Brazil, for example, nonstate actors have initiated legal actions since the 1970s, during and after the military regime, before and after the establishment of the Amnesty Law of 1979 (Law 6,683/79). The interpretation of this law—whether or not it grants amnesty to state agents who committed serious human rights violations—continues to be an object of political and judicial debate. Although nonstate actors have not initiated a large number of legal actions, as in the cases of Argentina and Chile, their legal mobilization practices have focused on emblematic cases, and have been important for challenging the limits of transitional justice policies in Brazil. Since the 1970s, they have not been alone in these legal actions either. Both domestic and international non-governmental organizations and, most recently, agents of the state, such as a group of federal prosecutors at the Federal Office of the Public Prosecutor (*Ministério Público Federal*), have become allies of families of the disappeared and former political prisoners, and have initiated a number of legal actions to promote state and individual civil and criminal liability.

Both domestic and international forces contributed to the creation of reparation commissions in the 1990s and early 2000s, such as the Special Commission on Political Deaths and Disappearances of Persons (*Comissão Especial sobre Mortos e Desaparecidos Políticos*, hereafter CEMDP), housed at the Secretariat on Human Rights (*Secretaria de Direitos Humanos*, or SDH), and the Amnesty Commission (*Comissão de Anistia*, herafter CA), housed in the Ministry of Justice. Domestic and international forces also pressured the Brazilian government to establish in 2012 the country's first National Truth Commission (*Comissão Nacional da Verdade*, hereafter CNV).[2] It should be noted that the CEMDP and the CA are hybrid institutions, in the sense that they are composed of state officials representing different state departments or ministries, on one hand, and civil society actors selected due to their recognized knowledge of and commitment to human rights, on the other hand. The CEMDP includes one representative of families of the disappeared. Some civil society members of the CA are also victims of political repression, even though they do not serve on this commission as representatives of the victims. The CNV commissioners, on the other hand, were only civil society actors selected by President Dilma Rousseff on the basis of their knowledge of and commitment to promoting human rights. None of these commissioners represented families of the disappeared.

In sum, the case of Brazil cannot be characterized as "post-transitional justice." In fact, it is more productive to examine the role played by both domestic and international forces, as well state and nonstate actors, to understand the power relations and the processes of negotiation and contestation involved in the establishment of transitional justice policies over time. Before illustrating how legal mobilization by nonstate actors has been an important aspect of Brazilian politics concerning memory, truth and justice since the 1970s, I shall first provide evidence of official accounts of transitional justice that have either made invisible or understated the political role of the legal actions initiated by families of the disappeared and former political prisoners throughout the past forty years.

OFFICIAL REPRESENTATION OF LEGAL MOBILIZATION BY NONSTATE ACTORS

In her critical narrative analysis of what is made visible and invisible in Brazil's first official truth report, *Direito à Memória e à Verdade: Comissão Especial sobre Mortos e Desaparecidos Políticos* (The Right to Memory and Truth: Special Commission on Political Deaths and Disappearances of Persons), published in 2007 by the CEMDP, Rebecca Atencio argues that,

> It is important to attend critically to the question of visibility because this report is a foundational narrative of the Brazilian state's new politics of memory: it marks the first time the state has officially and systematically laid out its vision of what transitional justice means in the Brazilian context. (Atencio 2014, 85)

This was the final report on the work of the CEMDP, created in 1995 by then President Fernando Henrique Cardoso to grant financial reparations to families of the persons who were killed or disappeared during the dictatorship. Atencio (2014, 85) argues that this report makes visible political disappearance and the "rights to memory and truth," "but renders justice invisible." She notes that the report uses the term "justice" only on one occasion. The meaning of justice is also redefined. "The authors of the report do not equate justice with criminal punishment (nor with the identification of perpetrators)." (Atencio 2014, 86). Instead, referring to the work of the CEMDP and the CA, the report equates justice with "financial reparations," which become, in the report's words, "natural and legal consequences" (Atencio 2014, 86).

Another important aspect of what is made visible and invisible in this report, according to Atencio, is the representation of the struggle waged by families of the disappeared. The report acknowledges these families' pressure in favor of amnesty and the right to truth in the 1970s, acknowledging their critiques of the Amnesty Law of 1979. However, "A close reading reveals that this history largely suppresses the existence of demands for punishment" (Atencio 2014, 86). Indeed, Atencio points out that the critiques on the limits of the CEMDP and the demands for criminal and civil accountability made by some families of the disappeared are briefly and superficially addressed in the report. "By omitting the fact that at least some families also pressured for punishment, the report not only silences those demands but also implies that even if they exist, they weren't legitimate" (Atencio 2014, 86). In sum, this report "embraces the discourse of reconciliation by memory, giving its culturally dominant approach to the past political hegemony" (Atencio 2014, 86). Although the term "transitional justice" was not used in this first official report on Brazilian policies on truth and memory, Atencio's critical reading brings to light how certain nonstate actors' practices and awareness are made invisible by hegemonic thinking.

A year after this report was published, one agency of the state—the CA—began to publicly defend not only policies on "truth and memory" (e.g., educational and memorial projects) but also "justice" (in the sense of state and individual civil and criminal accountability). The SDH and a group of federal prosecutors at the Federal Office of the Public Prosecutor also adopted this position, which aroused much reaction from the military and then dominant civilian sectors of the state and society. This shows that the state is not a homogenous actor and that transitional justice politics does not take a progressive, linear path (Santos 2010). Yet, despite the political shift in one sector of the state, which culminated in the creation of Brazil's CNV in 2012, I want to reiterate Atencio's critical reading and further argue that the legal mobilization practices waged by families of the disappeared and former political prisoners continued to be represented by hegemonic political thinking as marginal. Most of the legal actions initiated by these families are not mentioned in the 2007 CEMDP report. The official and scholarly publications using the term "transitional justice" often place at the margins these civil legal actions and struggles for justice.

A case in point are the publications organized by the CA. The CA was created in 2001 by President Cardoso to provide financial reparations to civilians and military officials who were persecuted (e.g., arbitrarily arrested, fired, forced to leave the country in exile, and so on) by the military regime for political reasons. This reparation commission became more active and efficient only after 2007, under the leadership of its new president Paulo Abrão, selected for this position during President Lula's second term (2007–2010). Paulo Abrão and Marcelo Torelly, the CA's special advisor until 2011, expanded the work of this commission and greatly contributed to the promotion of "transitional justice" debates and policies in Brazil. In their capacity as heads of the CA, they looked for guidance from and engaged in dialogue with national and international scholars and practitioners, such as the International Center for Transitional Justice (ICTJ) based in New York, as well as other organizations based in Latin American countries. In 2008, the CA began to officially use the term "transitional justice," signing an international cooperation program with the United Nations and incorporating into its projects the paradigm of transitional justice promoted by the UN and the ICTJ (Marcelo Torelly, e-mail message to author, August 7, 2013).[3] Thanks to this international cooperation program, the CA was able to organize a series of international conferences on transitional justice in partnership with renowned universities in Brazil, European countries, and the United States.[4] Since 2009 the CA has published the journal *Revista Anistia Política e Justiça de Transição* (Political Amnesty and Transitional Justice Journal) and a series of books on the issue of transitional justice (see, for example, Payne, Abrão, and Torelly 2011).

Overall, these publications on "transitional justice" in Brazil tend to focus on the actions taken by the state, portraying memory politics mainly "from above" and from a linear, progressive, and static-phase perspective. Abrão and Torelly (2013), for example, describe the development of "transitional justice" policies in Brazil based on the changing meaning of amnesty across three separated phases. The first phase started with the establishment of the Amnesty Law in 1979. It corresponded to a dominant political, cultural, and social culture that forged "forgetting" and "impunity" in opposition to the fight for "memory and truth" carried out by families of the disappeared and political prisoners. The second phase started with the creation of the CEMDP in 1995, followed by the CA in 2001. The authors point out that this phase was characterized by the politics of "reparation," which indirectly also promoted a politics of "memory and truth," as illustrated by the educational and memorial projects promoted by the CA. According to the authors, this second phase also sparked "new" mobilizations by families of the disappeared, former political prisoners, civilian and military public officials persecuted by the military regime, among other actors. The third phase began with the creation of the CNV in 2012. It is characterized by the politics of "truth," fostering "new" social mobilizations and political conflicts over the end of impunity.

Abrão and Torelly (2011) acknowledge the role of social mobilization in all of these phases. As they report, the 1979 Amnesty Law was a result of strong social mobilization carried out by diverse social movements which opposed the military regime. The reparation commissions created during the second phase also resulted from social mobilizations waged by two movements: the first movement was formed by what the authors describe as a "small group of families of the disappeared," resulting in the creation of the CEMDP in 1995; and the second movement was formed by workers who had been fired or prevented from working during the dictatorship due to their exercise of the right to association. This movement led to the creation of the CA in 2001. Drawing on existing historical research, the authors persuasively note that after the passage of the 1979 Amnesty Law, new social movements did not include in their agenda any demand for "transitional justice" in Brazil, and society at large did not care about this issue either. Thus, they aptly argue that the "low level of social mobilization" by society at large is one of the factors that explain the persistence of impunity (Abrão and Torelly 2011, 237–39).

The authors situate the third phase within the context of "new" social movements formed by a new generation of activists who have embraced the pro-accountability cause, such as the youth movement called *Levante Popular da Juventude* (Youth Popular Uprising). These are not direct victims or family members of the disappeared or former political prisoners. Although their mobilizations are socially relevant, the authors explain the recent change in the position of the Brazilian government—in favor of some transitional justice measures, such as the creation of the CNV—as a result of two institutional factors: changes in the national political forces within the state, thanks to the new directions taken by the reparation commissions since 2007, and changes in the international forces, including the 2010 decision by the Inter-American Court of Human Rights (IACtHR) that condemned Brazil in the Araguaia Guerrilla case (Abrão and Torelly 2013).

The importance of this account from inside the state on the development of transitional justice policies in Brazil is undeniable. The identification of these three policy phases does not contradict but rather complements my reading on transitional justice from the standpoint of nonstate actors. However, this state-centered analysis of separated phases ends up making invisible or placing at the margins of transitional justice politics the *ongoing* struggles and legal mobilization practices waged by families of the disappeared and by former political prisoners. In this perspective, the families are viewed as "old" actors and as "victims," not as political subjects actively involved in transitional justice politics in Brazil today. Not surprisingly, the authors overlook the fact that the 2010 IACtHR decision was a result of transnational legal mobilization initiated by civil society actors, namely by the alliance formed between organized groups of families of the disappeared and international human rights NGOs. They also overlook the alliances made between the "old" (family victims) and the "new" (non-family) activists who are fighting for civil and criminal accountability in contemporary Brazil.

The 2014 CNV final report is another example of the hegemonic representation of legal mobilization practices by the families of the disappeared and former political prisoners as marginal. The CNV was established in 2012 to uncover the "serious human rights violations" that took place in Brazil between 1946 and 1988 (Law 12,528/2011).[5] The CNV worked for two years and seven months, focusing on the state apparatus, ideologies and practices of repression during the military dictatorship (1964–1985). Despite its limited mandate, restricted to finding "truth," not "justice," and the initial criticisms raised by families of the disappeared claiming that the CNV was not efficient and transparent, this unprecedented truth commission was an important advancement in the politics of transitional justice in Brazil. It is not within the scope of this chapter to discuss the process of creation and operation of the CNV. It is also too early to evaluate its effects on Brazilian society and on transitional justice politics. But it is important to highlight a few advancements brought about by the CNV final report, released on December 10, 2014, and discuss how this report relates to and portrays the organized groups of families of the disappeared and former political prisoners.

The CNV final report is the first official acknowledgment that the Brazilian state created a repressive apparatus during the military dictatorship. This report reiterates official statements and knowledge already made public in the 2007 CEMDP report. It largely relies on secondary sources, especially on the research previously conducted by national and international scholars and the data collected for the *Brasil: Nunca Mais* project.[6] It also builds on the "dossiers" about the persons killed and disappeared during the military regime, which were organized by non-governmental organizations composed of families of the disappeared.[7] Yet the CNV report, which includes three volumes and is over 4,000 pages in length, also collected unprecedented testimonies by victims and agents of repression alike, and counted on the complementary work conducted by numerous truth commissions established by states' assemblies and universities, among other institutions.

Contrary to the "reconciliation by memory" approach of the 2007 CEMDP report, the CNV final report goes further by laying out the repressive institutions and clandestine centers of repression and torture created during the dictatorship, naming 377 state officials from all levels of state administration, who are cited as responsible for designing and implementing a repressive regime based on forced disappearances, extrajudicial executions, arbitrary arrests, and the systematic practice of torture. Moreover, the CNV final report makes explicit its support of transitional justice measures relating not only to "truth and memory," but also to "justice" (civil and criminal accountability) and "institutional reform," as recommended by the United Nations and the Organization of American States. One of the CNV's 29 recommendations to the Brazilian state is that public agents who committed "serious violations of human rights" during the military dictatorship be held responsible and subjected to the appropriate criminal, civil and administrative sanctions. The CNV also called for the Judiciary to disregard the Amnesty Law of 1979 with respect to these types of violations (CNV 2014, 966). However, one of the seven commissioners, the former Minister of Justice José Paulo Cavalcanti Filho, did not support this recommendation, a position that is shared by the Armed Forces and many civilians in government and in the Judiciary. In her emotional speech made at the official delivery of the CNV final report, President Dilma Rousseff signaled her lack of support to this recommendation and emphasized the continuation of the "reconciliation by truth" approach to transitional justice: "Truth does not mean revenge. Truth does not need to be a reason for hate or reckoning."[8]

Due to lack of cooperation on the part of the Armed Forces, the CNV was not able to advance much official knowledge or confirm unofficial data on the number of persons arbitrarily arrested, disappeared and tortured under the military regime. But there is clear evidence that "The repressive system improved and became institutionalized" (CNV 2014, 105). Drawing on information from the American Embassy in Brazil, the CNV indicates that over 5,000 individuals were arrested on the days that immediately followed the military coup of 1964 (CNV 2014, 98). Indeed, according to the 2007 CEMDP report, over 50,000 individuals were arrested in the first months after the coup, and approximately 10,000 individuals lived in exile during the military regime (CEMDP 2007, 30). As of September 2014, the Amnesty Commission had received 62,000 petitions requesting financial reparations, out of which 35,000 were approved. This number attests to the pervasive and massive level of political persecution undertaken by the repressive regime (CNV 2014, 27). From 1964 until 1985, agents of repression systematically used torture to extract information from political prisoners, even after the repressive state eliminated armed groups of resistance (CNV 2014, 349).

Regarding the number of political deaths and forced disappearances, the CNV final report confirmed a few less cases (434) than those indicated in the 2007 CEMDP report and in the last dossier organized by the families of the disappeared (see Almeida et al. 2009). It is interesting to note that the CNV final report acknowledges that this number does not correspond to the total number of deaths and disappearances but rather to what the CNV was able to confirm. The CNV final report also dedicates two chapters in the second volume to serious human rights violations perpetrated against peasants and indigenous people, and suggests an "expressive number of victims" (CNV 2014, 964). The third volume of the CNV final report is dedicated to listing a short bio of each individual who died or disappeared for political reasons during the dictatorship. This volume, as noted, draws on the 2009 dossier organized by families of the disappeared.

Although the CNV final report largely recognizes and draws on the work of "memory" and the struggle for "truth" waged by civil society actors and organized groups of families of the disappeared, these actors' legal mobilization practices and struggles for "justice" are marginalized in this report. The CNV final report dedicates one chapter to the Araguaia Guerrilla movement that took place in the late 1960s and early 1970s. The then clandestine Communist Party of Brazil (PCdoB) sent sixty-nine members to organize a guerrilla movement in the Araguaia region in the north of Brazil. The armed forces used 10,000 troops to decimate the movement, killing and disappearing the bodies of most guerrilla members. Local peasants and indigenous people also faced repression and torture perpetrated by military soldiers. The CNV final report includes information on the local and transnational legal actions initiated by twenty-two relatives of disappeared members of the Araguaia Guerrilla, but it does not give sufficient attention to this legal mobilization practice as part of civil society actors' struggles for "memory, truth and justice" (see CNV 2014, Vol. 1, Book II, Chapter 14). The Araguaia Guerrilla legal case and a few other legal actions initiated by families of the disappeared are also cited in one of the chapters specifically dedicated to the Judiciary. Yet, this chapter of the CNV report does not fully acknowledge the important role of legal and political mobilization enacted by these civil society actors (see CNV 2014, Vol. 1, Book II, Chapter 17). In fact, similarly to the 2007 CEMDP report, the families of the disappeared and former political prisoners are portrayed as "victims," not as political subjects, let alone activists. Even though not all victims engage in politics and are activists, there are former political prisoners who have continuously engaged in activism after the end of the dictatorship, and there are families of the disappeared who have become activists involved in varying causes, including the struggles for memory, truth, and justice, as illustrated below by the legal actions initiated by members of the NGOs *Grupo Tortura Nunca Mais* in Rio de Janeiro (GTNM/RJ) and *Comissão de Familiares de Mortos e Desaparecidos Políticos* in São Paulo (CFMDP).

LEGAL MOBILIZATION IN STRUGGLES FOR MEMORY, TRUTH, AND JUSTICE

Before addressing the main legal actions initiated by nonstate actors in their struggles for memory, truth, and justice in Brazil, I shall present the approach to legal mobilization that is used in this chapter to shed light on studies of transitional justice on the ground and from the margins. Law and society scholarship broadly defines legal mobilization as a variety of practices such as litigation, legal campaigns, lobbying to change laws, rights talk, popular legal education, legal consciousness raising, and so on (McCann 2008). Legal mobilization can involve individual or collective actors. Litigation is just one among many possible dimensions of legal mobilization. The use of courts or litigation can be individual or collective, and might be directly or indirectly linked to social and political mobilization. Legal mobilization in general and litigation in particular can take place at different scales—local, national, transnational.

Reviewing law and social movement scholarship, McCann (2006) refers to the fact that the "process-based approaches to studying law in social movements" emphasize "various contextual factors." As noted by the author, "Opportunity structures, movement resources, and discursive terrains or legal consciousness are familiar organizing categories for such analyses. Some of the most interesting and important contributions of scholarship on social movements derive from this attention" (McCann 2006, 25). McCann (2006) observes that the literature on law and social movements has expanded in the United States since the mid-1990s. Even though most research focuses on legal mobilization at the local and national scales, international and transnational legal mobilization has also gained increased attention in studies of law and social movements since the early 2000s.

Going beyond the limits of the nation-state and of individualistic uses of law, Santos and Rodríguez-Garavito (2005) propose an approach that they call "subaltern cosmopolitan legality" to refer to the transnational, counter-hegemonic mobilization of law by social movements in the global South. "Subaltern cosmopolitan legality" is characterized by four expansions of the conception of law and of the politics of legality. First, there must be a combination of political and legal mobilization. In fact, subaltern cosmopolitan legality is a form of political mobilization of law. It presupposes the politicization of the use of law and courts. Legal mobilization, in turn, may involve legal, illegal, and non-legal actions. Second, the politics of legal mobilization needs to be conceived of at three different scales—the local, the national, and the global, so that the struggles are linked across borders. Third, there must be an expansion of professional legal knowledge, of the nation-state law, and of the legal canon that privileges individual rights. This does not mean that individual rights are abandoned by subaltern cosmopolitan politics and legality, even though there is an emphasis on collective rights. Finally, the time frame of the legal struggle must be expanded to include the time frame of the social struggle that serves to politicize the legal dispute. This means that the social conflicts are conceived of as structural problems related to capitalism, colonialism, patriarchy, authoritarian political regimes, and so on (Santos 2005, 30).

The legal defense of leaders and causes of social movements by "popular advocacy" in Brazil is an example of the political mobilization of law. This can be illustrated by the struggles for agrarian reform and counter-hegemonic globalization waged by the Movement of Landless Rural Workers (Santos and Carlet 2010). The so-called "strategic litigation" (*litígio estratégico*), carried out in Latin America by human rights NGOs that specialize in litigation to defend a cause, is also an example of the political mobilization of law that can go beyond the limits of the nation-state (Cardoso 2012). The "transnational legal activism" practices by NGOs and social movement actors that use the Inter-American system of human rights to pressure states to promote legal and policy changes at the domestic level might also serve as an example of subaltern cosmopolitan legality (Santos 2007).

The legal actions initiated by families of the disappeared and former political prisoners illustrate practices of local and transnational legal mobilization that gain a political meaning, even if these actors do not specialize in the "strategic" use of courts and do not fight for the causes of others. They fight for their own individual rights and rely on the support of attorneys and/or NGOs. Yet, many times their individual struggles are linked to larger social and political mobilizations (Teles 2005; 2010; Santos 2007; 2010). The legal mobilization and subaltern cosmopolitan legality approaches are useful to understand and make sense of these legal actions. These actions depend on the material and emotional resources available to the litigants, and influence the level of their rights consciousness to demand "memory, truth, and justice." Not all families of the disappeared and former political prisoners engage with legal mobilization. Not all who initiate legal actions view themselves as "political actors" and "activists." But there are groups of families of the disappeared and former political prisoners who have continuously struggled for justice and social change since the dictatorship, and there are some who have become activists in the collective struggles for the rights to memory, truth, and justice.

This chapter does not intend to discuss the frames and the outcomes of legal actions, but mainly to show that this type of legal mobilization practice existed before and after the Amnesty Law of 1979, which marked the beginning of the long "transition" from military to civilian rule in 1985. Contrary to a vision of separated "phases" of transitional and post-transitional justice, the existence of these legal actions illustrates continuity in struggles for memory, truth, and justice. Nonstate actors have made accountability claims before and after the so-called "transition." And the new legal and political opportunities and contexts have allowed for the emergence of new legal actions initiated by a pro-accountability group of federal prosecutor officers. New civil society and state actors have also joined the pro-accountability cause, as noted by Abrão and Torelly (2013). Moreover, some of these actors, such as the movement called *Levante Popular da Juventude*, have enacted legal mobilization practices outside of courts (e.g., *escrachos*) and in coordination with groups of families of the disappeared.[9]

Transnational and Local Legal Actions Against the State (1970s–1980s)

In her approach to "post-transitional justice" in Latin America, Collins (2010) argues that the strategies and frames to articulate rights claims to memory, truth, and justice have to be examined in each particular context. Indeed, then and now, as noted by legal mobilization scholars (McCann 2006), legal actions are shaped by the legal and political opportunities and contexts in which they take place. According to Collins (2010, 44), the legal actions initiated in Latin America before transitions might have been primarily intended "to expose HRV patterns, to reduce or end ongoing abuse, or to protect detained individuals via legal injunctions or international publicity."

In contrast with Collins' (2010) argument about possible differences between the goals of legal actions before and after transitional periods, this chapter shows that in the case of Brazil there are continuities in nonstate actors' struggles for memory, truth, and justice. In the early 1970s, both local and transnational legal actions were initiated by families of the disappeared and/or by relatives of political prisoners. The repressive political context and the overall lack of access to domestic courts required the transnationalization of legal action. At the time, several petitions denouncing arbitrary detentions and practices of torture and political deaths committed by state agents were sent to the Inter-American Commission on Human Rights (IACHR). Most cases ended up being dismissed by the IACHR (Teles 2005; 2010; Santos 2009; 2010). Yet, families of the disappeared and former political prisoners continued to struggle for the rights to memory, truth, and justice at the domestic level and used the courts according to the resources and legal opportunities available at the time.

prisoners, 1970s and 1980s[a]

Case	*Year of petition*	*Type of legal action*	*Complainant(s)*	*Year and content of decision on merit*	*Last decision on appeals or current status*
Mãos Amarradas (Hands Tied Up) Case (Case n. 88.0009436-8, Federal Court of Rio Grande do Sul)	1973	Civil legal action against the state and agents of the state, demanding reparations for moral and material harms due to the death of Manoel Raimundo Soares.	Elizabeth Challup Soares (wife) – she died in June 2009, but her daughter can replace her in the legal action (Teles 2010; CNV 2014).	2000 – Decision found the state responsible for death and torture of the victim, condemning the state to pay reparations. State agents were excluded because the complainant withdrew the charges against them.	Civil Appeal n. 2001.04.01.085202-9/RS, decided by the Federal Regional Court in 2005, confirming the original decision. However, as of December 10, 2014, the state had not paid reparations yet (CNV 2014).
Vladimir Herzog Case (Case n. 136/76, Federal Court of São Paulo)	1976	Civil legal action against the state, requesting declaration of civil responsibility, not demanding financial reparations.	Clarice Herzog (wife) and two sons	1978 – Decision in favor of the complainants, declaring civil responsibility of the state for the "death and torture" of journalist Herzog.	Last decision on appeal in 1994, maintaining the original decision.
Manoel Fiel Filho Case (Case n. 0129866-13.1979.4.03.6100, Federal Court of São Paulo)	1978	Civil legal action against the state, demanding financial reparations.	Thereza de Lourdes M. Fiel (wife) and daughters	1981 – Decision in favor of complainants, ordering the state to pay reparations due to arbitrary arrest and torture leading to death of the union leader Manoel Fiel Filho.	Last decision on the appeal in 1987, confirming the original decision, except the payment for "moral harm."
Mário Alves de Souza Vieira Case (Case n. 2678420, Federal Court of Rio de Janeiro)	1979	Civil legal action against the state, demanding recognition of civil responsibility but not financial reparations.	Dilma Borges Vieira (wife) and daughter, Lúcia Caldas Vieira	1981 – Decision in favor of complainants	Civil appeal decided in 1987, confirming the original decision that found the state responsible (civil) for the arbitrary arrest, death, and disappearance of the victim.

Raul Amaro Ferreira Case (Case n. 241.0087/99, Federal Court of Rio de Janeiro)	1979	Civil legal action against the state, demanding recognition of civil responsibility but not financial reparations (CEMDP 2007, 173).	Mariana Lanari Ferreira (mother)	1982 - Decision in favor of complainant	In 1994, decision on the last appeal confirmed the first decision; the state was held responsible for the arbitrary arrest, torture, and death of Raul Ferreira.
Inês Etienne Romeu Case (1) (Case n. 0000166-68.1981.8.19.0042, Civil Court of Petrópolis)	1981	Civil legal action against the owner of a clandestine torture center known as "Casa da Morte" (Death House, a clandestine torture center), demanding declaration of civil responsibility.	Inês Etienne Romeu, the only survivor of the "Death House"	1981 – Decision against complainant, not recognizing responsibility, alleging that the owner of the house did not have knowledge of what was happening in the house (CNV 2014, 954).	Inês Romeu also reported the crimes to the Bar Association. The Federal Council of the Bar Association and the Brazilian Press Association requested an investigation by the Council for the Defense of the Rights of Human Beings in the Ministry of Justice, which closed the case without investigation (case MJ 7252/1981, cited in CNV 2014).
Araguaia Guerrilla Case (Case n. I-108/83, Federal Court of the Federal District of Brasília)	1982	Civil legal action against the state, demanding information allegedly in possession of the Army on the disappearance of guerrilla members; requested the localization of their remains, and the right to bury them.	22 relatives of disappeared members of the Araguaia Guerrilla movement	2003 – Decision on the merit in favor of complainants	In 2007, after a number of appeals, the final decision confirmed the 2003 decision.
Ruy Frazão Soares Case (Case n. 10.980-0, Federal Court of Pernambuco)	1983	Civil legal action against the state, demanding declaration of civil responsibility, not financial reparations.	Felicia Moraes (wife) and Henrique Ruy	1991 – Decision declared state responsible for arbitrary arrest, death and disappearance of Ruy F. Soares.	After a series of appeals, the case was finally decided in 2002, confirming the first decision.

[a] This table draws on data cited in Teles' thesis (2005) and on the websites of the Federal Courts where each legal action was initiated. I am grateful to Crimeia Schmidt de Almeida, survivor of the Araguaia Guerrilla massacre and founding member of the CFMDP, for

As table 3.1 indicates, the main local legal actions initiated in the 1970s and 1980s targeted the state and demanded civil accountability for the arbitrary detentions, torture and political deaths, and forced disappearances.[10] These legal actions started during the military regime. All of them were initiated by families of the disappeared, former political prisoners, or relatives of political prisoners tortured and killed by the repressive state. All but two—the *Mãos Amarradas* (Tied Up Hands) and the Inês Etienne Romeu cases—were against the state, not against individuals and/or state agents of repression. The complainants in all of these legal cases sought the courts to have the rights to "truth," "memory," and "justice" (civil accountability) recognized. Only one case—the *Mãos Amarradas*—demanded financial reparations in addition to the recognition claims of truth, memory, and civil accountability.

It is important to note that the *Mãos Amarradas* case and two other legal actions (Herzog and Fiel Filho cases) were initiated before the Amnesty Law of 1979. The *Mãos Amarradas* case was filed in 1973 in the state of Rio Grande do Sul by Elizabeth Soares, the wife of the victim Manoel Soares, a former military officer who was killed by the state due to his political position against the regime. His body was found in a river with his hands tied up to his back, hence the naming of the case as "Tied Up Hands." Until recently, this case had not attracted any social and political attention (Teles 2010). According to Teles (2010), the complainant was not connected to other families' struggles for truth, memory, and justice. That is why the pattern of her isolated legal action was unique. Her case is the only one from that period that demanded state and individual civil responsibility, as well as reparations. Yet the complainant ended up withdrawing the charges against individual state agents, as indicated in table 3.1.

The Herzog case, although not the first, received at the time large support from social movements and human rights organizations, including the groups of mothers and families of the disappeared (Moraes 2006, 15).[11] Vladimir Herzog was a well-known journalist living in the city of São Paulo. In October 1975, he was arbitrarily arrested, submitted to torture and killed in the São Paulo station house of DOPS-*Departamento de Ordem Política e Social* (Department of Political and Social Order, an organ of the army). His death sparked widespread social mobilization that attracted great media attention. In 1976, his wife, Clarice Herzog, and their two sons filed a civil legal action against the state, demanding the judicial recognition that the victim had not committed "suicide," contrary to what his death certificate indicated, but rather that the state was responsible for his death as a result of torture. No financial reparation was demanded. In 1978, the decision on the merit was published, favoring the complainants. This was an important and courageous decision in face of the repressive context in which it occurred. This decision was made by a young judge then appointed to preside over this case in lieu of an elder judge who was forced to retire due to the armed forces' suspicion that the original judge was going to decide against the state. This unprecedented ruling, holding the state responsible for the death of the journalist as a result of torture, was widely covered by the media and challenged the legitimacy of the military regime. Yet, Herzog family's struggle for justice did not end in 1978. The state appealed to the superior courts, as it did in all of the other cases where the judges decided against the state, and the case ended only in 1994. The family continued to fight in courts to change Vladimir Herzog's death certificate until 2013. In addition to the struggle for civil accountability, in 2009 the family and their human rights NGO allies also decided to demand in court the criminal accountability of state agents who tortured and killed Herzog, as indicated in table 3.2.

Immediately after the enactment of the 1979 Amnesty Law, families of the disappeared and/or former political prisoners initiated new legal actions. All were against the state and all demanded the recognition of state's civil accountability. The Araguaia Guerrilla case, initiated in 1982 by twenty-two relatives of guerrilla members who disappeared as a result of state repression, requested that a report allegedly in the hands of the Army be disclosed to reveal information on the circumstances of the deaths and disappearances of the victims. In addition to such demand for the "truth," this legal action also intended to restore the "history" of the Araguaia Guerrilla movement and the "memory" of the victims. And it demanded civil accountability of the state. This legal action is unique because of its collective initiative (twenty-two complaintants). It is a clear example of the continued struggle for memory, truth and justice waged by families of the disappeared. This is also a landmark case that has served to pressure the Brazilian state to do the work of memory, truth, and (civil) justice since the early 1980s (Teles 2005; Santos 2010). This legal case was pending in the domestic courts until 2007, as noted in table 3.1, and until the end of 2014 the state had not yet fully complied with the judge's decision.

The fact that all the legal actions initiated in the 1970s and 1980s did not demand criminal accountability does not mean that there was no consciousness of the right to admission of criminal responsibility for serious human rights violations. The 1979 Amnesty Law was a result of social and political mobilization waged by various social movements and clandestine political parties. At that time the *Comissão de Familiares de Mortos e Desaparecidos Políticos* (Commission of Families of the Disappeared and Killed for Political Reasons, or CFMDP), the *Grupo Tortura Nunca Mais-São Paulo* (Group Torture Never Again-São Paulo, or GTNM/SP), and the *Comitê Brasileiro pela Anistia* (Brazilian Amnesty Committee, or CBA) were formed. These groups held different views regarding civil and criminal accountability of state agents. The CFMDP and the GTNM/SP, which remain active nowadays, have always defended the pursuit of justice (civil and criminal), whereas the CBA, which ended soon after the Amnesty Law was enacted, did not support criminal accountability claims. Thus, there were some groups that did articulate a political discourse in favor of criminal accountability in the 1970s (Atencio 2014, 86). At the end of the 1970s, the project *Brasil: Nunca Mais* was created. This project report, published in 1985, documented thousands of cases of torture based on copies of trials of political prisoners sentenced by the Military Courts. But this report did not advocate criminal accountability, considering it to mean "revenge," not "justice" (Arquidiocese de São Paulo 2003, 26). In the mid-1980s, new organizations composed of families of the disappeared were created, such as *Grupos Tortura Nunca Mais* (Torture Never Again Groups, or GTNM) in the cities of Rio de Janeiro, Recife, and Belo Horizonte. The GTNM of Rio de Janeiro is still active and continues to defend the rights to memory, truth, and justice, including civil and criminal accountability. In 1988, in the context of redemocratization and under a civilian regime, the National Constituent Assembly enacted the new Brazilian Constitution, which incorporated important demands of social movement actors for the recognition of new rights. As Abrão and Torelly (2011) point out, the new social movements did not continue to support the struggle for memory, truth, and justice waged by families of the disappeared and former political prisoners. But these families did not give up in their struggle.

Transnational Legal Mobilization in the Context of Redemocratization (1990s)

In the 1990s, families of the disappeared and former political prisoners initiated only two new legal actions. But this does not mean that legal mobilization ended. In fact, most of the legal actions filed in the 1980s continued for more than twenty years, as illustrated by the Araguaia Guerrilla case depicted in tables 3.1 and 3.2. These legal cases served as complementary weapons for the social and political mobilization waged by families of the disappeared and former political prisoners. The most important case was the transnationalization of the legal action relating to the Araguaia Guerrilla movement. In 1995, families of the disappeared during the Araguaia Guerrilla were able to forge alliances with human rights NGOs and sent this case to the IACHR.

Table 3.2. Transnational and local legal actions against the state, by families of the disappeared, human rights NGOs, and former political prisoners, 1990s[a]

Cases	*Year of petition*	*Type of legal action*	*Complainant(s)*	*Year and content of decision on merit*	*Last decision on appeals or current status*
Araguaia Guerrilla Case (transnational) (Case 11552 - Gomes Lund and Others versus Brazil)	1995	Petition sent to the Inter-American Commission on Human Rights.	CEJIL-Center for Justice and International Law, Human Rights Watch, Comissão de Familiares de Mortos e Desaparecidos Políticos (CFMDP), Grupo Tortura Nunca Mais-RJ (GNTM/RJ).	2001 – IACHR published the admissibility report (n. 33/01).	IACHR sent the case to the IACtHR in 2009. The IACtHR condemned the Brazilian state in 2010.
Inês Etienne Romeu Case (2) (Case n. 0027857-69.1999.4.03.6100, 17th Federal Civil District Court of São Paulo)	1999	Civil legal action against the state, demanding declaration of civil responsibility not financial reparations.	Inês Etienne Romeu (only survivor of a clandestine torture center known as "Casa da Morte" (Death House) in Petrópolis, near the city of Rio de Janeiro).	2003 – Decision in favor of complainant found the state responsible for her arbitrary arrest and torture.	The case was appealed by the state. The General Legal Consultant of the state recommended that the state withdraw the appeal. The case was closed in 2007.

[a] Data on the Araguaia Guerrilla case in the IACHR was generously provided by Crimeia Schmidt de Almeida. Information on this case is also based on interviews that I conducted with petitioners, attorneys, and state officials in São Paulo, Rio de Janeiro, and Brasília, and with a legal officer in the IACHR in Washington DC. Data on the Inês Etienne Romeu case was gathered from the website of the Federal Court of São Paulo and from the 2014 CNV final report.

The transnationalization of the Araguaia Guerrilla case must be situated within the political and legal opportunities and context in which it is embedded. This context favored the development of the mobilizing strategy to forge *transnational* legal alliances between the families of the disappeared and human rights NGOs. Brazil ratified the American Convention on Human Rights in 1992 and recognized the jurisdiction of the IACtHR in 1998. In the mid-1990s, domestic human rights NGOs began to develop the strategy of transnational legal activism (Santos 2007). The Araguaia Guerrilla case pending in the Brazilian courts did not reach a decision on merit until 2003 (see table 3.1). Thus, it was necessary to resort to transnational advocacy networks to provoke a "boomerang effect" (Keck and Sikkink 1998).

The law on access to public documents was indirectly under dispute in the legal battle over the Araguaia Guerrilla case. In 1991, then President Fernando Collor de Melo signed the Law 8,159/1991, establishing the National Policy on Public Archives. This law classified the degrees of secrecy for public documents and the statute of limitations for declassifying them. Documents that threatened "National Security" were classified as "top secret" (*alto grau de sigilo*). This law was an impediment to accessing information on the dictatorship that was in the hands of the army. The presidency of Fernando Henrique Cardoso (1995–2002) also established laws on access to public documents and extended the statutes of limitation for declassifying documents considered "top secret." The Lula government (2003–2010) maintained the same approach and established new decrees to extend the statute of limitation for declassifying those documents. Thus, the transnationalization of the Araguaia Guerrilla case was an attempt to change this kind of policy and gain access to "truth and justice." The petitioners and their allies used this case to mobilize for a new legislation on access to public information. In 2011, during Dilma Rousseff's presidency, a new legislation was enacted to grant citizens the right to ample and free access to public information (Law 12.527/2011). This law was signed together with the law that determined the creation of the CNV (Law 12.528/2011). Both laws were the result of a long-term struggle waged by pro-accountability actors, including old and new nonstate and state actors.

The CEMDP, as noted above, was created by then President Cardoso in 1995 and established an important transitional justice measure focusing on financial reparations. However, the Araguaia Guerrilla case was sent to the IACHR *before* the creation of the CEMDP. The families who were fighting for the rights to memory, truth and justice did not restrict their demands to financial reparations. Indeed, the families continued their social and legal mobilizations, as demonstrated by the dossier and the book they organized at the time to challenge the limits of the reparation commission created by Cardoso. The "Dossier of Political Deaths and Disappearances since 1964" (*Dossiê dos Mortos e Desaparecidos Políticos a Partir de 1964*) was published in 1995 and was based on several years of research by nonstate actors (CFMDP et al. 1995). In the mid-1990s, Janaína de Almeida Teles, who holds a Ph.D. in History and is a daughter of former political prisoners and niece of an Araguaia Guerrilla survivor, organized a conference at the University of São Paulo bringing together scholars, attorneys and activists to challenge the limited scope of the new reparation commission. This conference resulted in the publication of the book, *Mortos e Desaparecidos Políticos: Reparação ou Impunidade?* (Political Deaths and Disappearances: Reparation or Impunity?) (Teles 2001).

In addition to these publications and other social mobilization practices, organized groups of families of the disappeared and former political prisoners looked for new allies, domestic and international, inside and outside of the state. For instance, they forged an alliance with CEJIL-Center for Justice and International Law, an international human rights NGO that specializes in "strategic litigation" in the Inter-American system of human rights. In alliance with CEJIL and the international NGO Human Rights Watch, the CFMDP and GTNM/RJ sent a petition on the Araguaia Guerrilla case to the IACHR in 1995, as noted in table 3.2. At the domestic and governmental level, they also sought to establish alliances with politicians, such as Miguel Arraes, then governor of Pernambuco who had been in exile. Arraes sponsored the publication of the dossier in 1995 (CFMDP et al. 1995). They also looked for the support of members of the Federal Public Attorney Office (*Ministério Público Federal*, or MPF) of Rio de Janeiro and São Paulo, as federal prosecutor Marlon Weichert reported to me in an interview conducted in São Paulo on August 15, 2005. It was thanks to the provocation by the GTNM/RJ and the CFMDP that federal prosecutors learned about the social struggles for access to public information, the search for the remains of the disappeared in the Araguaia Guerrilla, and the search for and identification of the remains that had been found in a clandestine pit in the Perus Cemetery in São Paulo. In 1999, a group of federal prosecutors began to study legal strategies to defend the rights to memory, truth, and justice in relation to the crimes committed by the military regime, and they then initiated the first public civil legal actions against the state (Fávero 2009).

New Legal Actions in the Era of Individual Accountability (since 2005)

In the 2000s, a new international legal and political context conducive to individual accountability opened up the path for new legal actions initiated by two families (the Teles and Merlino families) against one state agent, namely Colonel Carlos Alberto Brilhante Ustra. This colonel was accused of torture. He had been the head of the Center of Operations for Internal Defense (*Centro de Operações de Defesa Interna*, or DOI-CODI) in São Paulo, from 1970 to 1974. These legal actions are important because they focus on *individual* liability, not on *state* accountability. Both are civil legal actions, as indicated in table 3.3.[12]

The political and ethical significance of these legal actions is well illustrated by the words of Maria Amélia Teles, one of the complainants in the Teles family case. As she writes,

> This legal action is declaratory in nature, we do not demand any financial reparations, nor punishment. The condemnation of Colonel Ustra is in the moral and ethical realm of justice. The recovering of history has a practical function: to repudiate hideous facts, to recover the credibility of society, transforming it into an active force, capable of following new paths and blocking backward movements. This is denied to the Brazilian people. We came out of a dictatorship without investigating the responsibilities for the torture, deaths, kidnapping and forced disappearances committed by agents of the Brazilian state. Brazilian people have the right to know who kidnapped, tortured and eliminated the lives of militants who dared to fight against the dictatorship. It is not possible to compromise with the practice of torture. Confronting it is a matter of justice, not a private issue. The legal action of the Teles family is an action of the Brazilian people.[13]

The new legal actions against Colonel Ustra were initiated in the context of favorable political and legal opportunities. The IACtHR ruled on cases that established a firm jurisprudence considering as "self-amnesty" the amnesty laws that were in effect in several countries in Latin America.[14] In 2003, Argentina revoked its laws of "Punto Final" (Full Stop Law) and of "Obediencia Devida" (Law of Due Obedience). This immediately sparked a number of new trials, and since then hundreds of state agents have been convicted and sentenced by Argentine courts for crimes against humanity.

Given this favorable international legal context, it is not surprising that the Teles family was able to win their case at all courts and levels of litigation, as indicated in table 3.3. In 2008, the judge presiding over this case ruled in favor of three of the five family member complainants. In 2012, the Superior State Court of São Paulo denied the appeal filed by Colonel Ustra. The day of this ruling, Crimeia Schmidt de Almeida, one of the winning complainants, made the following statement in celebration with the crowd that mobilized in front of the court: "This victory is not only of the Teles family, it's of the whole Brazil."[15] On December 9, 2014, one day before the public release of the CNV final report, the Superior Court of Justice based in Brasília, the federal capital, rejected again the last appeal filed by Colonel Ustra.

Table 3.3. Local and transnational legal actions against state agents, by families of the disappeared, former political prisoners, and human rights NGOs, since 2005

Case	*Year of petition*	*Type of legal action*	*Complainant(s)*	*Year and content of decision on merit*	*Last decision on appeals or current status*
Teles Family Case (Case n. 583002005202853-5, 23rd Civil District Court of São Paulo)	2005	Civil legal action against state agent Colonel Carlos Alberto Brilhante Ustra, demanding declaration of his civil responsibility for torture.	Former political prisoners Crimeia Schmidt de Almeida, Maria Amélia de Almeida Teles and César Augusto Teles, and the children of Maria Amélia and César, Janaína Teles and Edson Teles.	2008 – Decision declared Ustra responsible for the practice of torture, causing moral harms and physical injury to three petitioners (excluding the children Janaina and Edson).	2012 – State Superior Court decided unanimously against the appeal by Ustra. Another appeal was presented to the Superior Court of Justice and the majority of justices (3 against 2 votes) decided against Ustra on December 9, 2014.
Merlino Family Case (1) (Case n. 583.00.2007.241711-9, State Court of São Paulo)	2007	Civil legal action against state agent Colonel Carlos Alberto Brilhante Ustra, demanding declaration of his civil responsibility for torture and death of Merlino.	Family of Luiz Eduardo da Rocha Merlino (Angela Maria Mendes de Almeida and Regina Maria Merlin de Almeida).	2008 – Decision in favor of complainants.	Appeal decided in 2008 in favor of Ustra. The court considered that the family should request reparations due to moral harms.
Herzog Case (transnational) (Petition P-859-09)	2009	Petition sent to the Inter-American Commission on Human Rights, demanding criminal responsibility of	Center for Justice and International Law-CEJIL, Inter-American Foundation for the Defense of Human Rights (FIDDH), Center Santo Dias of the	2010 – IACHR published the admissibility report (n. 80/12).	Pending decision on the merit.

		arbitrary detention, torture, and death of Vladimir Herzog.	Paulo, and Tortura Nunca Mais/São Paulo.		
Merlino Family (2) (20th Civil District Court of the São Paulo Central Forum)	2010	Civil action against state agent Colonel Carlos Alberto Brilhante Ustra demanding financial reparations for moral harm.	Family of Luiz Eduardo da Rocha Merlino (Angela Maria Mendes de Almeida and Regina Maria Merlin de Almeida)	2012 – Decision in favor of complainants.	Pending appeal.

It is important to recall that even though the Brazilian Amnesty Commission (CA) had been created in 2001, it became more effective only after 2007, as noted above. Thus, this commission did not influence nonstate actors to use the courts in 2005 as a strategy to seek civil accountability of state agents. In fact, it is more likely that the legal actions initiated by the Teles and Merlino families served to pressure the state. As Janaína de Almeida Teles writes, "The novelty and the paradigmatic character of this action provoked the restarting of the debate on torture and on the scope of the Amnesty Law of 1979."[16] Furthermore, only after 2008 did a group of federal prosecutors begin to take legal actions in pursuit of individual and state civil and criminal accountability (Ministério Público Federal 2013; 2014).

At the transnational level, CEJIL and other human rights NGOs sent a petition in 2009 on behalf of the Herzog family to demand criminal accountability of state agents for the torture and killing of the journalist Vladimir Herzog.[17] In the same year, the CFMDP published a new edition of the dossier on the deaths and political disappearances (Almeida et al. 2009). It was also in 2009 that the Araguaia Guerrilla case was sent by the IACHR to the IACtHR. Pressures coming from the families of the disappeared and their allies sparked the IACHR initiative. In response to CEJIL's request, in 2008 the IACHR held the thematic session entitled "The Amnesty Law as an Impediment to Justice in Brazil" (*A Lei de Anistia como Obstáculo à Justiça no Brasil*).

At the same time, sectors of the government, such as the CA, the SDH and the pro-accountability group of federal prosecutors, began to promote public debates on the limits of the 1979 Amnesty Law. For example, in the first semester of 2008, the CA and the SDH held a public hearing on the "Limits and Possibilities for Legal Responsibility of Agents Who Violated Human Rights During the State of Exception in Brazil" (*Limites e Possibilidades para a Responsabilização Jurídica dos Agentes Violadores de Direitos Humanos durante o Estado de Exceção no Brasil*). This was an unprecedented initiative by state actors to bring to the center of the governmental agenda a public debate on the revision of the 1979 Amnesty Law. This public hearing sparked an internal division within the Executive branch of the state. On one side were the pro-accountability actors, such as the Ministry of Justice, the CA, the SDH, and the group of federal prosecutors, who defended the non-application of the Amnesty Law to perpetrators of serious human rights violations. On the other side were the con-accountability actors, such as the General Attorney Office and the Ministry of Defense, who advocated that the Amnesty Law be applied not only to the "political crimes" committed by dissidents of the authoritarian regime, but also the "connected crimes" (interpreted as crimes perpetrated by agents of the state), as prescribed in the provisions of the Amnesty Law. This political division within the executive power became even more accentuated when President Lula signed the third

National Human Rights Plan, which included for the first time a thematic area dedicated to the "right to truth and memory," and determined the creation of a National Truth Commission.

Another important actor that joined the pro-accountability cause in 2008 was the Brazilian Bar Association, which initiated a legal action before the Federal Supreme Court—the ADPF-Non-Compliance Action of the Fundamental Principle no. 153, demanding that the Court interpret the Amnesty Law in a manner that would suspend the application of the law to state agents who committed serious violations of human rights. The Federal Supreme Court ruled this action inadmissible and confirmed, by seven to two votes, the validity of the 1979 Amnesty Law. This certainly contributed to the 2010 decision by the IACtHR, condemning Brazil in the Araguaia Guerrilla case.[18] The IACtHR decided unanimously that the crimes committed by the Brazilian state to repress the Araguaia Guerrilla—such as forced disappearance, extrajudicial summary executions, and torture—constituted "crimes against humanity." And decided in line with its established jurisprudence on "self-amnesty" laws that,

> Par. 147—Amnesties or similar forms have been one of the obstacles alleged by some States in the investigation, and where applicable, punishment of those responsible for serious human rights violations. This Court, the Inter-American Commission on Human Rights, the organs of the United Nations, and other universal and regional organs for the protection of human rights have ruled on the non-compatibility of amnesty laws related to serious human rights violations with international law and the international obligations of States.[19]

This unprecedented decision has helped to strengthen the pro-accountability mobilization practices in Brazil. The IACtHR made clear that the creation of a national truth commission would not be sufficient to address the serious human rights violations committed by the Brazilian state and its agents in the repression of the Araguaia Guerrilla. This emblematic case is an example of enduring legal and political mobilization practices by nonstate actors since the early 1980s. This case has also helped to redefine the agenda of certain state actors, such as the reparation and truth commissions and the group of federal prosecutors who have been taking legal initiatives to force the Brazilian state to fully comply with this international decision (Ministério Público Federal 2014). Yet, Brazilian media, state sectors, and civil society actors are divided about the validity of this decision and Brazil's duty to comply with it (Cardia, Possas, Blotta, and Bastos 2014).

CONCLUSION

As demonstrated throughout this chapter, the case of Brazil challenges the concept of "post-transitional justice." Legal actions have been initiated by domestic nonstate actors since the 1970s. They are part of a larger struggle for the rights to memory, truth, and justice. These actions have preceded and succeeded each of the three phases of transitional justice described by Abrão and Torelly (2011; 2013). Thus, the history of transitional justice politics needs to be reread from the margins to account for the multiple processes, actors, and strategies of struggle that occur within particular political and social contexts. More recently, state actors, such as federal prosecutors, have also initiated a new wave of civil and criminal legal actions against the state and individual state agents. Even though the families of the disappeared and new pro-accountability social movements have been critical of the state, there have been mutual exchanges of experiences between state and nonstate actors, and some pro-accountability sectors of the state have been more open to incorporate demands from nonstate actors into the governmental agenda on transitional justice. State and civil society actors are not as separated as the literature on transitional and post-transitional justice seems to imply. In addition, both domestic and international forces have shaped the politics of transitional justice in Brazil.

Uncovering legal mobilization practices sheds light on transitional justice politics on the ground and from the margins, helping to legitimize marginalized subjects of history, memory, and justice. Legal mobilization by nonstate actors, as part of larger struggles for the rights to truth, memory, and justice, has been marginalized in official accounts of transitional justice in Brazil. Families of the disappeared and former political prisoners are portrayed mainly as "victims," not as activists and political subjects. Yet, these families have been struggling and developing collective strategies to promote justice since the early 1970s. In fact, the legal and political battles over "truth" and "memory" are part of the work of "justice." As noted by James Booth (2006, 128), "In our time, this connection between memory-truth-justice has become, if anything, even more compelling. For one of the goals of the perpetrators of mass crime in this past century has been the obliteration of the memory of the victims." In this sense, "Writing history and doing justice, the labor of historians and of courts, are both forms of memory work" (Booth 2006, 114).

McCann (2008, 35) argues that, "Legal mobilization tactics do not inherently empower or disempower citizens. Legal institutions and norms tend to be Janus-faced, at once securing the status quo of hierarchical power while sometimes providing limited opportunities for episodic challenges to and transformations in that reigning order." Indeed, in the case of Brazil, legal mobilization practices by nonstate actors face many challenges and cannot be sustained without the support of domestic and international allies inside and outside of governmental institutions. As Teles (2010, 280) points out, the legal actions take too long; the judicial outcomes are often limited and frustrating for the families, and may have demobilizing effects on their organizations; the economic and emotional costs of initiating a legal action are huge. It is no accident that the number of legal actions by nonstate actors is not significant in comparison with the recent legal actions undertaken by the pro-accountability group of federal prosecutors. The CNV's recommendations to the Brazilian government regarding the pursuit of civil and criminal accountability will probably spark a new wave of legal actions initiated by federal prosecutors.

Finally, it is important to note that the "memory-truth-justice" work carried out by the families of the disappeared and former political prisoners is not the only narrative that has been placed at the margins. The meaning of "political deaths and disappearances," for example, changes over time. The 2014 CNV report recognizes that indigenous groups, peasants, and LGBT people were subjected to persecution for political reasons during the military dictatorship. Yet, the CNV was unable to confirm or "prove" the scope of such political repression. Thus, the uncovering of the history of serious human rights violations and struggles for truth, memory and justice in relation to the military dictatorship is not over in Brazil. The politics of truth-memory-justice will continue. And legal mobilization will probably continue to be used as a strategy in the struggles for memory, truth, and justice.

NOTES

I am grateful to the editors of this book and Marcelo Torelly for their careful and constructive comments on earlier drafts of this chapter. Special thanks are due to the members of the Teles family and federal prosecutor Marlon Weichert for our ongoing conversations and for providing me with information and copies of documents relating to their legal actions. I am also grateful to the members of human rights NGOs and state agents, especially Marcelo Torelly, for sharing information on their work. Data collection on the legal cases addressed in this chapter was conducted in 2013 and 2014. Some data and ideas also draw from a research project on transnational legal mobilization and human rights in Brazil, particularly on the Araguaia Guerrilla case, carried out in 2006–2010, funded by the Faculty Development Fund and the Jesuit Foundation at the University of San Francisco (Santos 2007; 2009; 2010).

1. The term "political opportunity structure" is used in the social movement literature to refer to the macro, external, institutional structure and socio-political context in which social movements are embedded (McAdam, McCarthy, and Mayer 1996; Benford and Snow 2000). The term "legal opportunity structure" is generally used in the law and social movement literature "to describe both the stable and contingent factors that influence whether social movements are able and willing to pursue their goals through the courts." (Vanhala 2012, 527). The factors mostly addressed by "legal opportunity structure" scholars include procedural rules, material resources, legal resources, judicial receptivity of claims, cultural frames, and the presence of allies or counter-mobilizing forces (Vanhala 2012). Given that "structural" features are many times "contingent," some authors prefer the terms "political opportunities" and "legal opportunities" (Hilson 2002). This chapter builds on this critical literature.

2. The CEMDP was created in 1995 (Law 10,559/02). The CA was created in 2001 (Law 10,559/02). These two reparation commissions were established under the presidency of Fernando Henrique Cardoso, elected for two terms (1995–1998 and 1999–2002). The CNV was created in 2012 (Law 12,528/11) under the presidency of Dilma Rousseff, also elected for two terms (2011–2014 and 2015–2018).

3. In an e-mail message to the author on August 7, 2013, Marcelo Torelly revealed that in 2008 the CA began to negotiate a program with the Brazilian Agency of Cooperation of the Foreign Relations Ministry (*Agência Brasileira de Cooperação do Ministério das Relações Exteriores*) and the United Nations Development Program (UNDP). The goal was to create an international cooperation program on transitional justice to advance this agenda in Brazil. The program was signed in December of 2008, titled "Cooperation for the International Exchange, Development, and Expansion of Transitional Justice in Brazil" (*Cooperação para o Intercâmbio Internacional, Desenvolvimento e Ampliação da Justiça de Transição no Brasil*), and received the number BRA/08/021 in the United Nations' Atlas system.

4. In November 2008, the CA organized the first "International Seminar on Transitional Justice," held at the State University of Rio de Janeiro, in partnership with CLACSO-Latin American Council of Social Sciences. I was invited to participate in this seminar as presenter and representative of the Center for Social Studies (CES) at the University of Coimbra. The following year, the CA and CES co-organized a seminar on transitional justice, held in Coimbra, which resulted in the publication of a book (Santos et al. 2010). In addition to this event, from 2009 to 2014 the CA organized international seminars at the following universities: University of Carlos III (Spain), Oxford University and King's College (UK), Frankfurt University (Germany), Pablo de Olavide University (Spain), Catholic University of Porto Alegre-PUC (Brazil), as well as Brown University and Columbia University (USA). The CA also engaged in a series of encounters with civil society actors from different countries in Latin America, Africa, and Europe, with the goal of exchanging knowledge and training governmental and non-governmental agents (Marcelo Torelly, e-message to the author, August 7, 2013).

5. This official mandate went beyond the period of the 1964–1985 military regime to dissipate the reactions on the part of the Armed Forces and other state and nonstate actors who oppose any type of transitional justice measures in Brazil. However, once the seven commissioners nominated by President Rousseff initiated their work in the CNV, they decided to restrict their mandate to examining only the period of the military regime corresponding to April 1, 1964, until the end of 1985.

6. This project was initiated in 1979 and concluded in 1985. The goal was to document the practices of torture and the political deaths and disappearances perpetrated by agents of repression during the military regime. The project compiled copies of over 707 trials against political dissidents decided by the Military Tribunal and dozens of cases pending before this tribunal in the period of April 1964 until March 1979 (see Arquidiocese de São Paulo 2003).

7. For these dossiers, see Almeida, Almeida, Almeida, and Lisboa (2009) and CFMDP (1995).

8. In her speech, President Rousseff was moved by the CNV final report and showed strong emotions, certainly accentuated by the fact that she herself had been imprisoned and tortured by agents of repression, as she recounted in her testimony to the CNV, cited in the final report. Yet, her speech also made clear remarks about preserving a "pact of reconciliation." Available at: http://www.brasil.gov.br/governo/2014/12/dilma-recebe-relatorio-final-da-comissao-nacional-da-verdade (Accessed December 20, 2014).

9. The "escrachos" appeared in Argentina and Chile as a public manifestation in the streets (through theater, placing posters, protests, and so on) to denounce perpetrators of serious human rights violation. These public manifestations intend to name and shame, uncover history that is not acknowledged by the courts, and perform the work of memory, truth, and justice through public exposure of torturers. In Brazil, the *Levante Popular da Juventude* has successfully adopted this model of collective legal mobilization outside of courts to expose agents of the state who committed serious violations of human rights during the military dictatorship (Soares and Quinalha 2013).

10. This and the following tables do not intend to list all of the legal actions initiated by nonstate actors. This selection does not intend to be comprehensive but rather exemplary of

emblematic cases and/or of cases that I could find. The data was gathered from the following types of sources: the websites of courts where the cases were initiated, decided, and/or are pending; newspaper and magazine articles (mostly online); academic and official publications on transitional justice and struggles for truth, memory and justice in Brazil; semi-structured interviews and conversations with one family of the disappeared and former political prisoners, attorneys, prosecutors, members of NGOs, and state officials. The interviews and conversations are especially related to the Araguaia Guerrilla case and the Teles family case.

11. The Manoel Fiel Filho case also sparked social mobilization and protests against the military regime. Mário Sérgio de Moraes (2006) argues, however, that the socioeconomic and political background of the victims influenced the different repercussions of the Herzog and the Fiel Filho cases. Vladimir Herzog was a middle-class journalist well known in São Paulo. Manoel Fiel Filho was a working-class union organizer. Herzog's death sparked a wave of protests and mobilization by middle-class intellectuals and students who united to fight for liberal democracy, human rights, and citizenship rights. For them, the meaning of "citizenship rights" did not refer to socioeconomic rights, but rather to political and civil rights.

12. Data on these legal actions can be found in the website of the São Paulo State Court of Justice (http://www.tjsp.jus.br/).

13. Maria Amélia de Almeida Teles, "O Torturador no Banco dos Réus." Available at: http://www2.sinal.org.br/informativos/show_sumula.asp?codigo=43652andtema=andtipo=Randdata=anddt_dia=5anddt_mes=12anddt_ano=2006 (Accessed December 16, 2006. My translation from the original in Portuguese).

14. Among other cases, see Case of Almonacid Arellano et al. versus Chile. Preliminary Objections, Merits, Reparations and Costs. Judgment of September 26, 2006. Series C No. 154, para. 94. Available at: http://www.corteidh.or.cr/docs/supervisiones/almonacid_18_11_10_ing.pdf (Accessed December 10, 2014).

15. Cited in Isabel Harari, "Essa Vitória Não É Só da Família Teles, É de Todo Brasil," *Carta Maior* (August 14, 2012). Available at: http://cartamaior.com.br/?/Editoria/Direitos-Humanos/ percent27Essa-vitoria-nao-e-so-da-familia-Teles-e-de-todo-o-Brasil percent27 percent0D percent0A/5/25677 (Accessed December 15, 2014. My translation from the original in Portuguese.)

16. Janaína de Almeida Teles, "O Torturador no Banco dos Réus: A Ofensa aos Direitos Humanos Não Prescreve." Available at: https://hannaharendt.wordpress.com/2009/11/16/o-torturador-no-banco-dos-reus-a-ofensa-aos-direitos-humanos-nao-prescreve-1/ (Accessed December 18, 2014. My translation from the original in Portuguese.)

17. Cf. Inter-American Commission on Human Rights, Report n. 80/12 (Admissibility), Petition P-859-09, Vladimir Herzog et al. v. Brazil, November 8, 2012.

18. Cf. Case of Gomes Lund et al. ("Guerrilha do Araguaia") v. Brazil. Preliminary Objections, Merits, Reparations, and Costs. Judgment of November 24, 2010. Available at: http://www.corteidh.or.cr/docs/casos/articulos/seriec_219_ing.pdf (Accessed January 6, 2014).

19. Cf. Case of Gomes Lund et al. ("Guerrilha do Araguaia") v. Brazil. Preliminary Objections, Merits, Reparations, and Costs. Judgment of November 24, 2010. Available at: http://www.corteidh.or.cr/docs/casos/articulos/seriec_219_ing.pdf (Accessed January 6, 2014).

SELECTED BIBLIOGRAPHY

Abrão, Paulo, and Marcelo D. Torelly. 2011. "As Dimensões da Justiça de Transição no Brasil, a Eficácia da Lei de Anistia e as Alternativas para a Verdade e a Justiça." In *A Anistia na Era da Responsabilidade: O Brasil em Perspectiva Internacional e Comparada*, edited by Leigh A. Payne, Paulo Abrão, and Marcelo Torelly, 212–49. Brasília: Ministério da Justiça, Comissão de Anistia; Oxford: Oxford University, Latin American Centre.

———. 2013. "Transformaciones del Concepto de Amnistía en la Justicia de Transición Brasileña: La Tercera Etapa de la Lucha por la Amnistía." *Jueces para la Democracia* 77: 95–109.

Almeida, Crimeia Schmidt de, Janaína de Almeida Teles, Maria Amélia de Almeida Teles, and Suzana Lisboa. 2009. *Dossiê Ditadura: Mortos e Desaparecidos Políticos no Brasil, 1964–1985*. São Paulo: IEVE/Imprensa Oficial.

Arquidiocese de São Paulo. 2003. *Brasil: Nunca Mais*. Petrópolis: Vozes, 33a edtion.

Atencio, Rebecca J. 2014. *Memory's Turn: Reckoning with Dictatorship in Brazil*. Madison, WI: The University of Wisconsin Press.

Benford, Robert D., and David A. Snow. 2000. "Framing Processes and Social Movements: An Overview and Assessment." *Annual Review of Sociology* 26: 611–39.

Booth, W. James. 2006. *Communities of Memory, Witness, Identity, and Justice*. Ithaca, NY: Cornell University Press.

Brito, Alexandra B. de, Carmen González-Enríquez, and Paloma Aguilar, ed. 2001. *The Politics of Memory: Transitional Justice in Democratizing Societies*. Oxford: Oxford University Press.

Burt, Jo-Marie, Gabriela Fried-Amilivia, and Francesca Lessa. 2013. "Civil Society and the Resurgent Struggle Against Impunity in Uruguay (1986–2012)." *International Journal of Transitional Justice* 7: 306–27.

Cardia, Nancy, Mariana Thorstensen Possas, Vitor Blotta, and Lucia Elena Arantes Ferreira Bastos. 2014. "A Cobertura da Mídia sobre a Decisão da Corte Inter-Americana de Direitos Humanos no Caso Araguaia: Promovendo Mudança ou Mantendo a Negação?" In *Direitos Humanos Atual*, edited by Inês Virgínia Prado and Flávia Piovesan, 406–49. Rio de Janeiro: Elsevier.

Cardoso, Evorah L. C. 2012. *Litígio Estratégico e Sistema Interamericano de Direitos Humanos*. Belo Horizonte: Editora Fórum.

CEMDP (Comissão Especial sobre Mortos e Desaparecidos Políticos). 2007. *Direito à Memória e à Verdade*. Brasília: Secretaria de Direitos Humanos da Presidência da República.

CFMDP (Comissão de Familiares de Mortos e Desaparecidos Políticos), IEVE (Instituto de Estudo da Violência do Estado), and Grupo Tortura Nunca Mais-RJ/SP. 1995. *Dossiê dos Mortos e Desaparecidos Políticos a Partir de 1964*. Recife: CEPE-Companhia Editora de Pernambuco, Governo do Estado de Pernambuco.

CNV (Comissão Nacional da Verdade). 2014. *Relatório*. Brasília: Comissão Nacional da Verdade. 3 Volumes.

Collins, Cath. 2006. "Grounding Global Justice: International Networks and Domestic Human Rights Accountability in Chile and El Salvador." *Journal of Latin American Studies* 38 (4): 711–38.

———. 2008. "State Terror and the Law: The (Re)judicialization of Human Rights Accountability in Chile and El Salvador." *Latin American Perspectives* 35 (5): 20–37.

———. 2010. *Post-Transitional Justice: Human Rights Trials in Chile and El Salvador*. University Park: The Pennsylvania University Press.

Fávero, Eugênea A. G. 2009. "Crimes da Ditadura: Iniciativas do Ministério Público Federal em São Paulo." In *Memória e Verdade: A Justiça de Transição no Estado Democrático Brasileiro*, edited by Inês Virgínia P. Soares, and Sandra A. S. Kishi, 213–32. Belo Horizonte: Editora Fórum.

Hilson, Chris. 2002. "New Social Movements: The Role of Legal Opportunity." *Journal of European Public Policy* 9 (2): 238–55.

hooks, bell. 1984. *Feminist Theory: From Margin to Center*. New York: South End Press.

Keck, Margaret E., and Kathryn Sikkink. 1998. *Activists beyond Borders: Advocacy Networks in International Politics*. Ithaca, NY: Cornell University Press.

Kobalec, Kobi. 2014. "Memory and Periphery: An Introduction." *Hagar – Studies in Culture, Polity and Identities* 12: 7–22.

Lorde, Audre. 1984. "An Open Letter to Mary Daly." In *Sister Outsider*, 66–71. Freedom, CA: Crossing Press.

Lutz, Ellen, and Kathryn Sikkink. 2001. "The Justice Cascade: The Evolution and Impact of Human Rights Trials in Latin America." *Chicago Journal of International Law* 2 (1): 1–33.

Maeso, Silvia R. 2010. "Política del Testimonio y Reconocimiento en las Comisiones de la Verdad Guatemalteca y Peruana: En torno a la Figura del 'Indio Subversivo'." *Revista Crítica de Ciências Sociais* 88: 23–56.

McAdam, Doug, John D. McCarthy, and N. Zald Mayer. 1996. "Introduction: Opportunities, Mobilizing Structures, and Framing Processes—Toward a Synthetic, Comparative Perspective on Social Movements." In *Comparative Perspectives on Social Movements Opportunities, Mobilizing Structures, and Framing*, eds. D. McAdam, J. D. McCarthy, and M. N. Zald, 1–20. Cambridge, UK: Cambridge University Press.

McCann, Michael. 2006. "Law and Social Movements: Contemporary Perspectives." *Annual Review of Law and Social Science* 2: 17–38.

———. 2008. "Litigation and Legal Mobilization." In *The Oxford Handbook of Law and Politics*, eds. K. E. Whittington, R. D. Kelemen, and G. A. Caldeira, 522–40. New York: Oxford University Press.

McEvoy, Kieran. 2008. "Letting Go of Legalism: Developing a 'Thicker' Version of Transitional Justice." In *Transitional Justice from Below: Grassroots Activism and the Struggle for Change*, eds. Kieran McEvoy and Lorna McGregor, 15–45. Oxford and Portland, Oregon: Hart Publishing.

McEvoy, Kieran, and Lorna McGregor. 2008. "Transitional Justice from Below: An Agenda for Research, Policy and Praxis." In *Transitional Justice from Below: Grassroots Activism and the Struggle for Change*, eds. Kieran McEvoy and Lorna McGregor, 1–13. Oxford and Portland, Oregon: Hart Publishing.

Ministério Público Federal. 2013. *Crimes da Ditadura: Relatório Preliminar de Atos de Persecução Penal desenvolvidos pelo MPF acerca de graves violações de direitos humanos cometidas por agentes do Estado durante a ditadura*. Brasília: Procuradoria Geral da República.

Ministério Público Federal. Câmara de Coordenação e Revisão, 2. 2014. *Grupo de Trabalho Justiça de Transição: Atividades de Persecução Penal Desenvolvidas pelo Ministério Público Federal: 2011–2013*. Brasília: Ministério Público Federal.

Moraes, Mário Sérgio de. 2006. *O Caso da Ditadura: Caso Herzog*. São Paulo: Barcarolla.

Olsen, Tricia D., Leigh A. Payne, and Andrew G. Reiter. 2010. *Transitional Justice in Balance: Comparing Processes, Weighing Efficacy*. Washington DC: United States Institute for Peace.

Payne, Leigh A., Paulo Abrão, and Marcelo Torelly, eds. 2011. *A Anistia na Era da Responsabilidade: O Brasil em Perspectiva Internacional e Comparada*. Brasília: Ministério da Justiça, Comissão de Anistia; Oxford: Oxford University, Latin American Centre.

Reátegui, Felix, ed. 2011. *Transitional Justice Handbook for Latin America*. Brasília: Brazilian Amnesty Commission, Ministry of Justice and International; New York: Center for Transitional Justice.

Roht-Ariaza, Naomi, and Javier Mariezcurrena, eds. 2006. *Transitional Justice in the Twenty-First Century: Beyond Truth versus Justice*. Cambridge: Cambridge University Press.

Santos, Boaventura de Sousa. 2005. "Beyond Neoliberal Governance: The World Social Forum as Subaltern Cosmopolitan Politics and Legality". In *Law and Globalization from Below: Towards a Cosmopolitan Legality*, eds. Boaventura de Sousa Santos and Cesar A. Rodriguez-Garavito, 29–63. Cambridge, UK: Cambridge University Press.

———. 2014. "A Critique of Lazy Reason: Against the Waste of Experience and Toward the Sociology of Absences and the Sociology of Emergences." In *Epistemologies of the South: Justice Against Epistemicide*, 164–87. Boulder and London: Paradigm Publishers.

Santos, Boaventura de Sousa, and César A. Rodríguez-Garavito. 2005. "Law, Politics, and the Subaltern in Counter-Hegemonic Globalization." In *Law and Globalization from Below: Towards a Cosmopolitan Legality*, eds. Boaventura de Sousa Santos and César A. Rodríguez-Garavito, 1–26. Cambridge, UK: Cambridge University Press.

Santos, Boaventura de Sousa, and Flávia Carlet. 2010. "Movement of Landless Rural Workers in Brazil and Their Struggles for Access to Law and Justice." In Marginalized Communities and Access to Justice, eds. Yash Ghai and Jill Cottrell, 60–82. Abingdon: Routledge.

Santos, Boaventura de Sousa, Paulo Abrão, Cecília MacDowell Santos, and Marcelo Torelly, eds. 2010. *Repressão e Memória Política no Contexto Íbero-Brasileiro: Estudos sobre*

Brasil, Guatemala, Moçambique, Peru e Portugal. Brasília: Ministry of Justice, Amnesty Commission; Coimbra: Center for Social Justice, University of Coimbra.

Santos, Cecília MacDowell. 2007. "Transnational Legal Activism and the State: Reflections on Cases Against Brazil in the Inter-American Commission on Human Rights." *Sur-International Journal on Human Rights* 4 (7): 29–59.

———. 2009. "A Justiça ao Serviço da Memória: Mobilização Jurídica Transnacional, Direitos Humanos e Memória da Ditadura." In *Desarquivando a Ditadura: Memória e Justiça no Brasil*, vol. II, eds. Cecília MacDowell Santos, Edson Teles, and Janaína de Almeida Teles, 472–95. São Paulo: Hucitec Press.

———. 2010. "Memória na Justiça: A Mobilização dos Direitos Humanos e a Construção da Memória da Ditadura no Brasil." *Revista Crítica de Ciências Sociais* 88: 127–54.

Schneider, Nina. 2011. "Impunity in Post-Authoritarian Brazil: The Supreme Court's Recent Verdict on the Amnesty Law." *European Review of Latin American and Caribbean Studies* 90: 39–54.

Sikkink, Kathryn. 2012. *The Justice Cascade: How Human Rights Prosecutions Are Changing World Politics*. New York: W.W. Norton and Company.

Soares, Inês V. Prado, and Renan H. Quinalha. 2013. "Os Escrachos e a Luta por Verdade e Justiça: O Que Esperar em 2013?" *Correio da Cidadania* (January 3, 2013). Available at: http://www.correiocidadania.com.br/index.php?option=com_contentandview=articleandid=7968:dicionario030113andcatid=19:dicionario-da-cidadaniaandItemid=56 (Accessed January 6, 2014).

Teitel, Ruti. 2003. "Transitional Justice Genealogy." *Harvard Human Rights Journal* 16: 69–94.

Teles, Janaína de Almeida, ed. 2001. *Mortos e Desaparecidos Políticos: Reparação ou Impunidade?* São Paulo, Humanitas/FFLCH/USP. [2nd ed.].

———. 2005. "Os Herdeiros da Memória: A Luta dos Familiares de Mortos e Desaparecidos Políticos por "Verdade e Justiça" no Brasil." Master Thesis, University of São Paulo.

———. 2010. "Os Familiares de Mortos e Desaparecidos Políticos e a Luta por "Verdade e Justiça" no Brasil." In *O Que Resta da Ditadura: A Exceção Brasileira*, edited by Edson Teles and Vladimir Safatle, 253–98. São Paulo: Boitempo.

Vanhala, Lisa. 2012. "Legal Opportunity Structures and the Paradox of Legal Mobilization by the Environmental Movement in the UK." *Law and Society Review* 46 (3): 523–56.

Part III

El Salvador

Chapter Four

Toward Reconsidering the Root Causes of Violence

Free Trade, Mining, and Transitional Justice in Central America

Steve Dobransky

Transitional justice has been one of the dominant frameworks in many countries since the 1990s and has energized grassroots organizations and academia. The idea that political transformation should encompass instruments such as truth and reconciliation commissions, amnesty, trials without punishment, lustration and vetting, reparations, and other strategies became a popular and often necessary substitute for the desire for stronger punishment (Hinton 2011, 4). The general population and in particular the victims were told that this was the only way to ensure a peaceful transition from dictatorships to democracy and that life under a new and properly enforced rule of law was much better (Teitel 2000, 223–25).

What may have been intended as a permanent solution has been challenged recently by a new generation of activists as well as older critics who are part of what many now call the "post-transitional justice" school (Collins 2010). Post-transitional justice research has emphasized how societies entered a *new* political phase (one that followed the formal transition), and pinpointed weaknesses in what I call the "transitional justice prescription." They argue that societies are strong enough to reexamine past human rights violations and seek greater justice through various means, including arrests, trials, and other punishments of the culprits that have been avoided previously (Collins 2010, 21–23; Almqvist and Espósito 2012, 1, 9). A number of scholars have started to recognize that the idea of transitional justice was conceived too narrowly toward political ends and often ignored the socio-economic aspects that are the root causes of mass poverty, misery, and violence (Mani 2008; McEvoy and McGregor 2008; Miller 2008; Stahler-Sholk, Vanden, and Kuecker 2008). Much of the violence in the past was predicated on inequality and the maintenance of the existing elites, rather than on specific leaders. Hence, the question is raised as to how justice can be achieved if the root causes of previous violence and dictatorships still exist to a large extent in these transitional countries (Mani 2008; Miller 2008; De Greiff and Duthie 2009, 84).

This chapter argues that transitional justice failed to capture the most important elements of "justice" and the root causes of violence—mass poverty and inequality. Many Latin American countries today, especially in Central America, are facing serious challenges to peace and stable political systems. As I will show, the transitional justice paradigm has also proven inadequate for its environmental destruction. This chapter highlights the case of foreign corporate mining in Latin America and, in particular, Central America and El Salvador. The consequences of foreign mining help to explain why many civilians in Central American and, especially, El Salvador are dissatisfied with the transitional justice movement and are leading protests on a regular basis. Reports show that thousands of people protest against and resist foreign mining companies, and these corporations have also been increasingly challenged by scholars (Stahler-Shalk, Vanden, and Kuecker 2008; Archibold 2011; Broad and Cavanagh 2011; Llewellyn 2012; Solis 2012; Karunananthan 2013; Moore, Broad, and Cavanagh 2014). The opponents include a wide range of citizens—often poor villagers and farmers near the mines, but also the people living along the river systems. Protest groups include: environmental organizations, human rights groups, church leaders, political authorities (up to the Salvadoran president), scholars, and journalists.

The movement against foreign mining emerged around 2005 with the intensifying debate over the Central American Free Trade Agreement (CAFTA) and, especially, after its implementation in 2006. There had been prior protests on a local level, but the national resistance coincided with CAFTA. The clash between grassroots organizations and foreign mining escalated greatly when the Pacific Rim Mining Corporation took the Salvadoran government to international court when it was denied a mining permit for the El Dorado mine in the Cabañas region, which it had been seeking since 2002. The widespread protests were supported by extensive data and experiences from the Commerce Group's mine in the San Sebastian area that had been closed down since 1999 but continued to contaminate the rivers and land with high levels of toxic chemicals. The environmental damages remained and became well documented by citizens challenging Pacific Rim (Broad and Cavanagh 2011; Llewellyn 2012; Karunananthan 2013; Moore, Broad, and Cavanagh 2014). The public anger was exacerbated when the Commerce

Group pursued legal measures with Pacific Rim for a combined total of more than $400 million.

Overall, a number of Central American regions now head toward the brink of widespread violence, as their governments are unable or unwilling to protect their people from foreign mining corporations and the likely negative effects. In short, after decades of implementation, transitional justice policies have failed to provide average citizens with the necessary conditions to live a decent life. This highlights the need for a new post-transitional justice approach that includes greater socio-economic equality and strong environmental protections.

TRANSITIONAL JUSTICE: ORIGINS, EVOLUTION, AND DEMISE

Transitional justice emphasizes the need to 1) address war crimes and human rights abuses (here the lessons of the post-World War Two movement were incorporated, the Nuremburg trials being the key example); 2) create stronger international laws and institutions; and 3) promote negotiated, peaceful democratic transitions in the 1980s and 1990s to protect citizens from physical harm by the old regime (Hinton 2011, 2–3). Although the term was coined in the early 1990s, the characteristics of it have often been traced to the lessons from WWII. The fundamental assumption of transitional justice is that in the aftermath of major human rights crimes, mechanisms are required to allow the general population to find a form of "closure" (Teitel 2000; McEvoy and McGregor 2008; De Greiff and Duthie 2009; Hinton 2011; Kent 2012; Williams, Nagy, and Elster 2012). The method of redress separates transitional justice from other policies. Transitional justice emphasizes communication, transparency, and other restorative elements over incarceration and physical punishment. It holds certain people accountable but highlights a path of reconciliation rather than vengeance, which led scholars to make the distinction between restorative and retributive justice (Minow 1998; Kent 2012, 4, 33).

Transitional justice stresses the psychological benefits of forgiveness, and the need to focus on the future, over retaliation. A leitmotif of transitional justice rhetoric is the reunion of the country, while the correction of major economic and land inequalities is considered often a separate issue (Teitel 2000, 223–25). The implication is that fundamental socio-economic problems can resolve themselves through the new democratic process of accountable government and free markets, instead of there being an alteration of fundamental structures that perpetuate mass inequality and conflicts (McEvoy and McGregor 2008; De Greiff and Duthie 2009, 84, 111).

Transitional justice omits specific socio-economic goals and, particularly, the means to achieve them. It also offers no clear socio-economic measurements or benchmarks to evaluate success, from financial and property holdings to overall standards of living and education. Nonetheless, it is understandable why these factors are excluded. Their incorporation would complicate the initial stages of any political transition and directly threaten the elites who expected no redistribution or reduction in their existing power and wealth (McEvoy and McGregor 2008, 129; Schmid and Nolan 2014, 7–9).

In a similar vein, transitional justice reaches out to the international community for advice and financial support. It links global economic integration with having democracy, the rule of law, human rights, and other political intangibles that major Western countries consider prerequisites to economic development (Kent 2012, 5–6). The United States, other countries, and international institutions, moreover, demand significant progress toward democracy and free markets as conditions for receiving substantial amounts of financial aid and technical assistance. Many of the new governments that consent to these policies, unfortunately, turn out to be very weak and open to undue influence, as the foreign mining case suggests (McEvoy and McGregor 2008, 104–5). Central America is a good example because the regimes have been historically dependent on foreign assistance to maintain order and their survival. Dependence in the last decade or two has led to much greater privatization, foreign multinational corporations (MNCs), and, ultimately, free trade agreements.

Transitional justice encourages globalization, defined here as the economic integration of countries under free market and comparative advantage principles, but ignores the exploitation and inequality that it often entails. The unwillingness to integrate socio-economic root causes of violence into the transitional justice paradigm has prevented the overcoming of old conflicts and may lead to new violence. This is why, for example, foreign governments are expected to welcome the multinational corporations, but when these foreign businesses demand economic changes to the detriment of the native population, the transitional governments are put in a double-bind between submission and violating the free trade agreements. Transitional justice, thus, has made governments vulnerable to certain concepts that start with idealized beliefs and then end with serious domestic inequalities and other problems like environmental destruction (Stahler-Sholk, Vanden, and Kuecker 2008, 100–102).

Throughout Central America, there is growing hostility toward foreign corporations who wish to seize certain lands and extract their precious resources. From poor and educated to individual farmers and organized urban groups, the terrible effects of mining that have been observed and documented by scholars like Broad and Cavanagh (2011), Llewellyn (2012), Karunananthan (2013), Treat (2013), Moore, Broad, and Cavanagh (2014), and Torres-Valverde (2014) have led to intense opposition. In El Salvador, popular resistance was motivated by the potential catastrophic outcome of extreme contamination. Much of the population and animals living along rivers were at risk, because the drinking water was being polluted. The people rose up by organizing groups such as the National Roundtable Against Metallic Mining (MESA), which united hundreds of communities (Karunananthan 2013; Moore, Broad, and Cavanagh 2014). Many environmental groups inside and outside El Salvador conducted extensive tests to expose the mining companies and their false claims. By 2008 a national poll showed that 62.4 percent of people potentially affected opposed the mining (Moore, Broad, and Cavanagh 2014).

All in all, the general population may not care about free trade's promotion of service and retail industries operating within their countries, but mining corporations threaten their livelihood, let alone their traditional beliefs and values. In societies in which the vast majority of the land and natural resources are seen as being owned by the public, even if there is no official documentation, there is a growing resistance to corporate claims of the right to own and exploit the land (De Greiff and Duthie 2009, 338–39, 342–43, 352).

Local empowerment movements have emerged to confront the foreign corporate giants and have challenged the constraints, I argue, of previous transitional justice models. These grassroots movements have in many cases substantially increased the costs of corporate operations, from finances to prestige. Many domestic and foreign nongovernmental organizations (NGOs) have forced mining companies to spend extraordinary amounts of money trying to bribe local communities in the face of overwhelming evidence of the dangers, as well as produce more studies defending their projects. The popular resistance, moreover, has pressured mining companies to promise even greater efforts at preventing environmental damage, which in turn increases their costs and thus reduces their profit margins.

These intense and broad-based efforts appear to challenge the top-bottom authority structure that transitional justice relies upon. The local populations are not waiting for government legislation to protect them but, instead, are targeting mining corporations from every angle, from public opinion to highly technical research studies. They also recognize that some of their own elites have sided with and benefited from foreign corporations; the betrayal for profits is nothing new. They, furthermore, are uniting with others in neighboring countries to produce a stronger regional force against mining. They have attracted substantial support from groups in advanced industrialized countries, who have criticized the mining corporations within their home countries (Stahler-Sholk, Vanden, and Kuecker 2008, 97–98, 100–101, 108–9; Archibold 2011; Llewellyn 2012; Solis 2012; Kaunananthan 2013; Treat 2013; Moore, Broad, and Cavanagh 2014).

These grassroots movements have led to new organizational techniques and approaches that have been very effective in mobilizing opposition to the mining corporations. They have been able to counter the marketing and propaganda from the mining interests, and to show first-hand the terrible damages of previous locations like San Sebastian and their long-term effects. The San Sebastian River, which was once clear before the U.S.-based Commerce Group began operating a gold mine nearby, is reported to this day to be orange like the sun despite the project shutting down in 1999 (Karunananthan 2013). The Salvadoran government tested the river in 2012 and revealed that the water had extreme levels of cyanide and iron. Even though some people in the area who can afford it drink bottled water, the river is still used by the general population for bathing and washing dishes, as well as by farm animals (Karunananthan 2013). According to Lita Trejo, a native Salvadoran, there are substantial numbers of people with kidney problems and other diseases that can be attributed to the contaminated water (Torres-Valverde 2014). The local movements, as a result, have united to fight back against foreign corporate exploitation and the existing free trade practices (Stahler-Sholk, Vanden, and Kuecker 2008, 102, 111–12).

The free trade ideals which underlie the transitional justice paradigm clash with local popular interests. The post-transitional justice perspective is moving beyond legal questions and empowerment to a level in which local communities are learning how to engage politically. This causes foreign mining companies and even the countries' own governments headaches and escalating costs. New grassroots protest methods, therefore, have translated into effective instruments to defend local communities (Stahler-Sholk, Vanden, and Kuecker 2008; Broad and Cavanagh 2011; Llewellyn 2012; Moore, Broad, and Cavanagh 2014).

The Salvadoran people have become ever more confident that the time is right to re-address previous disputes rooted in socio-economic inequalities and the lack of full basic rights. They are starting to believe that they can make a difference. This new form of local and decentralized politics has created dynamics and uncertainties that contrast with traditional transitional justice approaches. A whole new variable has to be included that free trade advocates and even many transitional justice proponents previously treated as weak and submissive, insignificant and hopeless. On September 15, 2014, for example, more than 200 Salvadorans staged a protest against mining in front of the World Bank, in order to highlight the environmental damage on Salvadoran rivers, including San Sebastian (Torres-Valverde 2014). Unlike their indecisive governments, they reclaim what they consider is theirs. The post-transitional justice movement, I suggest, should incorporate this new popular organizational element and consider the root causes of the uprisings, particularly the socio-economic factors.

CAFTA AND THE ADJUDICATION OF SOVEREIGNTY: A BRIEF HISTORY

In order to demonstrate the necessity for expanding the post-transitional justice framework toward socio-economic and environmental concerns—my core argument in this chapter—I will briefly introduce the Central American Free Trade Agreement (CAFTA) in more depth. CAFTA has become the primary lever for shifting domestic economic decisions from national governments to foreign corporations via the World Bank. The World Bank is well known for demanding fundamental changes in poor countries that can be very painful and are seen often as promoting Western economic values and interests. Transitional justice tends to promote or accept neutrally this drive toward modernization through Western institutions. It is understandable, since Western countries like the United States present themselves as the sole alternative to the previous dictatorships. The new transitional governments have needed desperately to stabilize themselves. Western multinational corporations and investors have entered these countries that are undergoing transitions, and, over time, generated many problems while not improving substantially the well-being of most of the general population. This is now threatening millions of people, and, I argue, it is in part the result of the failures of a flawed transitional justice paradigm, which weakened Central American countries. The vulnerability of these countries made negotiations a one-sided deal from 2003 to 2005 when they debated, signed, and approved the 2,400-page document.

The CAFTA members included the United States, Honduras, Guatemala, Costa Rica, El Salvador, Nicaragua, and the Dominican Republic. The Central American countries had been improving economic relations with each other for decades, but a complete reduction of barriers and the inclusion of the United States caused a series of problems (Jaramillo, Lederman, Bussolo et al. 2006, 18–22). They, however, were desperate to generate significant economic growth and raise their citizens' standard of living. And complete, unadulterated access to the United States' markets was essential to achieve their ends.

While foreign mining companies benefited substantially from CAFTA (Jaramillo, Lederman, Bussolo, et. al 2006, 22), the aggregate GDP of the Central American countries was around $70 billion at the time, which was miniscule (Spotts 2005, 39). Foreign companies were supposed to achieve unhindered access to the valuable resources deep down in the natural vaults. They had the technology and determination to extract these resources, especially gold. The local communities, however, quickly figured out that gold mining and other similar activities usually led to the use of toxic chemicals like cyanide. The general population saw that with the nearby rivers, land, and other highly sensitive parts of the ecosystem, the toxins were bound to seep into soil and water and cause massive, long-term damage (Stahler-Sholk, Vanden, and Kuecker 2008, 98–104). As a result, the local population and the foreign mining companies opposed each other. I argue that this would never have occurred if transitional justice had addressed the socio-economic problems that lead to violence.

Moreover, the Central American governments learned that they were not able to maintain their own sovereignty over the natural resources. They found out that the thousands of pages of the CAFTA agreement included chapters and clauses, especially chapter 10 (Investment), which required all national citizens and foreign conglomerates to have equal access to a member's resources. Chapter 9 (Government Procurement) of CAFTA opened up the possibility that government services, including mining and land maintenance, could be put into the arms of private companies, whether foreign or domestic. CAFTA pitted governments against private corporations in a competition to determine who could deliver existing public services at the best price (CAFTA 2005; Spotts 2005, 57–58). Since private industry was bound to win at least on paper in the statistical calculations, many Central American governments resisted and sought to protect their public services and ownership.

As this chapter focuses on the reception of the transitional justice paradigm in Central America, it is beyond its scope to explore in more depth why CAFTA has become one of the greatest threats to millions of people in Central America and has redefined state sovereignty. Yet, it is important to show that CAFTA has made Central America vulnerable to the exploitation of all natural resources and minerals. If Central American governments seek to defend their people and resources, then the issue is brought before the World Bank, more specifically the International Centre for Settlement of Investment Disputes (ICSID), or possibly the United Nations Commission on International Trade Law (UNCITRAL) (CAFTA 2005). Whether or not the original signatories truly understood the implications of designating a highly biased arbiter to decide their fates is unknown. This institution was rigged heavily in favor of the foreign corporations, especially when less than ten percent of the World Bank's representation was from Latin America (Archibold 2011).

To illustrate the dimensions of the problem, I will briefly explain what may be regarded as its climax—a lawsuit by a U.S. mining firm against a Latin American government. A legal precedent was established when the U.S. company Metalclad sued the Mexican government under the North American Free Trade Agreement (NAFTA) and won $15.6 million in damages for not being allowed to construct a hazardous waste treatment plant. NAFTA eliminated all economic barriers between the United States, Canada, and Mexico. Much of NAFTA's basic text and rules were transferred exactly to CAFTA and thus, its influence is indicative of what will happen to Central

American countries. From this point onward, foreign corporations have been suing Latin American governments to gain access to all types of operations, even if it means destroying the environment and potentially harming millions of people (Archibold 2011). It is an amazing instrument of new free trade agreements that only seems to be applied selectively to the poorer and weaker members.

For the first time, corporations can sue national governments and win in a court system for being denied permits for certain operations that could harm citizens. It is a novelty that corporations can sue before a contract even exists or goes into effect. Never before could corporations sue for monetary damages for lost operations and stock value using a future and hypothetical calculation of acquisitions. Overall, based upon the actions since 2005, the foreign private corporations and the United States appear to have understood every word and sentence of CAFTA, particularly Chapter 10, Article 4 (Most-Favored-Nation Treatment) and Section B (Investor-State Dispute Settlement, Articles 15-27) (CAFTA 2005). The Central American governments, however, signed a deal that guarantees all current and future governments a constant wave of attacks against those who fail to allow private industries to take over anything publicly related that could be done better by the private sector. Foreign corporations, by far, are the most likely legal threats to Central American governments and are the key beneficiaries of CAFTA.

To this day, the United States government seems to be completely unwilling to alter the terms of the agreement and correct this dispute resolution mechanism. It was the United States' government who supported strongly the insertion of this section into the agreement as it did with NAFTA, and U.S. interest groups benefited from these clauses. Latin American countries have found out how they were being manipulated but seem to feel powerless given the free trade problem. They appear to be trapped between the desire for rapid economic development and the tough realities of CAFTA's capitalistic system.

THE CURRENT CONTEXT OF TRANSITIONAL JUSTICE AND THE MINING CHALLENGE

CAFTA can be seen as giving a vivid demonstration of how free trade agreements have threatened the population's health and the natural environment, as well as fueled poverty by directing the profits to foreign companies rather than the local population. It is important to make the connection between transitional justice and the mining issue. The transitional justice paradigm based itself on the consummate argument that all people should agree to certain global principles, including free trade policies. These values, often, have contrasted with economic realities (Harvey 2003; Stahler-Sholk, Vanden, and Kuecker 2008, 97–112; De Greiff and Duthie 2009, 132–34, 145; Collins 2010, 21–23; Kent 2012: 6). "Democracy" and "freedom" mean little to Central American citizens if their vital water sources are polluted dangerously by mining companies, with profits outweighing the importance of lives and land. The glossing over and wishful thinking of the transitional justice discourses will hopefully, in my view, make free trade's existence a temporary phenomenon. It was only a matter of time before many people realized that free trade ideas were not addressing but threatening fundamental aspects of their lives, providing grounds for new violence.

What was implied by the transitional justice movement never translated into greater prosperity and equality. The link with international institutions inevitably brought the violence-torn Central American countries into the free trade system that attached many other elements to the relationship beyond reconciliation and human rights laws. What started out as a potential goodwill paradigm to help countries transition with economic assistance led to these countries becoming increasingly dependent on the capitalist framework and, thereafter, made them susceptible to its demands, or more specifically, to the United States and foreign corporations.

Could there have been an alternative to free trade principles? Yes, I believe, if there had been politically strong governments at the time and they made the socio-economic issue a critical part of their policies. Transitional justice could have assisted in this, if it only had incorporated a socio-economic dimension. The historical reality is that the transitional governments were relatively weak and divided and their leaders were aligned closely to the political and financial support of the major Western powers. By delegating a significant portion of their transition to Western governments and institutions like the World Bank, the Central American governments were expected to integrate with the free trade system, with rewards and punishments for subsequent compliance or non-compliance. The overall results have been generally inadequate and dismal. Transitional justice's failure to offer a better alternative to laissez-faire principles is at the heart of the existing dilemma.

It should be recognized that transitional justice also triggered positive developments in Central America, including more competitive elections, greater free speech and press, and less state violence in certain countries. In El Salvador, the Farabundo Martí Liberation Front (FMLN), which had been made up of socialist rebel insurgents during the Salvdoran civil war from 1980–1992, competed politically for years and eventually won the elections in 2009. The FMLN is an example of how political negotiations can integrate former political opponents who once used violence as a means of political change. It also demonstrates more recently that even socialists and former insurgents have not been able to substantially change the main conditions in

Central American societies, even when they are in government. This confirms that socio-economic powers can still dominate or counteract political pressures to change, which highlights again one of the key missing pieces in the transitional justice paradigm. For the social and economic dimensions, very little was done. Mass poverty, inequality, and low-level education continued, largely due to the fact that the economic structures remained intact. The vast majority of private wealth has continued primarily in the hands of a few individuals while the public wealth in certain sectors ensured the stability and electability of the new governments. Thus, no significant increases in public funding have occurred to alter the status quo, leaving a high degree of misery, crime, hopelessness, and violence to fill in the gap. And, the failure of transitional justice should take at least some of the blame for the grave injustices that exist to this very day.

THE END OF TRANSITIONAL JUSTICE AND THE NEW POST-TRANSITIONAL JUSTICE FRONTIER

Whatever positive elements transitional justice achieved, it was within a narrow political and personal confine that failed to address the fundamentals of justice. Some of the core questions underlying the transitional justice critique are: What is justice? How do we define democracy, and who defines it? I argue that both definitions should include the socio-economic dimension of human beings, and even animals and the environment. The inability of transitional justice to acknowledge such a basic cornerstone of justice (and democracy) is critical to understanding why Central America and many other countries may in the medium-term reject the transitional justice paradigm. Democracy can be regarded as a threat when it leads to a government unable or unwilling to protect its people from economic exploitation and environmental destruction. For corporations, these kinds of "democratic" systems are convenient.

Overall, transitional justice may have been appealing for a while, but practical critical analysis reveals that it ignored the most essential rights and the basics of justice in Central America. Furthermore, it promoted cosmetic changes and failed to develop a more substantive approach to achieve the declared goals. It is time to improve the transitional justice concept. Scholars can do so by examining in more detail the local mobilization and the domestic and international networking of anti-mining groups. Scholars, I propose, can contribute to moving beyond the transitional justice model and developing a comprehensive approach with due attention to socio-economic problems. It is of greatest importance to the future peace and stability of Central America and the rest of the world.

SELECTED BIBLIOGRAPHY

Almqvist, Jessica, and Carlos Espósito, eds. 2012. *The Role of Courts in Transitional Justice: Voices from Latin America and Spain*. New York: Routledge.

Archibold, Randal C. 2011. "First a Gold Rush, Then the Lawyers." *New York Times* (June 25, 2011). Available at: www.nytimes.com/2011/06/26/world/americas/26mine.html ?ref=central

americanfreetradeagreement (accessed May 20, 2012).

Audley, John J. 1997. *Green Politics and Global Trade: NAFTA and the Future of Environmental Politics*. Washington DC: Georgetown University Press.

Broad, Robin, and John Cavanagh. 2011. "Like Water for Gold in El Salvador: Activists Are Risking Their Lives in the Fight Against US and Canadian Mining Companies." *The Nation* (August 1, 2011): 26–30.

Central American Free Trade Agreement (CAFTA). 2005. Available at: http://www.ustr.gov/trade-agreements/free-trade-agreements/cafta-dr-dominican-republic-central-america-fta/final-text (accessed May 1, 2012).

Collins, Cath. 2010. *Post-Transitional Justice: Human Rights Trials in Chile and El Salvador*. University Park, Pennsylvania: Pennsylvania State University Press.

Cornell, Drucilla, and Karin van Marle, with Albie Sachs. 2014. *Albie Sachs and Transformation in South Africa: From Revolutionary Activist to Constitutional Court Judge*. New York: Birbeck Law Press.

De Greiff, Pablo, and Roger Duthie, eds. 2009. *Transitional Justice and Development: Making Connections*. New York: Social Science Research Council.

Harvey, David. 2003. *The New Imperialism*. New York: Oxford University Press.

Hayner, Priscilla B. 2002. *Unspeakable Truths: Facing the Challenge of Truth Commissions*. New York: Routledge.

Hinton, Alexander Laban, ed. 2011. *Transitional Justice: Global Mechanisms and Local Realities after Genocide and Mass Violence*. New Brunswick, NJ: Rutgers University Press.

Jaramillo, Carlos Felipe, Daniel Lederman, Maurizio Bussolo, David Gould, and Andrew Mason, eds. 2006. *Challenges of CAFTA: Maximizing the Benefits for Central America*. Washington DC: World Bank.

Karunananthan, Meera. 2013. "El Salvador Mining Ban Could Establish a Vital Water Security Precedent." *The Guardian* (June 10, 2013). Available at: www.theguardian.com/global-development/Poverty-matters/2013/jun/10/el-salvador-mining-ban-water-security (accessed May 2, 2014).

Kent, Lia. 2012. *The Dynamics of Transitional Justice: International Models and Local Realities in East Timor*. New York: Routledge.

Langford, Malcolm, Ben Cousins, Jackie Dugard, and Tshepo Madlingozi. 2014. *Socio-Economic Rights in South Africa: Symbols or Substance?* New York: Cambridge University Press.

Llewellyn, Robin Oisín. 2012. "El Salvador Mulls Total Ban on Mining." *Mongabay* (October 22, 2012). Available at: http://news.mongabay.com/2012/1022-mining-el-salvador-llewellyn.html (accessed May 3, 2013).

Mani, Rama. 2008. "Editorial: Dilemmas of Expanding Transitional Justice, or Forging the Nexus Between Transitional Justice and Development." *International Journal of Transitional Justice* 2 (3): 253–65.

McEvoy, Kieran and Lorna McGregor, eds. 2008. *Transitional Justice from Below: Grassroots Activism and the Struggle for Change*. Portland, Oregon: Hart Publishing.

Miller, Zinaida. 2008. "Effects of Invisibility: In Search of the 'Economic' in Transitional Justice." *International Journal of Transitional Justice* 2 (3): 266–91.

Minow, Martha. 1998. *Between Vengeance and Forgiveness: Facing History After Genocide and Mass Violence*. Boston: Beacon Press.

Moore, Jen, Robin Broad, and John Cavanagh et al., eds. 2014. "Debunking Eight Falsehoods by Pacific Rim Mining / OceanaGold in El Salvador." Available at: www.ips-dc.org/reports/debunking_eight_falsehoods_by_pacific_rim_mining (accessed March 2, 2014).

North American Free Trade Agreement (NAFTA). 1994. Available at: https://www.nafta-sec-alena.org/Default.aspx?tabid=97andlanguage=en-US (accessed March 2, 2014).

Olsen, Tricia D., Leigh A. Payne, and Andrew G. Reiter. 2010. *Transitional Justice in Balance: Comparing Processes, Weighing Efficacy*. Washington DC: United States Institute of Peace Press.

Popovski, Vesselin, and Mónica Serrano, eds. 2012. *After Oppression: Transitional Justice in Latin America and Eastern Europe*. New York: United Nations University Press.

Schmid, Evelyne, and Aoife Nolan. 2014. "'Do No Harm'? Exploring the Scope of Economic and Social Rights in Transitional Justice." *International Journal of Transitional Justice* 8 (3): 362–82.

Solis, Domingo. 2012. "(Under) Mining Human Rights in El Salvador." Speech to the InterReligious Task Force on Central America, 32nd Annual Commemoration of the Martyrs of Central America and Columbia, Cleveland Heights, Ohio (November 4, 2012).

Spotts, Greg. 2005. *CAFTA and Free Trade: What Every American Should Know*. New York: Disinformation Company.

Stahler-Sholk, Richard, Harry E. Vanden, and Glen David Kuecker. 2008. *Latin American Social Movements in the Twenty-First Century: Resistance, Power, and Democracy*. New York: Rowman and Littlefield.

Teitel, Ruti G. 2000. *Transitional Justice*. New York: Oxford University Press.

Torres-Valverde, Diana Anahi. 2014. "The Fight to Keep Toxic Mining—and the World Bank—Out of El Salvador." *Foreign Policy In Focus* (September 24, 2014). Available at: http://fpif.org/fight-keep-toxic-mining-world-bank-el-salvador/ (accessed May 2, 2015).

Treat, Jonathan. 2013. "Mexico: International Meeting Unites Movements Against Destructive Mining Projects" (February 6, 2013). Available at: http://upsidedownworld.org/main/news-briefs-archives-68/4117-mexico-international-meeting-unites-movements-against-destructive-mining-projects (accessed May 4, 2015).

Van Der Merwe, Hugo, Victoria Baxter, and Audrey R. Chapman, eds. 2009. *Assessing the Impact of Transitional Justice: Challenges for Empirical Research*. Washington DC: United States Institute of Peace Press.

Williams, Melissa S., Rosemary Nagy, and Jon Elster, eds. 2012. *Transitional Justice*. New York: New York University Press.

Part IV

Peru

Chapter Five

First Empowerment, Then Disillusion

The Ambivalent Legacy of the Transitional Justice Process in Local Peru

Laura Tejero Tabernero

> We have come here from the 15 regions most affected by the period of political violence to demand the fulfillment of all commitments that were assumed by the Peruvian state. We raise our voice as no advances have been made. We have norms, supreme decrees, we have a Reparations Program but nothing has been implemented. Until today, we can say that only minimum advances have been achieved in implementing the seven different components that the Truth and Reconciliation Commission delivered to the state. This is why we are here today, to claim our rights and to ask for all those commitments to be finally and fully implemented. We keep waiting but . . . how much longer do we have to wait?[1]

August 28, 2013, marked the tenth anniversary of the submission of the Final Report of the Peruvian Truth and Reconciliation Commission.[2] As in previous years, victims' organizations and human rights NGOs organized different activities in Lima to commemorate the outcomes of this report and to draw attention to the significance of this date through marches, awareness raising events, public exhibitions, religious activities, and concerts. Considered the national day of the victims of the armed conflict, August 28 is not only the day Peru remembers all those who died and had disappeared but also the day they rallied to demand access to the rights that have been continuously denied them since the start of the internal armed conflict in 1980.

Busloads of people from different regions poured into the capital from early in the morning. Relatives and members of different organizations all across the country had been convened to meet at "el ojo que llora," Lima's main memorial site.[3] After a short snack and greetings, hundreds of men and women started their march to the Congress of the Republic. Led by their representatives, the people carried a set of proposals to be delivered to the members of Congress. For the most part, these proposals and demands resulted from the lack of implementation and the lack of funding with regard to the Reparation Programme, which was established in 2005 as part of the recommendations made by the Truth and Reconciliation Commission. The protesters also demanded new memory initiatives, a national plan for the search for the disappeared and judicial guarantees in a context of growing impunity at the national level.

While accompanying some of the members of CONAVIP (Coordinadora Nacional de Organizaciones de Afectados por la Violencia Política), I was able to experience and observe how, after many years of marches, negotiations and protests, the streets of the country's capital were once again awash with indignation, frustration, anger and exhaustion.[4] "We want reparation, not discrimination"; "More budget for reparations"; "Twenty-nine years asking for justice"; or "Enforcement of Law 28,592" were some of the demands that were clamored for and written on posters that day. Demands and claims which expose the ways transitional justice practices have evolved in this specific historical scenario, reveal the role played by victims' organizations and their relationship with the Peruvian state, and uncover a maze of unmet expectations and unfinished processes.

Among the raw data I collected during fieldwork in Peru, images of disillusionment and frustration are very common. These images operate as windows into the complex web of actors, discourses and practices that characterized the everyday operation of transitional justice in Peru. Drawing from extended fieldwork, conducted between 2010 and 2013, this chapter examines the impact the transitional justice project has had on post-conflict Peru, by looking closely at the social and political practices developed by different victims' organizations across the country. These practices that can be considered as privileged ethnographic cases to empirically apprehend the type of power relations built and displayed in specific transitional scenarios.

I will demonstrate that the role of the transitional justice paradigm was ambiguous and changed over time. Introduced by different local and international human rights organizations, the transitional justice framework was at first helpful for victims and survivors in Peru. As was the case in many different places around the world, human rights NGOs and social movement activists played a crucial role, operating as they did as intermediaries, translating and interpreting the transnational discourse of human rights and transitional justice for local victims. We can speak of this process as one of vernacularization (Merry 2006) insofar as the transitional justice rhetoric was appropriated, translated, and remade into the vernacular.[5] This was a rhetoric that victims' organizations adopted and used to mobilize and claim rights, especially once the Truth and Reconciliation Commission was established in 2001, opening a new space of opportunities and expectations. However, by now they have become disillusioned, or perhaps even victimized for a second time. As I will show throughout these pages, the way transitional justice programs and mechanisms have evolved has provided no consistent support for the communities most affected by the period of political violence, and the programs ultimately failed to deliver meaningful forms of justice and reparation.

Transitional justice is often defined as justice associated with periods of political change, characterized by legal responses to confront the wrongdoings of repressive predecessor regimes (Teitel 2003). In this sense, transitional justice can be understood as a normative framework but also as a range of processes and mechanisms associated with a society's attempt to come to terms with a legacy of large-scale past abuses, in order to ensure accountability, serve justice and achieve reconciliation (UN 2010). Since the origins of transitional justice, which authors such as Teitel date back to the Nuremberg Trials, we have witnessed an unprecedented expansion of a unique network of knowledge and legal practices that has contributed to the transnationalization and institutionalization of this framework, now constituted a field in itself.[6] It has become a professional and academic inquiry linked to a set of practices (prosecutions, truth commissions, memorialization, lustration and vetting, reparations, amnesties, or pardons), and involves institutional structures such as international humanitarian law, international tribunals and courts, the United Nations Development Program (UNDP) and nongovernmental organizations (Hinton 2010, 4). Due to this rapid growth, transitional justice has also come to be defined as an industry, composed of teams of expert consultants, standardized software packages for data management, and a set of assumptions regarding how to "do memory" and why memory matters (Theidon 2009, 296). It is an industry that moves quickly from one country to another, importing and exporting a globally prescribed set of measures and assumptions on how to best deal with violent pasts.

I will therefore refer to transitional justice not only as a normative framework but also as a rhetoric, a practice, and a materialized institutional-professional industry. But more specifically, I will refer to transitional justice as a new technology of government (governing as understood in the Foucauldian sense of conducting our conduct). This technology of government incites subjects to make use of truth discourses and expand frameworks of rights to express their political and social discontent and to channel their dissenting practices (Odysseos 2010). It is a form of power that produces new subjects—the victims of human rights violations—and shapes the moral, social, and political grounds that sustain their actions within this specific field of interaction.

ON THE CONSTRUCTION OF THE TRANSITIONAL JUSTICE FIELD IN PERU

The possibility of a Truth and Reconciliation Commission in Peru was the result of a historical momentum created by the collapse of the Fujimori regime in 2000, when a series of videos were publicly aired providing evidence for the corruption of the government. As a result of social pressure and the total loss of credibility, the president flew to Japan and resigned from office. This situation lead to the constitution of a transitional government chaired by the interim president, Valentin Paniagua, who, among other major challenges, had to face the legacies of the political violence that had ravaged the country since Shining Path troops initiated their attack on the Peruvian state in May of 1980.[7]

The human rights movement perceived this new political juncture as a space of opportunity to take concrete steps to clarify the mechanisms of political violence and to compensate victims by granting their rights to truth, justice and reparation. Drawing from experiences learned in other Latin American and Africa countries, their political advocacy work began, finally materializing in a series of political commitments that led to the setting up of a working group of government officials and civil society representatives to develop a proposal for a truth commission.

The Peruvian Truth and Reconciliation Commission was tasked to investigate the origins and responsibilities for human rights violations between May 1980 and November 2000 (PCM 2001). Importantly, these crimes were attributed both to the terrorist organizations and to state agents. The commission collected nearly 17,000 testimonies, organized thirteen public hearings, created multiple working groups and revised the information gathered and published by different human rights NGOs that had been operating in this arena since the beginning of the internal armed conflict. The results were published in a Final Report in August of 2003.[8]

This report became the roadmap for further transitional justice mechanisms. The report's recommendations included the creation of a massive reparations program for victims, a series of institutional reforms, and the establishment of a national plan for the search for the disappeared. Informed by international human rights standards and principles, the Peruvian state had the moral and legal obligation to compensate for the psychical, material, and psychological damages committed against a large part of its population.

The global framework of transitional justice thus met national politics, in a context that was of course not free from political contestation and conflicting interests and goals. Politicians and socio-economic elites directly linked to the former governments of Alan Garcia and Alberto Fujimori were not to accept the implantation of these processes; still less the meta-narrative that emerged once the Final Report was submitted. Taking advantage of the ideology that had been widely spread during the years of political violence, they were able to retain the support of a huge part of the general public who still often excused human rights violations as "excesses" of the conflict and as the cost of defeating the terrorist threat (Laplante 2008, 82). According to this interpretation, transitional justice mechanisms were not only not needed but also not desirable; there was nothing to investigate and nothing to repair. There were several attempts to delegitimize the experience of the Truth and Reconciliation Commission—some of which remain to date—but no matter these resistances, the transitional justice paradigm finally managed to enter official discourse and practice in Peru. As had happened in other local and national settings, it became increasingly difficult for local governments and political elites to fight against the credibility of human rights and transitional justice concepts, supported by the international community and by a growing body of treaties and resolutions that have strengthened their international legal basis (Merry 2006, 2).

Although the concept of transitional justice did not permeate the discourses of most stakeholders involved in this scenario (government officials, human rights activists, and victims), all of them rapidly incorporated the narrative of national reconciliation and the language of right to truth, justice, and reparation. These languages and narratives also became embedded in new public policies, normative frameworks, and institutional arrangements. Firstly, with the creation of the "Comisión Multisectorial de Alto Nivel" (CMAN), organ of the state in charge of the coordination and follow-up of the different governmental policies to promote peace, collective reparation, and national reconciliation. Secondly, with the promulgation of the Comprehensive Reparation Plan Law in July 2005. This law was almost entirely inspired by the Commissions' recommendations and was the result of an initiative led by the International Centre of Transitional Justice (ICTJ) in collaboration with some national human rights NGOs. Working as consultants, they actively participated in the design and definition of a comprehensive plan that could address the complexity of the victims' universe after twenty years of rampant violence and human rights violations.[9] This law provided for the first time a concrete definition of victims and beneficiaries, defined the different components of the reparations plan and ordered the creation of a Reparations Council in charge of coordinating the official registration of victims.

Different national and international consultants and experts also rapidly intervened in different communities all across the country: lawyers and legal advisers, psychologists and psychiatrists in charge of protecting the mental health of "traumatized populations," forensic anthropologists, gender specialists, volunteers and social workers in charge of the collection of testimonies and registration of victims. The work performed by the Truth and Reconciliation Commission and by different NGOs linked to the process taught victims about their right to justice and reparations (Laplante 2008) and different ideas, values, discourses, and practices were thus transplanted into local scenarios.

VICTIMS' ORGANIZATIONS IN THE POST-TRC SCENARIO

At the end of August 2013, I was invited to participate in a workshop in Huamanga, capital of the region of Ayacucho.[10] The occasion was prompted by the thirtieth anniversary of "Asociación Nacional de Familiares de Secuestrados, Detenidos y Desaparecidos" (ANFASEP). The main purpose was to bring together members of different victims' organizations from across the country in an unprecedented forum to discuss the successes and failures in the field of transitional justice as well as the goals yet to be fulfilled ten years after the submission of the Final Report of the Truth and Reconciliation Commission. Different NGO workers, international donors, and state authorities publicly discussed different issues, from the lack of accountability to the recognition of successful experiences of memory work across the country.

While attending the different activities and observing the interactions that were taking place, I suddenly found myself taking notes compulsively. This workshop had become a unique ethnographic site for information gathering and refutation of some of the ideas and questions that had been guiding my research during the past three years, mainly: How is victimhood redefined and reinterpreted in specific transitional scenarios? What room for political agency has resulted from the implementation of transitional justice processes in Peru? What are the underlying power relationships that shape transitional justice scenarios and how do victims respond to them?

ANFASEP was the first victims' organization created in the country. Led by a group of Quechua-speaking indigenous women, they started to confront state power in their relentless search for their beloved ones: husbands, sons and brothers who had been forcibly disappeared since the beginning of the armed conflict in 1980. These women were followed by other organizations, started during the 1980s and the 1990s, mainly by relatives of people who had been imprisoned and/or disappeared and by members of different forcibly displaced communities who had resettled in the outskirts of the main cities across the country.

During the years of political violence, and as a consequence of what some authors have defined as a strategy of "instrumentalization of fear" (Burt 2009a, 317)—led not only by the government but also by the terrorist groups—Peruvian civil society was demobilized, collective identities were debilitated, and the moral and material foundations of different civil society organizations were destroyed (Burt 2009a, 327). Although some organizations and different human rights NGOs began to publicly denounce the violations that were committed during this period, it was not until the end of Fujimori's government in 2000 that they could actively put forward their demands of truth and justice in the public sphere without being considered and prosecuted as the "legal arm of terrorism." After the collapse of the Fujimori regime and with the advent of the new transitional government, these organizations could emerge. The transitional justice discourse and entrepreneurs weakened the climate of fear and raised expectations for truth and justice. People who had been imprisoned and/or tortured, women who had suffered sexual violence, displaced communities and relatives of people who had been murdered or disappeared soon created their own organizations. Generally speaking, we can refer to the setting up of most of these organizations as a strategic calculation of the social and political opportunities this new context was to offer. In creating these organizations they were turning an experience of victimhood, long denied and stigmatized, into a strategic political position from which to claim and mobilize rights.

This process of creation of new victims' organizations was encouraged and promoted by different human rights NGOs. Throughout the workshop it was common to hear participants speak about human rights NGOs as their main "allies." These organizations, along with other "transitional justice entrepreneurs" (Madlingozi 2010), helped victims tackle the formal institutional and sometimes economic requirements to build their organizations at the local, regional and national levels. They also actively participated in the identification of possible leaders, evaluated their communicational and organizational capacities and their ability to position themselves in the public sphere.[11]

> Once they incarcerated my daughter, I did many things. Every event that was organized about human rights, I was there. And I always invited the other mothers I had met when visiting my daughter . . . and they saw that I was able to reach these mothers; the NGO saw that I had some attitude, a fighting nature. And then they always took me from one event to the next. They said, "People from the United Nations are coming and you are going to talk." They saw my skills, my attitude, and finally they called me and we created our organization. . . . (Interview with woman, whose daughter was one of the many university students who were unjustly imprisoned during Fujimori's regime, Lima 2012)[12]

> I was asked to give an interview to a newspaper, to talk about my experience . . .. And the interview was published, and I talked about the difficulties we were facing and then the NGOs said "she is the spokesperson," she has a good approach to the problem, because she speaks from the human side. She will then be the referent. And that is how I gained mayor leadership. (Interview with woman 2012)

Different human rights NGOs also started to develop projects aimed at strengthening and empowering victims and their organizations, not only by providing know-how and legal assistance but also through constant training of their members and leaders. Below is from a personal interview with a human rights NGO worker when discussing their day-to-day activities:

> One of our main activities has been to train relatives in the field of forced disappearance because we thought. . . . Ok, they have a relative that was forcibly disappeared and they don't know what to do. But if they do know how to proceed, where to go, the legal framework, then the process will be at least a bit easier for them . . . we are interested in changing this. They have to know their rights once they knock on a door asking for something and it is also about the authorities, they need to know and see that the relatives are empowered. That is the starting point for everything else. (Interview with journalist and member of a local human rights organization, Lima 2011) [13]

It was then, with the creation of the transitional justice field that the figure of the victim finally appeared in the public discourse. After many years of persecution and denial, a discursive space was opened for them to share their experiences but also to politically participate in the process. Different victims' organizations soon became direct interlocutors with the Peruvian state and started participating in different consultancy committees and socio-political and legal platforms. In this specific context, victims had become recognized rights-holders and demanded to be assisted and listened to. [14] Demands for rights had been legitimized through certain types of discourses that were now available for victims to frame and express their experiences of violence and their social and political discontent.

Throughout the workshop, there were different sessions and presentations that animated heated debates. Some of the participants who took part in these discussions, mainly victims and relatives from different communities in Ayacucho, directly addressed the audience in Quechua. Of course, their messages were utterly unintelligible for me and for some of the other guests. [15] However, it was striking to hear and observe how they were squeezing into their discourses some concrete terms in Spanish: "human rights," "reparations" or "victim," among many others. These are terms that are not part of the Quechua vocabulary, as they had only come to be used in this specific historical context when interacting with the state and with other social and political actors present in this field. It shows how victims have incorporated the framework established by the Truth and Reconciliation Commission (and the collective languages instituted by subsequent laws and policies) to articulate their demands, while at the same time they resignified them according to the social and economic realities from which they spoke, those of historical inequality and discrimination.

To provide an example, the very use of the "victim" label was only pressed onto those who had suffered from violence once the reparations plan was finally established in 2005, along with a set of new laws and institutional arrangements. Once the "victim" became the subject of concrete public policies, other forms of identification that had been previously used to define and present their experiences in the public sphere were rapidly abandoned. As Maria Eugenia Ulfe states in her research on the politics of reparation in the community of Lucanamarca, the first term used during the period of political violence was the "displaced"—as a way of naming one of the most visible experiences resulting from violence: the massive migrations of entire communities from the Peruvian highlands to the main cities of the country. Once the Commission was established, "displaced" was replaced by the term "affected," which was incorporated by different social and political agents (mainly, human rights organizations and activists involved in this process) to refer to other experiences of violence and to avoid further victimization (Ulfe 2013, 19). In the same vein, and following the experience of mobilization in countries like Argentina and Chile, the term "relatives" also appeared, especially to refer to those who had experienced the death or disappearance of their family members. But once the field of transitional justice became institutionalized and bureaucratized, the "victim" label came to dominate this field as well as the social and political subjectivities emerging from it.

Victimhood was the common feature that had that day brought together people from different places all across the country, men and women, Quechua and Spanish speakers, people from rural and urban areas.[16] There were people who had experienced not only violence and extreme suffering but also an identity transformation that directly correlated to the reframing of the history of political violence in the country as well as to the new rights framework defined and legitimized by the work of the Truth and Reconciliation Commission. The new transitional justice scenario and new (mainly imagined) benefits that had become available were pushing actors to redefine themselves and their most intimate experiences according to a new set of rules and principles (international human rights law, classifications of crimes), relationships (manifested through their interactions with government officials and NGO workers) and expectations (final outcomes of the process). A certain way of being a "victim," of mobilizing victimhood and claiming rights was being defined in the process, in so far as certain discourses and modes of action were being celebrated and performed while others simultaneously discarded. Following Butler's (1997, 2) notion of subjection, understood as the fundamental dependency on a discourse we never chose but that, paradoxically, initiates and sustains our agency, we can thus speak of a process in which transitional justice entrepreneurs directly impacted the production of new political subjectivities. From this perspective, transitional justice should also be considered a new form of power, one that is produced and reproduced within and outside the state. A form of power that, in many different post-conflict settings around the globe, is raised to prescribe certain forms of legitimate discourse, producing a particular modality of subjectification that is imposed on individuals but through which it is also possible for them to make their cause heard (Fassin 2012, 203).

WHAT WE ARE LEFT WITH WHEN TRANSITIONAL JUSTICE FAILS

It was October 2013 and we were heading to Huaycan, a place on the outskirts of the city where a huge community of displaced people live. I had been invited to join an informal meeting of CONAVIP ("un día para bajar a las bases") and engage with the members of different smaller organizations who are part of this huge umbrella organization. Once we arrived in Huaycan, we were gently welcomed with snacks and refreshments. After the usual formal presentations, members of the organization could ask questions to their leaders and express their most urgent and painful concerns.

Lidia was the first to share her personal experience that day. Originally from a small community in the highlands, she had to flee to Lima in 1988 after both of her parents were shot dead by Shining Path troops.[17] Followed by her six younger brothers and sisters, and thanks to the help of relatives, she was able to reach the city and join some of the members of her community who had also been forced to abandon their homes. At the time of her speaking, Lidia was one among the nearly 30,000 registered victims who had already benefited from economic compensation.[18] As established by Supreme Decree 51-2011-PCM, final economic compensation amounts to 10,000 soles (or $3,450) to be delivered in one-time cash payment to victims of rape, victims of torture suffering from some sort of disability, and relatives who had forcibly disappeared family members or deceased victims. In the case of families, the total amount needs to be divided: 50 percent to the wife, spouse or partner, and the remaining 50 percent to be distributed among the rest of the family, such as children or parents of the victim. Once this form of distribution was applied, Lidia received nearly 1,500 soles from the Peruvian state (something less than $520). Predictably, she was not satisfied with this amount but rather outraged. With tears in her eyes she told us how she considered this amount a direct "insult to her suffering," a symbol of ongoing discrimination. She had only been compensated for the death of her father and it was yet unclear whether she would also be compensated for the death of her mother or for the loss of her family house.

Lidia was not an exception. Many other participants were still waiting for their reparation payments. Rocío, for example, had not even been able to properly register as a victim as her case was still pending final confirmation after more than eleven months. Once the registration process was opened, she was forced to travel back to her community to ask for some documents from local authorities that could prove the alleged violations. Others, who had already navigated the long registration process to be granted their victims' certificate, were not even aware of the specific benefits associated with this recognized condition. As questions began to arise, members from CONAVIP had to carefully explain how reparations had materialized, from specific health care to scholarships for higher education.

Conversations lasted more than three hours until it was time for us to return to Lima. During the journey, one CONAVIP member told me how exhausting it had become for him to face this type of situation. It was hard not only hearing the stories of violence and suffering but mainly to observe how people were losing faith in the process.

This experience exemplifies the multiple types of social, political, economical and institutional frictions that have come to define most of the transitional justice process since the submission of the Final Report of the Truth and Reconciliation Commission in 2003. Although most conversations held that day revolved around reparations, similar tensions occur when victims discuss the specific dynamics and outcomes of transitional justice processes in relation to prosecutions of perpetrators or to the search of the bodies of the disappeared. They allude to difficulties that range from the mere rejection of a document in an institutional office to feelings of humiliation associated with derisory economic compensations, from disinformation to the feeling of institutional and social abandonment while waiting for commitments to be fully met and for their right to be finally acknowledged.

As mentioned above, victims' organizations had actively incorporated the transitional justice framework to claim a series of rights long denied. Once the Truth and Reconciliation Commission was established in 2001, and especially after the Reparation Plan in 2005, victims felt they were being granted a unique opportunity not only to fulfill their needs for justice but also to improve their living conditions. This was especially the case for those suffering from poverty, historical exclusion, and institutional marginalization. These people had envisioned reparations as a practical solution to some of their most basic needs: health and education for them and their children, and new economic opportunities to restart life projects that had been destroyed. But, no matter these expectations, the reality of the process became a new source of despair and disenfranchisement.

Designed with the help of national and international consultants, the Peruvian Reparation Plan provides for individual and collective reparation. These range from specialized health care and education to memorialization and monetary compensation. However, and despite the impressive advances in the normative framework described previously, the implementation of these programs has been slow, uneven, and inefficient. Different bureaucratic and administrative hurdles have come to define the process, from the need of documents to be officially registered by a victim to different economical assessments to be granted concerning university scholarships, or the lack of knowledge of public health officials leading to the denial of health care in different local settings. Hurdles that have now become too much of a deterrent for many victims to keep struggling for rights and recognition.

The technical and political withdrawals identified by authors like Laplante and Theidon (2007) only two years after the formal launching of the Peruvian Reparations Plan remain unchanged. In 2014, the Reparation Council was still underbudgeted and understaffed and there was a clear lack of consistency and coordination between the different institutions linked to the implementation of the Reparation Plan. Final decisions and outcomes were still subject to the political will of successive elected governments who had remained reluctant to properly fund this plan and to establish mechanisms that could properly fulfill the demands and expectations of those affected by violence. Furthermore, there had been a clear withdrawal of international support, which had also worsened the situation and limited the chances of success.

At the beginning of the process, Peru, with its violent and tragic recent past, managed to attract the attention of the international community and funds were provided by different international agencies through the signing of cooperation agreements. According to the financial information made public by the commissioners, almost 40 percent of the total costs associated with work of the Truth and Reconciliation Commission were covered by international financial sources.[19] Funds were also provided to enable the work that was yet to follow. The Reparations Plan and its institutions had the support of the Spanish Agency for International Development Cooperation (AECID) and the German Technical Cooperation Agency (GTZ). These agencies also supported the work to be delivered by different human rights organizations, whose projects and programs became directly dependent on the funds provided by the international community. However, ten years after the submission of the Final Report, Peru is no longer a priority for international agencies and donors. There are new scenarios that have now become the target of transitional justice interventions. This withdrawal of international support has both limited the capacity of the Peruvian government to follow the transitional justice plan outlined and weakened human rights organizations, which have now lost their capacity for advocacy and mobilization. Projects and activities directly aimed at monitoring the advances made in this field have been shut down, as new problems are on the Peruvian human rights agenda, like environmental conflicts, and sexual and reproductive rights.

In the meantime, victims' organizations keep playing a significant role by mobilizing for punishment and developing different forms of intra- and extra-institutional mobilization, from marches and sit-ins to lobbying, litigation or active participation in different consultancy committees. Their actions are important for reaching their often-remote members and providing them with know-how about their rights and suitable political strategies. But it is still proving difficult for them to retain the support of their members. People and communities start to lose faith in this process, leading to the disarticulation and disempowerment of victims' organizations—a disarticulation that has been exacerbated as the result of a widespread feeling of disappointment, even of anger against not only the government but also human rights NGOs.

Leaders and members of victims' organizations still work closely with human rights NGOs, especially with those who played a key role in shaping the practices and strategic direction of the victims' movement. However, it has also become common, when conducting fieldwork in communities directly affected by violence, to hear comments and discourses that relate to what some authors have defined as the "theft of victims' pain." This occurs when NGOs speak about and for victims with the aim of involving others to do something to end victims' suffering (Madlingozi 2010, 211). This is felt as a theft by men and women who have shared their stories of suffering and violence, who have incorporated the language of victimization and the discourses of legalism and human rights and who, at the end, have not experienced any positive impact on their socioeconomic needs.

CONCLUDING COMMENTS

"We want reparations not discrimination" has become one of the victims' main discourses in different marches and sit-ins. For years, members of different victims' organizations had come to accept the transitional justice agenda as defined since the establishment of the Truth and Reconciliation Commission.[20] The invocation of a new institutionalized rights framework had incited victims as rights-holding subjects, empowered through the adoption of transitional justice ideas which have led to specific aspirations and new popular demands (Anderson 1993, 186). However, after years with this process many of those who initially welcomed the transitional justice rhetoric and policies now reject it and even show resistance. As in many other places, the supposed deliverance turned out to be a relative continuity of historically rooted political and socioeconomic inequalities and forms of discrimination. These inequalities are expressed through problematic or even offensive monetary payments, and the lack of political will to properly implement programs and to improve the living conditions of these populations. Also, the inequalities are reproduced through underlying forms of power that transcend the relationships between the victims and the Peruvian state. By considering transitional justice as a new form of government, we have attempted to displace our analysis to those relationships that occur outside the state and its institutions. We have intended to show the ways in which power relationships unfold in so-called transitional societies, imposing and legitimizing certain ways of managing experiences of inequality and injustice while simultaneously delegitimizing others, avoiding any alternative reinterpretations and ultimately contributing to the production of rightlessness.

At the end of the day, what seems to be clear is the way in which transitional justice rhetoric mismatches the Peruvian sociopolitical reality, particularly at the local level. Victims are still suffering the consequences of structural and symbolic violence, sometimes reinforced when transitional justice mechanisms are imported and exported from one place to another without their long-term impact on the lives of the people in whose names they are said to be put in place being carefully handled.

NOTES

1. Fragment of the speech delivered by a representative of the victims' movement during the commemoration of the tenth anniversary of the Final Report of the Peruvian Truth and Reconciliation Commission. Woman in her forties, whose husband was a victim of enforced disappearance in 1986. Translated by the author.

2. This paper is part of a PhD project on the politics of victimhood in the Peruvian context of post-conflict recovery, based at the Complutense University of Madrid. It has been partially funded by the European Union "Sustainable Peace Building" Initial Training Network, Marie Cure Actions of the Seventh Framework Programme. Some of the ideas in this essay have already been developed in a previous paper published in the journal *Papeles del CEIC* (Tejero 2014). The author would especially like to thank all members of the different victims' organizations with whom she has worked, for their invaluable generosity and for allowing her to accompany them in their struggle. She would also like to thank Marie José Devillard for her patience and support throughout this process.

3. Opened to the public in August 2005, "el ojo que llora" aims to commemorate the victims of the armed conflict and to foster awareness and reflection about Peru's violent past. Built by the Dutch-born sculptor Lika Mukal, it appears in the shape of a path made of thousands of small rocks with the names of those murdered and disappeared. For more information on the controversies surrounding this memorial site, see Saona (2014).

4. CONAVIP is the largest victims' organization in Peru. As an umbrella organization, it represents victims' support groups in fourteen different regions across the country. Since its constitution CONAVIP has acted as an interlocutor with the state, advocating for the right of victims to justice, truth, and reparation. Throughout these pages, I will refer specifically to those organizations represented under this umbrella. It is important to stress that the Peruvian victims' movement is not homogeneous. However, and despite the differences observed, it is believed there is a general pattern in terms of the role and positions assumed when interacting with human rights organizations, governmental bodies and, more broadly, with Peruvian society.

5. In Merry's (2006, 219) words, the process of *vernacularization* is one of appropriation and translation. Human rights ideas are appropriated by national elites and middle-level social activists and translated into local terms. Those who are most vulnerable, often the subjects of human rights, come to see the relevance of this framework for their lives only through the

mediation of middle-level and elite activists who reframe their everyday problems in human rights terms.

6. Defined as a field of struggles within which agents confront each other, with differentiated means and ends according to their position in the structure of the field of forces, thus contributing to conserving or transforming its structure (Reed-Danahay 2004, 32).

7. For a more detailed description and analysis of this specific context and challenges, see Burt 2009a.

8. According to this report, more than 69,000 people were killed or forcibly disappeared during the conflict, either by the armed forces or by the alleged terrorists groups. Nearly 75 percent of these victims were Quechua-speaking indigenous civilians, living in the Peruvian highlands and Amazon provinces. Thousands more were victims of torture, illegal detention, sexual violence, forced recruitment, and massive displacement (CVR 2003).

9. The International Centre for Transitional Justice (ICTJ) is a non-profit organization created in 2001 that provides technical expertise and knowledge of relevant comparative experiences in transitional justice from across the globe, see http://www.ictj.org/about (accessed April 8, 2014). The concrete proposal referenced in this text can be found in ICTJ and APRODEH (2002).

10. According to the Final Report of the Truth and Reconciliation Commission, Ayacucho was the region most affected by political violence. Fifty-four percent of the total victims were inhabitants of this region (CVR 2003).

11. I use the term "transitional justice entrepreneurs" to refer to the pool of international experts, donors, NGO workers, social movement activists, and researchers that operate in different transitional settings across the world.

12. Hereafter I will refer to this interview as "Interview with woman." Interview translated by the author.

13. Hereafter I will refer to this interview as "Interview with journalist." Interview translated by the author.

14. Or, as we will see, as rights-holders-in-waiting (Odysseos 2010).

15. An interesting approach to similar experiences of "unintelligibility" can be found in Castillejo (2013).

16. Victimhood is defined here not in terms of the condition resulting from an experience of suffering from an injurious and/or violent action—or as opposed to the condition of those considered perpetrators—but as a sociopolitical, legal, moral, and rhetorical construction. For a more detailed description and analysis of the process of social and legal construction of the figure of the victim, see Tejero (2014).

17. All original names and references to personal details have been replaced so as to guarantee full anonymity.

18. According to the information made public by the Ombudsman's office in its report N° 162, by June 2013 only 37.2 percent of the total number of registered beneficiaries had been awarded their compensation (Defensoría del Pueblo 2013, 41).

19. Eleven different cooperation agencies and private foundations economically participated in this endeavor. Among the main donors, we find the United States Agency for International Development (USAID) and its Office of Transition Initiatives (OTI). As stated in the Final Evaluation report of the OTI's Program in Peru, their strategy was intended to support peaceful democratic transition in Peru and to visibly associate the U.S. Government with these efforts. For a full list of international agencies, financial sources and percentages, see: http://www.cverdad.org.pe/ingles/lacomision/ifinanciera/financiamiento.php (accessed April 3, 2014).

20. Of course, exceptions exist, given the huge heterogeneity and diversity within and across these organizations. It should be stated that I am referring here specifically to those organizations which have gained mayoral support and which have become main interlocutors with the Peruvian state and its institutions.

SELECTED BIBLIOGRAPHY

Anderson, Michael R. 1993. "Litigation and Activism: The Bophal Case." *Third World Legal Studies* 12: 177–87.

Bebbington, Anthony, Claudia Bielich, and Martín Schurrah. 2009. *Los movimientos sociales y la política de la pobreza en el Perú*. Lima: IEP, CEPES y GPC.

Bourdieu, Pierre. 1984. *Distinction: a social critique of the judgment of taste*. London: Routledge.

Burt, Jo-Marie. 2009a. *Violencia y Autoritarismo en el Perú: Bajo la sombra de Sendero y la dictadura de Fujimori*. Lima: IEP, SER y EPAF. Available at: http://198.57.164.64/~ieporg/textos/DDT/violenciayautoritarismoenelperu.pdf (accessed May 4, 2015).

———. 2009b. "Guilty as Charged: The Trial of Former Peruvian President Alberto Fujimori for Human Rights Violations." *International Journal of Transitional Justice* 3: 384–405.

Butler, Judith. 1997. *The Psychic Life of Power. Theories in Subjection*. Standford: Standford University Press.

Castillejo Cuellar, Alejandro. 2013. "On the Question of Historical Injuries: Transitional Justice, Anthropology and the Vicissitudes of Listening." *Anthropology Today* 29 (1): 17-20.

Comisión de la Verdad y Reconciliación (CVR). 2003. *Informe Final*. Lima: CVR. Available at: http://cverdad.org.pe/ifinal/ (accessed May 4, 2015).

Defensoría del Pueblo. 2013. *A diez años de verdad, justicia y reparación. Avances, retrocesos y desafíos de un proceso inconcluso*. Lima: Serie Informes Defensoriales—Informe N° 162. Available at: http://www.gestionpublica.org.pe/plantilla/info_secpu/dp_281013_0005.pdf (accessed May 4, 2015).

EPAF. 2012. *De Víctimas a Ciudadanos. Memorias de la Violencia Política en Comunidades de la Cuenca del Río Pampas*. Lima: Equipo Peruano de Antropología Forense.

Fassin, Didier. 2008. "The Humanitarian Politics of Testimony." *Cultural Anthropology* 23 (2): 531–58.

———. 2012. *Humanitarian Reason: A Moral History of the Present*. Berkeley: University of California Press.

Foucault, Michel. 1982. "The Subject and Power." *Critical Inquiry* 8 (4): 777–95.

———. 1997. *Defender la Sociedad*. Buenos Aires: Fondo de Cultura Económica de Argentina S.A.

Hinton, Alexander L. 2010. "Introduction: Toward an Anthropology of Transitional Justice." In *Transitional Justice: Global Mechanisms and Local Realities After Genocide and Mass Violence,* ed. Alexander L. Hinton, 1–22. New Jersey: Rutgers University Press.

ICTJ and APRODEH. 2002. *Design Parameters for a Reparations Program in Peru*. Available at: https://ictj.org/sites/default/files/ICTJ-Peru-Reparations-Parameters-2002-English.pdf (accessed September 14, 2014).

Laplante, Lisa. 2008. "From Theory To Practice: Implementing Reparations in Post-Truth Commission Peru." In *Waging War, Making Peace: Reparations and Human Rights*, ed. Barbara Rose Johnston and Susan Slyomovics, 75–94. California: Left Coast Press Inc.

Laplante, Lisa, and Kimberly Theidon. 2007. "Truth with Consequences: Justice and Reparations in Post-Truth Commission Peru." *Human Rights Quarterly* 29 (1): 228–50.

Madlingozi, Tshepo. 2010. "On Transitional Justice Entrepreneurs and the Production of Victims." *Journal of Human Rights Practice* 2 (2): 208–28.

———. 2013. "Post-Apartheid Movements and Legal Mobilization." In *Socio-Economic Rights in South Africa: Symbol or Substance?* eds. Malcolm Langford, Ben Cousins, Jack Dugard, and Tshepo Madlingozi, 92–130. Cambridge: Cambridge University Press.

Merry, Sally Engle. 2006. *Human Rights and Gender Violence: Translating International Law into Local Justice*. Chicago: University of Chicago Press.

Odysseos, Louiza. 2010. "Human Rights, Liberal Ontogenesis and Freedom: Producing a Subject for Neoliberalism?" *Millenium: Journal of International Studies* 38 (3): 747–72.

———. 2011. "Governing Dissent in the Central Kalahari Game Reserve: 'Development,' Governmentality, and Subjectification amongst Botswana's Bushment." *Globalizations* 8 (4): 439–55.

Presidency of the Council of Ministers (PCM). 2001. *Decree N° 065-2001-PCM.* Lima: Presidency of the Council of Ministers. Available at: http://www.cverdad.org.pe/lacomision/nlabor/decsup01.php (accessed May 4, 2015).

Reed-Danahay, Deborah. 2004. *Locating Bourdieu.* Bloomington: Indiana University Press.

Saona, Margarita. 2014. *Memory Matters in Transitional Peru.* New York: Palgrave McMillian.

Teitel, Ruti. 2003. "Transitional Justice Genealogy." *Harvard Human Rights Journal* 16: 69–94.

Tejero Tabernero, Laura. 2014. "Nosotros, las víctimas: Violencia, justicia transicional y subjetividades políticas en el contexto peruano de recuperación posconflicto." *Papeles del CEIC* 1. Available at: http://www.ehu.eus/ojs/index.php/papelesCEIC/article/view/12431/11353 (accessed September 14, 2014).

Theidon, Kimberly. 2009. "Editorial Note." *International Journal of Transitional Justice* 3: 295–300.

Ulfe, Maria Eugenia. 2013. *¿Y después de la violencia qué queda? Víctimas, ciudadanos y reparaciones en el context post-CVR en el Perú.* Buenos Aires: CLACSO. Available at: http://biblioteca.clacso.edu.ar/clacso/becas/20130628122643/Ydespuesdelaviolencia.pdf (accessed February 2, 2015).

United Nations. 2010. *Guidance Note of the Secretary General. United Nations Approach to Transitional Justice.* Available at: http://www.unrol.org/files/TJ_Guidance_Note_March_2010FINAL.pdf (accessed February 2, 2015).

INTERVIEWS

Interview in Spanish with a woman in her fifties, member of CONAVIP (Coordinadora Nacional de Organizaciones de Afectados por la Violencia Política), Lima, August 2012.

Interview in Spanish with a woman in her forties, member of CONAMUACAI (Coordinadora Nacional de Mujeres Afectadas por el Conflicto Armado Interno), Lima, September 2012.

Interview in Spanish with a woman in her fifties, journalist and member of a local human rights organization, Lima, September 2011.

Chapter Six

How Transitional Is Justice?

Peru's Post-Conflict Revisited

José Pablo Baraybar, Jesús Peña, and Percy Rojas

Far from being an academic exercise, this contribution is rather a collection of notes from the field and the eyewitness account of Human Rights practitioners. Consequently, we are aware that this text may be colored by personal experiences from an activist point of view and even by political discourse. The points of view presented herein reflect a non-governmental organization's fieldwork in forensics and Human Rights advocacy, especially regarding the forced disappearance of persons during the Internal Armed Conflict of Peru and with a strong emphasis on the restitution of citizenship, or civil and political rights, to long neglected victims. For us, members of the Peruvian Team of Forensic Anthropology (Equipo Peruano de Antropología Forense, EPAF), one of the crucial teachings fieldwork has left us is the fact that forensics can be an important means to confront people's memories with often controversial but factual findings. We like to call this the "illustrative" power of forensics (Baraybar and Blackwell 2014). EPAF, since its inception in 2001, applies forensic sciences to determine the whereabouts of missing persons as a consequence of the Internal Armed Conflict within a transitional justice framework.

Between 1980 and 2000, Peru experienced an internal armed conflict initiated by the Communist Party of Peru-Sendero Luminoso (PCP-SL) and the Tupac Amaru Revolutionary Movement (MRTA) against the Peruvian State. During the conflict, rebels, Armed Forces and paramilitary groups committed murder and other serious crimes: enforced disappearances, other forms of abductions, torture, arbitrary detentions, and various other sorts of human rights violations (CVR 2003). This period marked the most cruel and violent period in the history of the Peruvian Republic. The number of dead and disappeared has risen steadily since the last decade. According to the 2003 report of the Truth and Reconciliation Commission (TRC) 8,558 people disappeared in Peru during between 1980–2000, most of them indigenous, Quechua-speaking and from the poorest strata of society. Ten years later, EPAF (2007) presented a list with the names of 13,271 missing persons. More recently, the Institute of Legal Medicine (IML), a semi-autonomous branch of the Public Ministry, put forward the figure of 15,731, and the Peruvian Government in turn has accepted this figure as official (MRE 2012). In addition, an estimate of 6,462 clandestine graves has been calculated (COMISEDH 2012) and the Registro Unico de Victimas (RUV) responsible for assembling a registry of victims for reparations purposes documented 7,399 cases of disappearances, stopping at March 2013 (Ombudsman's Report 2013).

Between 2002–2012, the Peruvian State recovered the bodies of 2,407 victims, 1,574 of which were victims of extrajudicial killings who had known identity; the remaining 833 unidentified people could have been victims of detentions and disappearance. Out of these 833, the bodies of 157 have been successfully identified by civil society organizations (i.e., EPAF). EPAF has been working for several years now in the basin of the Pampas–Qaracha Rivers in southern Ayacucho.

The prime goal of this chapter is to assess—from our perspective as forensic experts—some of the elements that the transitional justice paradigm has delivered and what it has failed to address in the post-conflict Peruvian context, especially from the perspective of missing persons. After a brief introduction to the conflict and the transitional justice steps employed in Peru, we demonstrate that while the concept (and literature) of transitional justice promised noble goals, it failed to tackle the structural problems that led to violence in the first place. We will focus on the TRC, the first and one of the most important Peruvian instruments, whose final report suggested many mechanisms that were not implemented. We argue that both the collective and individual reparation payments were highly problematic and that attempts for criminal prosecutions overall failed, because the limited number of processes held had high acquittal rates. Our main critique, however, is that the transitional justice paradigm failed to tackle the root causes of violence—structural poverty—and in contrast to its promises failed to grant universal citizenship. It is therefore necessary to question whether a transition did occur in Peru, when structural violence and social and legal inequality persist. We from EPAF advocate a more comprehensive perspective by which the enforcement of political and civil rights should also include social and economic rights. Such perspective could among other things include families in participating and overseeing the process of search, recovery, identification, and restitution of the remains of their loved ones, an exercise that would transform them into subjects and not objects in a process that occurs despite them.

THE CONFLICT

According to the Truth and Reconciliation Commission (TRC), the immediate as well as root cause of the armed conflict was the decision of the Communist Party of Peru-Sendero Luminoso (PCP-SL, by its initials in Spanish) to start a "people's war" against the Peruvian State.[1] The PCP-SL made this decision when Peru was undergoing a process of transition to democracy widely supported by the people and political groups that led to the establishment of a democratic constituent assembly, after more than a decade of military dictatorships (Willakuy 2008). When Peru 's military government allowed elections in 1980, the Shining Path was one of the few leftist political groups that declined to participate and waged war against the State instead. The Shining Path's first "act of war" was burning the ballot boxes at a polling station in the remote village of Chuschi, Ayacucho in May 1980. The Shining Path grew fast, especially in the Andean region as it filled the political vacuum left by the absent central government. What it termed "people's justice" often ended with summary executions or corporal punishments.

Based on testimonies, field investigation, and document analysis, the TRC determined that, during the conflict, crimes against humanity were committed by both the rebel groups—especially the PCP-SL—as well as by the Peruvian government.[2] In Peru, unlike in other Latin American dictatorships, such as those of Chile or Argentina, the main perpetrators of crimes against civilians were not State agents but "subversive" armed groups. Some 54 percent of victims were caused by the PCP-SL, which deliberately broke the basic rules of war and the principles of human rights. They systematically caused a permanent state of terror by using extreme violence with the purpose of gaining power. Through the use of violent means such as the annihilation of communities, razing villages, keeping defenseless communities in captivity and the systematic abuse and murder of prisoners, among other tactics, they meant to set examples which were intended to strike terror into the population.

Faced with the violence unleashed by the PCP-SL, the democratically elected Peruvian government had a duty to protect the people and uphold the constitutional order in the framework of respect for the law and fundamental rights.[3] However, law enforcement agencies frequently also incurred systematic and widespread violations of human rights; that paradoxically occurred more intensely during periods when the country was ruled by democratically elected civilian regimes; that is, between 1980 and 1992. Some attribute this fact to the problem of exclusion and socio-economic gaps that democratic governments were not able to confront and that dictatorships, on the other hand, have used to their advantage through populist politics of welfare.[4]

The ruling political class, made up by the State and political parties, was not able to cope with such a challenge and simply opted to give the armed forces the responsibility to lead the fight against "subversion." According to the TRC, "given the seriousness of the facts, it was inevitable and legitimate that constitutional governments resorted to declaring a state of emergency and to use military force to deal with armed subversion, [yet] this was done without taking steps to prevent that the fundamental rights of people were trampled" (Willakuy 2008). Thus, there have been thousands of reports of various kinds of human rights violations committed by state agents, including but not limited to extrajudicial executions, disappearances, torture, massacres, sexual violence against women, and other crimes. State agents, self-defense committees and military groups were responsible for 37 percent of deaths and disappearances reported to the TRC. Besides the crimes themselves, thousands of allegations of human rights violations were ignored, a common practice of the State to ensure impunity. The conflict affected mainly populations living in areas distant from the country's political and economic power centers. Statistics confirm that 75 percent of the victims were Quechua-speaking peasants, a segment of the population that has been historically ignored by the State and excluded from the benefits of development as well as from the political community (CVR 2003).

A SHORT OVERVIEW OF TRANSITIONAL JUSTICE MECHANISMS IN PERU

Overall, in Peru the degree of implementation of transitional policies is undoubtedly low, when compared with Argentina and Chile (Reátegui 2012). Transitional justice mechanisms adopted in Peru were: a Truth and Reconciliation Commission (TRC), individual and collective reparation mechanisms, and attempts to prosecute perpetrators. The TRC was of special importance, because it was the first measure to face the violent past and it recommended further accountability measures. After the fall of the authoritarian regime of Alberto Fujimori Fujimori in 2000, Peru began—after two decades of violence—a challenging transition to democracy. On June 4, 2001, the Transitional Government created the Truth Commission (later renamed Truth and Reconciliation Commission) mandated to investigate human rights violations, restore justice, and to propose initiatives to support and promote peace and national reconciliation among all Peruvians (PCM 2001). The TRC itself acknowledged that its narrative was only a start and that additional research was required (Gonzales Cueva 2013). Public hearings were held providing victims the space to discuss the atrocities that occurred between 1980 and 2000—stories that for years could not be told (Ulfe 2013, 57). In two years of investigations, the TRC collected more than 16,000 testimonies, and compiled a report of nine volumes. On August 28, 2003, President Alejandro Toledo presented the final report in a public ceremony.

In the aftermath of this war, the greatest challenge was to implement public policies to address, let alone fulfill, the demands of truth and justice. "Transitional Justice" is nowadays broadly known as the set of public policies, strategies and programs designed to address problems associated with past violence, aimed at addressing at least two rather broad objectives: achieving justice for the victims and attaining a more just and democratic order. As we will argue, neither goal was achieved in Peru. The so-called transitional justice process in Peru began with the final report of the TRC and its recommendations—a start, however, that did not have the expected impact.

In what follows we will assess the impact of transitional justice in Peru, focusing on its ability to: first, challenge historical narratives of the conflict; second, to fight impunity (related to retributive justice as well as the promised restitution or establishment of rule of law); and third and most important in our view, the continuing social and legal inequality and the failure of the transitional justice paradigm to grant universal citizenship.

HISTORICAL NARRATIVES AND MEMORY

One benefit of the TRC report was to correct a historical narrative that downplayed the systematic human rights violations committed by the Peruvian State; however, the new historical account was unsuccessful in changing the discourse about the violent past among many state officials and the majority of the Peruvian population.[5] The report of the TRC declared Alberto Fujimori's government and the armed forces fully responsible for defeating the rebel groups and obstructing peace. It delegitimized authoritarianism, showed the systematic policy of state violence, and refuted the prevailing myth that human rights violations were mere "excesses" or "the necessary cost of war" (Barrantes and Peña 2006, 22).[6]

Certain political groups, primarily Fujimori and APRA supporters, "sought to invalidate and discredit the claims outlined in the report [of the TRC]" (Ford Deza 2004, 143–56). Perhaps the expression that epitomizes such argument is "nosotros matamos menos" (we killed less), said by a Fujimorista congressman during a television interview (Trelles 2011). The meaning of such an expression was twofold—Sendero Luminoso was the main killer (a conclusion already established by the TRC) and there were fewer violations to Human Rights during the Fujimori regime, compared, for example, to Alan Garcia's. Those arguments led to a reification of Human Rights defenders and civil society groups supporting the TRC's conclusions as well as fighting the legacy of impunity as "caviars" (caviar; originally an expression born during France's Mitterrand used by working-class communists and socialists who viewed with suspicion young, bourgeois intellectuals who called themselves leftists) (Quintanilla 2012). So, with the publication of the Final Report of the TRC, a "battle for memory" began, the outcome of which undoubtedly determined how transition policies were configured during the ten years following the publication of the Final Report of the TRC (Jelin 2002). A selective reading of the conclusions of the Final Report has led to an official memory of the past in which a denial that violations were systematic persists; this, in turn, weakens calls for reparations and strengthens impunity.[7] One of the explanations that could be provided is that the TRC constitutes an official memory or a narrative of the past that as expected cannot satisfy all parties to the conflict. In addition to being an official narrative it became the narrative of a particular government, inasmuch as once Alejandro Toledo's term expired and Alan Garcia became president for the second time he expressed his views against what the TRC concluded (Diario La Republica 2009). Garcia had the opinion that "our homeland is plagued with a desire of revenge, one against the other, the one who says 'my truth is this' and the one that says the opposite. There have been mistakes everywhere [and no one is the] prime responsible." Further in the same interview he pointed out that "memory is not the patrimony of a single group no matter how intelligent it is, memory is [a] national [patrimony]" (Diario La Republica 2009). Garcia addressed an issue that still remains thorny; whose memory is it anyway? The final report of the TRC presented a historical timeline based on interviews and data that presented a different narrative than those forged by subgroups that lived those processes in different roles (i.e., the military, political parties, civil society groups, etc). Therefore an "official narrative" or in this case a "government narrative" could never become a space for various transactions that crisscross perceptive and emotional issues.

REPARATIONS

During the administration of President Alejandro Toledo, a legal framework was set to implement the National Plan of Reparations (PIR). In 2006, the Council of Reparations was created with the responsibility of compiling a Registry of Victims (Registro Unico de Victimas-RUV) that in turn would be used to allocate economic reparations. In mid-2013, the Office of the Ombudsman (Ombudsman's Report 2013) issued an interim report that shows the shortcomings of ten years of reparations. The report distinguishes between individual victims on one hand and collective victims on the other. As of March 2013, the total accredited individual beneficiaries amount to 182,350, of whom 106,919 are direct victims (59 percent), and 75,431 are family of victims (41 percent). The large majority of the 106,919 direct victims, who received reparation payments, are civilians (96.4 percent; 103,115 victims). Only 1 percent (1,034) of the reparation beneficiaries are members of the National Police, 1.2 percent (1,254) belong to the Armed Forces, and 1.4 percent (1,516) are members of Defense Committees (rondas campesinas), a mechanism generated by native communities (comunidades campesinas) to mitigate the absence of the State in protecting their rights (Ombudsman's Report 2013, 12).[8] As collective victims, the report registers 5,697 communities (2,799 of which are pending), and forty-six displaced person's organizations (from a total of 120).

Prioritizing collective economic reparations was a political decision of the then President Alan García Pérez (2005–2010). In 2007, the collective economic reparations program was launched with an initial budget of 30 million soles. The collective reparations were based on information provided by the final report from the TRC and the Census for Peace, research conducted by the Ministry of Women and Social Development (MIMDES) and the Program for Support to Repopulation and Development to Emergency Areas (PAR) in order to determine the extent of families affected during the Internal Armed Conflict. Each community received 100,000 soles (approximately US $40,000) as reparation and was free to decide—through an assembly—on the type of project that would be beneficial for the community. This freedom to decide upon the investment of the reparation money turned out to be very problematic. The communities were unconscious that reparation was a right of restitution; collective economic reparations became instead a social development scheme. Collective reparations, far from representing reparations as such, were an expression of municipal or governmental works of infrastructure. Many mayors and other local authorities failed to invest the money in development work, undermined the framework of reparations, and mismanaged the money.

During our years-long fieldwork in the basin of the Pampas–Qaracha Rivers in southern Ayacucho, the Peruvian Forensic Anthropology Team has learned that many communities are frustrated about how the 100,000 soles for collective reparations have been spent. Some people consider that the decisions were not taken by consensus and that not enough information was shared with the community. Many people did not know whether the sum was a compensation for damage, and called attention to the fact that, at the time of the inauguration of development work, there was no reference to its reparatory nature. Here are some examples: In the Annex of Colcabamba, Sacsamarca district, Province of Huancasancos, a water reservoir was built using the funds of collective reparations.[9] In conversations with community leaders they expressed that they were never consulted about how they wanted to be collectively repaired. As we learned from Placida Huaccachi Cayampi, a villager of Sacsamarca, the municipal authorities, without any consultation with the community, made the decision. In the case of Sacsamarca, a water reservoir was built (Interview Huaccachi Cayampi 2011).

In Putaccasa, an annex of the same district, the authorities decided to invest the money of collective reparations in buying improved alpacas to strengthen the association of alpaca herders and earn more income (Interview Garcia Callampi 2012). They bought seventy female and ten male alpacas that were brought from the city of Puno. This initiative arose because they had knowledge of other communities who bought improved cattle or invested funds in improving pastureland. Currently, Putaccasa has over 120 alpacas. In this case, although the decision arose from a consensus, the problem was the lack of foresight on the concrete benefits of the acquisition. Currently, the villagers have no markets to sell the alpaca wool at a fair price. The few buyers coming to the area offer a very low price, way below the market; villagers, in turn, prefer not to sell, waiting for better offers. In the meanwhile, wool is being stored for three years without special care, with the likely risk of spoilage (Interview Bautista Lopez 2013). According to our investigations, similar misspending of the collective reparation money has also occurred in other regions. Another case is the district of Huamanquiquia located in the province of Víctor Fajardo, on the right bank of the river Qaracha. There, a local two-story auditorium for meetings and a training room on the first floor were built; the second floor has approximately seven spacious rooms, which serve as accommodation for passers-by. The purpose of this construction was to have a location serving as a district civic center and also as a gathering place for meetings and other activities organized by the victims association of the district.

The municipality, however, has administered the space since its inauguration. City officials hold the keys of the "civic center" and the space for the auditorium now houses a garage for vehicles recently acquired by the municipality. Worst of all, the entrance to the building had to be expanded in order to the let the vehicles in. As for the garage, the "training room" was transformed into a "wawa wasi," a day care program from the Government for children under the age of four. The rooms on the second floor house the district office of the governor and are sporadically used to accommodate visitors or professionals coming to Huamanquiquia.[10] To this date, the authorities have no accountability on the cost of the building or on the property's income, nor do they report to the association of families of the district or the community. According to one of the victims (Interview Aponte Mendoza 2013):

> The location was built at the request of the Association of Relatives of Huamanquiquia because we had no place where to have our meetings, which we used to have in my house. But the problem we have now is that the municipality manages the space, they have the keys and every time we want to use the auditorium for our meetings we have to apply beforehand.

While conceived as a reparative measure it became a political statement:

> We have heard that there are plans to move the City Council to the "civic centre" so the City would become a district library. The fact is that it is the local authority who decides what use to give the building, when it was built for reparation purposes; so the meaning for which it was built is lost, we cannot use it, others do.

In sum, during our fieldwork we have realized that the collective rights of restitution ultimately depend on the political will of local authorities. Frequently collective reparation payment is simply being misused to fund projects to the benefit of local politicians rather than the victims of human rights crimes.

In Peru, the Plan of Integral Reparations (Plan Integral de Reparaciones-PIR) establishes who is entitled to individual financial compensations namely, the missing (disappeared), killed, victims of sexual violence, and people with disabilities. According to Law 28,592, persons that belong to so-called subversive organizations are outright excluded from reparations benefits.[11] In mid-2011, the process of individual reparations started through the implementation of a Supreme Decree (DS 051-2011–PCM) from July 16, 2011, starting with a budget of some 3 million soles (US $1.2 million).

The majority of victims' organizations, however, rejected the reparation decree, because it fixed the single amounts for reparations at 10,000 soles per family (approximately $3,500), well below the 39,000 soles given as reparation to members of self-defense committees, thus prioritizing some victim groups over others. A second problem was that victims could only register for reparations until December 2011, reducing the reparation policy to a limited rather than a permanent state mechanism. Individual reparations would begin with widows/mothers over sixty-five and widowers/fathers over eighty years and payments would be a single, lump-sum payment.

For both widows and widowers, 50 percent of the total amount was paid directly to them and the other 50 percent was to be distributed between the orphan children. The arithmetic of this distribution generated yet another conflict; for example, in a family with seven children, how much would each child receive? Assuming the widow would receive 5,000 soles (US $2,000), each child would receive a bit more than 700 soles (US $280) for the loss of their father and the interrupted life they had to live. Needless to say, such reparation would arrive some thirty years later. The reparations for children only began in mid-2013. A fundamental problem with the Peruvian reparation policy is that no additional economic reparation can be paid in cases where a person had been subject to multiple forms of abuse.[12] Victims who suffered multiple abuses are thus dissatisfied with the regulations for individual reparations. As noted by the Ombudsman's Office, a constitutional and autonomous institution responsible for supervising the work of other state organizations, according to the regulatory framework, individual financial compensation should be delivered for each episode of abuse, and yet, this provision has not been applied (Ombudsman's Report 2013, 14).[13]

A poignant example of the shortcomings of individual reparations is the case of Guillermo Bravo del Pino, a native of the annex of Nazareth de Uchu, district of Huamanquiquia and province of Víctor Fajardo, whom we met during our fieldwork. Don Guillermo lost his father, mother, and older brother; the PCP-SL killed them all when they attacked his community on August 15, 1984, at dawn. Four other members of the community also died that day. Don Guillermo has six brothers and one sister who also is a widow because her husband was murdered during the conflict. Don Guillermo's sister has three different episodes of abuse; however, she has been given reparation only for one (5,000 soles) in June 2013 without taking into consideration the death of her father and mother.

When the brothers Bravo went to the National Bank to collect their reparation money, they found out that 10,000 soles were divided into seven parts. According to the Regulation of Law of Reparations No. 28592, Article No. 45 states, "the most beneficial remedy is granted." Accordingly, the division was made among seven siblings, but excluding the sister who had been paid as a widow. So, in practice, only six payments were made (Interview Bravo 2013, 2014). It should be noted that those 10,000 soles divided by seven siblings, but paid only to six, applied only to the reparation for the death of the father but not to the death of the mother. It is up to the CMAN to rule on such cases and clearly explain how the regulatory framework is playing on the involvement of victims and their right to compensation. Another problem that has yet to be resolved is the question of accredited persons in the RUV who have died without receiving financial compensation. By March 2013, 3,528 direct beneficiaries of the reparations program had died without receiving individual economic reparations as a consequence of the Government's delay in implementing this policy. Despite the repeated request of the their legal heirs, the Government decided that they are not eligible to claim such funds. This situation differs greatly from laws governing insurance payments, pensions and inheritances.So far, ten lists of beneficiaries have been approved; the last two include orphan children.

These lists are being processed slowly by four-year periods, starting with events that occurred between May 1980 and June 1984. According to the Report of the Ombudsman, by June 2013, compensation to 29,392 beneficiaries (i.e., 37.2 percent of the total) had been delivered. It is worth noting, however, that those reparations include symbolic reparations as well as reparations in health, education and housing. Taking into consideration the difficulties and delays in accessing decent financial reparation, so, in absolute terms, very little has been done.

According to the Ombudsman's Report No. 162, which collects information from the CMAN through March 2013, there are 146,705 beneficiaries of reparations in health accredited in the RUV, of which 66,303 (45 percent) are affiliated with the SIS.[14] However, since 2010, we know of a number of complaints from victims and relatives in Lima, Ayacucho and other communities that have not had access to the right to health care through the SIS. According to health officials within the SIS, they lack information on how to proceed regarding those cases. While the situation has been reported to the CMAN, it has not yet changed.

Additionally, the modification of the clause in DS 051, regarding the closure of registration of victims after December 31, 2011, is still pending. Due to pressure from victims' organizations, the enrollment of victims continued through early 2013. However, these newly registered victims, according to the State, are not entitled to individual economic reparations, but only to other types of reparations. At the end, what all these shortcomings basically mean is that the right of victims to reparation is being violated in various degrees.

The process of reparations, while consisting of many topics (restitution of rights, education, health, housing, economic, and symbolic reparations), has so far concentrated primarily on economic reparations. Those in turn have been used politically, depending on the government in place. In addition, the fact that other policies complementary to reparations were not successfully implemented made matters worse. For example, while the TRC (CVR 2003) recommended a plan of forensic anthropology interventions to deal with the problem of the missing, a plan of exhumations was implemented instead; considering that reparations also include relatives of missing persons, a de facto choice was presented to those people: to receive a sum or money (or not) or to have the remains of their loved one recovered and identified. Another contentious issue has been the exclusion of members of subversive organizations who in some cases were victims themselves.[15] Therefore the combination of an integral approach to reparations (for example, proper guarantees of non-repetition through deep reforms of the judiciary, military, police, etc.), their ad-hoc and political use and the exclusion of relatives of those involved in subversive activities, have cemented the perception of a government narrative.

SHORTCOMINGS OF CRIMINAL JUSTICE

Criminal justice overall remains wanting in Peru; since the successful trial of Alberto Fujimori for human rights abuses the trend has been less promising (Burt 2009). State institutions often refuse to deliver the information necessary to start trials, and even if trials occur, the acquittal rates are high. With regard to criminal justice, the TRC developed sets of tools based on international humanitarian law and criminal law and presented forty-seven cases to the Prosecutor's Office for investigation (Godoy 2012). The quality of the information and testimonies contained therein clearly revealed the manner and circumstances in which the crimes were committed. It was expected that the Prosecutor's Office, having sufficient information to initiate investigations, would immediately proceed to prosecute human rights criminals, but instead the balance is bleak: the overall number of acquittals was high. According to the Ombudsman's report, based on a sample of 194 cases of human rights violations, by July 2013, 40 percent of cases (seventy-seven in total) were temporarily or permanently closed; the remaining 60 percent (122 cases) remained in preliminary investigation or had judgments passed. Even in those cases where trials were over and judgment was passed, arrest warrants were not enforced; out of sixty-five defendants, fifty remain at large (Ombudsman's Report 2013). The State invested insufficient financial and staff resources in the justice system, thus weakening the investigation of crimes committed by members of the State.

To improve the role of the judiciary, the TRC also recommended the creation of specialized Criminal Chambers in judicial proceedings relating to violations of human rights (known as Sala Penal Nacional). Some of those chambers passed important judgments, such as those against the paramilitary group also known as the "Colina" group.[16] In recent years, however, the jurisdiction of the Chambers expanded to other topics, such as terrorism and drug trafficking, losing sight of their initial focus. Given the high number of cases filed on human rights violations, the justice system decided that the chambers, originally created to address the crimes of the authoritarian past, would now have to cover more numerous and diverse cases even if without being allocated more resources.

Another aspect to be considered in the field of criminal justice is the constant refusal of the Ministry of Defense to deliver information to prosecutors and the judiciary on suspects in crimes against humanity. One such case is the massacre of peasants in the village of Putis in 1984, when an army patrol killed more than 100 men, women, and children. EPAF conducted exhumations, analysis and identification of remains recovered therein, in May 2008. From a total of ninety-two victims found in the mass grave, twenty-eight were successfully identified by DNA analysis. It was not until 2012, decades after the fact, that the Third Supra-Provincial Court of Lima admitted the complaint of the Second Criminal Prosecutor's Office of Ayacucho for aggravated murder against five former senior military officers who where posted in Ayacucho on the year of the massacre. However, thirty years after this atrocity took place, the justice system has not yet been able to identify those directly responsible. The response of the Ministry of Defense is that it is impossible to identify the military personnel stationed in the military base in the jurisdiction of Putis. The argument presented was that records were not always kept, and that in some cases, high ranking officers would even have files burned, but the fact remains that not establishing both individual and command responsibilities for these crimes is yet another violation of the victims' rights.

Numerous cases have been closed and the number of acquittals is high. Attorney Carlos Rivera, from the Institute of Legal Defence—Ideele, points out that that the National Criminal Court (Sala Penal Nacional) developed a "jurisprudence designed to acquit" those accused of human rights crimes; excessive documentary evidence is required to prove cases of forced disappearance, delinquents are acquitted on formal grounds although documentary evidence exists, and the testimony of family witnesses is being ignored, because of their alleged "vested interest" (Rivera 2013).[17]

One of the latest acquittals granted by the National Criminal Court [Sala Penal Nacional] occurred in the case of Lucmahuayco (a community located in the region of Cusco, southeast of Lima) where the presiding judge, Mirta Gómez Bendezú, blamed the survivors of human rights crimes and the victims' families of accusing the security forces "out of revenge" (Diario la República 2014). The counsel representing the victims has appealed the judgment with the Supreme Court.

SOCIAL INEQUALITY AND EQUAL CITIZENSHIP

While on the positive side the TRC report pinpointed the fact that poverty and social inequality were root causes of human rights violence, the Peruvian State failed to meet its recommendation to promote socio-political equality. According to the Final Report of the Truth and Reconciliation Commission, during the internal armed conflict in Peru, about 75 percent of the victims were indigenous peasants, both from the highlands and the lowlands. The large socio-economic gaps in Peruvian society caused a differential impact of violence (CVR 2003), therefore people living in rural Andean areas suffered more intensely from the violence generated by the conflict than people in any other part of the country. It is not a coincidence that the majority of victims of disappearance and extrajudicial killings were concentrated in the Province of Ayacucho, at some 50 percent of the cases, while the provinces of Junín, Huánuco and Huancavelica each had between 15 percent and 10 percent of the cases (TRC 2003). Recent estimates have determined that the same provinces still remain among the poorest in Peru (Vasquez Huaman 2012). Although Peru has been one of the Latin America countries with the highest gross domestic product (GDP) per capita since 2000, at an average rate of 3.8 percent, the socio-economic gaps have remained the same: in the rural highlands 66 percent of the population is poor and one third lives in extreme poverty (World Bank 2011, 32–33). This in turns leads us to the conclusion that considering victims always belong to the same segment of the population, we could argue that victimhood is in fact deliberately constructed by others (i.e., not by the victims themselves but for example by the State that enforces the condition of exclusion and inequality that in turns facilitates the transformation of excluded people into victims) through a number of abuses that culminate, in many cases, with death. While for many Andean peasants social exclusion does not date to the period of violence, it was exclusion that transformed them into victims in the first place. If they are to go through a process referred to as transition, their original exclusion as well as the crimes that transformed them into victims must be addressed first. Hence, any transitional process needs to address issues crosscutting Civil, Political and Social, Cultural and Economic rights—the pillars of what constitutes full citizenship. When the TRC refers to the need to reshape the social contract, it is referring to the need for a better distribution of power and for equal opportunities for all Peruvians (CVR 2003, 38).

JUSTICE POLICIES ON FORCED DISAPPEARANCES

Our field experience has shown that the most important goal for many victims' families is to locate the remains of the missing persons and allow for a proper burial.[18]

In Peru, state actions have focused on criminal justice, which is why many of the bodies that have been recovered have not yet been returned to their families for proper burial and closure. The State's retributive justice, however, can also be considered two-sided. A critical reading of these official initiatives reveals that by fulfilling its obligations to investigate and prosecute, the State demonstrates that it reacts to human rights violations. The problem is, however, that it often results in acquittals or trials simply being not held. Peru's case is well suited to demonstrate the shortcomings of a predominantly retributive approach to a violent past, a framework that defines the term "justice" in the paradigm of "transitional justice" as too narrowly focused on criminal justice.

Many civil organizations are currently demanding the right to search for the disappeared and prioritizing knowing the fate of their loved ones through retributive justice. The aim is to help the families in their grief, through the identification, restitution, and proper burial of the remains of their loved ones, without neglecting research on the responsibility of the crime. Such an approach has been dubbed the "humanitarian umbrella" (Baraybar, Brasey, and Zadel 2007), implying that any humanitarian-driven initiative to enforce the right to truth of families does not exclude justice. On the other hand, however, justice as a formal exercise requires specific evidence. In Peru generally there are victims who provide evidence and prosecutors are willing to investigate as long as they know who the suspects are, where the victims are, and in what circumstances the crime took place. Hence, the lack of "evidence" (one may know a family member was taken by hooded men) has led to closing hundreds of cases.[19] In Peru families want closure and justice (in that order).

While in Argentina and Chile reparations were accompanied with other measures to determine the whereabouts of missing persons (see Guembe 2006; Lira 2006), in Peru the confusion started directly from the presentation of the Final Report of the TRC, where the number of dead was combined with the number of missing.[20] This led to two conclusions: 1) the missing are dead, even if no efforts were made to determine so and 2) it will be extremely complicated to search for the missing since, unlike the dead (read extrajudicially killed), who were accounted as such based on their location, they were taken through a complex itinerary that resulted in their death.

Paradoxically, the focus of regional and national associations of victims (i.e., CORAVIP or CONAVIP, respectively) spins around issues of economic or material reparation, rather than searching for the missing and enforcing the "right to know," which doesn't acknowledge that by neglecting this other aspect, they are supporting activities that eventually will put an end to establishing an active search strategy for the missing (Beristain 2010). For example, one such proposal is transforming the so-called area surrounding the infamous military base of Los Cabitos in Ayacucho (a notorious clandestine detention center where numerous extrajudicial executions were committed) into a memorial place. The problem is that exhumations in the area have not been completed.[21]

The State's refusal to implement a public policy to search for the missing is a major problem. In close cooperation with victims' associations and human rights organizations, EPAF has used its experience to lead the search, recovery, and identification of persons forcibly disappeared during the conflict.

WHAT THE VICTIMS NEED AND EPAF'S APPROACH AND SUGGESTIONS

Based on extensive interventions by EPAF in Ayacucho, a breadth of information on the psychosocial sequels and insufficient organizational capacity in the affected communities has been gathered. EPAF, from its experience in forensic anthropological research, has adopted a humanitarian approach by which the search for victims of enforced disappearance is carried out with special attention to the families. EPAF's work over the years is based on the premise that the search for the missing is primarily a humanitarian endeavor that does not exclude justice, but does not depend on the times and requisites set forth by the justice system. In addition, it is understood that any intervention stems from the desire of a community to remember and through that process recover and dignify the remains of their loved ones. However, such a process is not exempt from controversy since possessors of individual memories will be confronted with factual and incontrovertible elements such as those exposed by forensic investigations. Any intervention starts with an "invitation to remember"—an approach to the community to determine whether they want to undertake the long legal and emotional process that may culminate in the search, recovery, identification, and restitution of the remains of their loved ones. If the community accepts the challenge, EPAF assists them with getting organized into an association and gaining representation as plaintiffs in a lawsuit filed with the prosecutor's office. In parallel, EPAF collects ante mortem data of alleged victims, determines the most likely place where victims may be buried and undertakes psychosocial support of the victims' families through periodical visits. Such an approach integrates families into the search effort, allowing them to become active subjects of a process in which they have always been considered passive objects. Forensic anthropology, in this context, promotes mechanisms for citizen empowerment, for it is an efficient tool to elicit social change and to invite families to remember, to organize themselves, to relate to each other, and to combat forgetfulness and impunity.

While working in Andean communities, motivating people to remember, we have witnessed how memories become a rather strong mechanism of empowerment, perhaps because, among other reasons, they allow different groups of people to feel part of the same community. Having shared memories contrasted against incontrovertible facts, such as those established by forensic work, helps people feel validated and thus integrated, included; in addition, the "validation of existence" through the identification of otherwise nameless human remains disposed of in clandestine graves also constitutes an act of transition from victimhood without recognition to one of restoration of rights, the basis of citizenship.

Let's use as an example EPAF's intervention in the community of Putis that we outlined earlier in the chapter.[22] Following the exhumation and identification of the victims, the community claimed all remains as "sons and daughters" of the community despite the fact that only twenty-nine had been identified. While the Prosecutor refused at first, she had given in to the pressure from the community to dignify the remains as being part of a whole. The community then built a cemetery to house the remains, which arrived in an endless procession of caskets. The new impetus gained through the forensic process allowed the communities of Putis to demand the State be recognized as Centro Poblado Menor (the lowest denomination of the administrative organization of the State) and as such being a recipient of monetary aid and development investment from public funds. At the same time, the communities gathered in an assembly and asked EPAF to assist them with a development project. Such a request was unusual for a forensic team but it was clear the community had taken a path of transformation initiated with the recovery of the remains of some 30 percent of members of the communities killed during the Internal Armed Conflict. From those exchanges emerged Paradero Esperanza (bus stop hope), a project to create a seed bank of some of the twenty-five species of native potatoes that grow in the area.[23]

We believe that, particularly in the case of Peru, and within the framework of transitional justice, it is important to broaden the focus of rights to consider those related to the social and economic and cultural development of the victims. Overcoming the causes and consequences of conflict is a step that cannot be taken without an effective recognition of the socio-economic exclusion. In other words, those issues should also be part of the process of transition.

However, perhaps the most important question to ask is whether Peru is a country in transition and if so, then a country transitioning to what, exactly? In the community of Oronccoy, district of Chungui, Province of La Mar, Department of Ayacucho, in the so called region of "Oreja de Perro," a strategic location heavily affected both by the Shining Path and the Armed Forces, the actors in yet another conflict are no longer the Shining Path and the Armed Forces but drug traffickers and armed robbers who ambush, kill, and rob the traffickers. The population is again between two fires without any presence of the State to provide security. [24] Regrettably, Oronccoy is no exception. Macroeconomic indicators point to a sustained growth of the economy while other studies indicate that while overall poverty may be decreasing, areas of historical inequality remain the same or worse (Vasquez Huaman 2012). As can be seen, the results of the conflict are multidimensional: "It is legal and forensic, psychological, ritualistic and symbolic, it is material, familial and social" (Vasquez Huaman 2012, 40). As such they should be addressed from different angles.

CONCLUDING REMARKS

While the TRC recommended a series of restorative measures, the State chose the simple solutions; it displayed legitimacy by instating a problematic reparation scheme (both individual and collective) and applying only minimal retributive justice, allowing for the creation of a "jurisprudence of impunity."

To date, there is no official number of people killed in Los Cabitos, nor an account of what was the situation on the exchange of prisoners between Los Cabitos and other bases of the same rank.[25] Victims from Los Cabitos may be further affected by the strictly judicial approach of some of the Human Rights organizations that represent individual cases (legal proceedings attempt to establish individual rather than collective responsibility). Considering that trials rarely end in criminal punishment given the high rate of acquittals, these families may get neither justice nor answers on the whereabouts of their missing relatives.[26] A good example for impunity is the acquittal of the alleged perpetrators (military officers) of the killing of twelve civilians.[27] While most accounts have concentrated on judgments, few scholars criticized that out of the twelve victims, only four were recovered and identified (Best 2011).

This situation is, unfortunately, a common one. Some families are left only with reparations; they end up being forced to choose between continuing the hopeless search for justice and truth, and a possible, however unlikely, economic compensation that will by no means allow them to transcend their position of neglect and non-citizenship within society.

Citizenship is built along different lines, one of which being the enforcement of civil and political rights. The fact that trials end up, more often than not, acquitting alleged perpetrators based on bogus jurisprudence, and the fact that the social, cultural, and economic rights of families continue to be neglected, creates a state of perpetual victimhood. People's path to citizenship is still too far away. It remains clear, however, that the search for justice and truth is not a priority for the State. Justice and truth compete with urgent needs such as health, nutrition and economic reparations. This is not only true for Peru but for the Global South as a whole; victims tend to belong to the same groups (the poor, the indigenous, and the disenfranchised). These segments of the population—subjects to multiple violations—are not random victims.

Based on our fieldwork, we advocate a more comprehensive view of transitional justice—a concept that accounts for economic, social, and cultural rights, in accordance with the principle of indivisibility and interdependence of human rights (UN 2003, 2). In Peru, the comprehensive report of the TRC has been used by the State and its institutions in a clientelist fashion, tagging and discriminating those who can and those who cannot be subject of reparations, what the reparation is to be used for, not implementing public policies to search and account for the missing, and creating a perverse combination where the slogan "neither truth nor justice" would be accurately descriptive. [28]

ACKNOWLEDGMENTS

We wish to thank Ricardo Alvarado for his comments on an earlier manuscript and to Rebecca Blackwell for the final edition and comments on the manuscript.

NOTES

1. This section is based on the Final Report of the TRC (CVR 2003).
2. This fact was determined by the percentage of deaths attributed to state agents and to PCP-SL in which the latter would be responsible for 54 percent of deaths. More recent reviews of the data however have questioned this findings pointing to the fact that they may be the result of specific calculations not reflecting a factual truth, see Rendon (2013).
3. In Peru, some paradoxes arise from the use of the "transitional justice" framework: a) twelve of the twenty years of violence took place under the rule of democratically elected governments; b) the initiation of political violence coincided with the restoration of democracy in 1980. Would the Peruvian case be a "transition from the transition?"
4. The internal armed conflict in Peru took place against the background of democratic regimes unlike other countries such as Chile or Argentina, where the "dirty war" happened during military regimes.
5. Interestingly enough despite public trials and proven corruption and human rights abuses, *Fujimorismo,* nowadays represented by Alberto Fujimori's daughter Keiko, is the first parliamentary force in Congress and has some 30 percent of intention of vote in the upcoming general elections. In addition, the current minister of interior is a suspect in the assassination of a journalist in one of the provinces under martial law in 1988. Mr. Urresti, then a G2 officer under the alias of "Arturo" has been syndicated as one of the authors of the crime. Such case was reported by the TRC.
6. The definition of "excess" is also illustrative inasmuch all "excesses" are considered transgressions from a tolerable or accepted situation, therefore rather than qualifying an "excess" it may be more useful to determine what is the "acceptable limit" over which it becomes a transgression. Paradoxically Abimael Guzman, supreme leader of the PCP-SL also qualified the massacre at Lucanamarca as "excess." See the Final report of the TRC, volume V, section 3, Violencia en las comunidades de Lucanamarca, Sancos, y Sacasamarca (CVR 2003).
7. For a list of publications by the military or organizations supportive of the military institution challenging the "truth" of the TRC visit the site of the Asociacion Defensores de la Democracia contra el Terrorismo: http://www.defensoresdelademocracia.org/index.php?option=com_contentandtask=viewandid=21andItemid=46 (accessed May 2, 2014).
8. While law 27,980 regulates the acts of *rondas campesinas* their participation in the internal armed conflict on the side of the Armed Forces was notorious and in some cases they became the perpetrators of serious human rights abuses, see: http://www.onagi.gob.pe/portal/Uploads/normatividad/17_normativa.pdf (accessed May 2, 2014).
9. The term "anexo" denotes permanent settlements within community land and accepted as such by the general assembly of the community. See Law 24,656, Ley general de comunidades campesinas. Available at: http://www.justiciaviva.org.pe/acceso_justicia/justicia_comunal/3.pdf (accessed May 1, 2014).

10. In Peru the Governor is the direct representative of the President and the Executive branch in his or her jurisdiction. The Ministry of Interior appoints them. Governors are in turn classified as Regional, Provincial, and district. Peru is divided into twenty-four Departments (Provinces) that also became Regions, 194 Provinces (a subdivision of Departments) including the Constitutional Province of Callao, adjacent to Lima and 1828 districts.

11. The Law 28,592 is available at: http://docs.peru.justia.com/federales/leyes/28592-jul-28-2005.pdf (accessed November 15, 2014).

12. Article 3 of Decree 051-2011-PCM provides that: "the amount of financial compensation will amount to 10,000 soles per victim missing or deceased, or a victim of rape or a victim with disability," available at http://proyectocotabambas.files.wordpress.com/2011/07/ds-051-2011.pdf (accessed October 11, 2014).

13. The Office of the Ombudsman (Defensoria del Pueblo in Spanish) is a constitutional body and Congress elects the Ombudsman. The Office produces reports and recommendations indicating the state of issues not addressed or resolved by responsible institutions. It is important to notice however that Congress has not been able to appoint a new Ombudsman and the current seats ad interim since 2011.

14. The acronym SIS stands for Sistema Integral de Salud. According to their website, it is "an Executing Public Agency (OPE) part of the Ministry of Health, aims to protect the health of Peruvians who do not have health insurance, prioritizing those vulnerable populations in poverty and extreme poverty." More information available at http://www.sis.gob.pe/Portal/quienes_somos/index.html (accessed May 12, 2014).

15. As examples we could cite the inmates extra-judicially killed at the prisons of El Fronton, Lurigancho, and Santa Barbara in 1986 and in Canto Grande in 1992.

16. As a matter of fact, most of the historical judgments, such as that against former president Alberto Fujimori or the Colina group, were handled by the Sala Penal Especial, which used to be a Special Chamber of the Supreme Court that has now been deactivated.

17. See also judgment in case Los Laureles, available at: http://www.justiciaviva.org.pe/webpanel/doc_int/doc19112009-175433.pdf (accessed June 25, 2014).

18. A number of judgments from the Inter American Court of Human Rights (IACHR) stress the need to identify and return the mortal remains to the their loved ones (see for example, Durand and Ugarte versus Peru, available at: http://www.corteidh.or.cr/docs/casos/articulos/Seriec_68_esp.pdf (accessed May 2, 2014); Anzualdo Castro versus Peru, available at: http://www.corteidh.or.cr/docs/casos/articulos/seriec_202_ing.pdf (accessed May 10, 2014); La Cantuta versus Peru, available at: http://www.corteidh.or.cr/docs/casos/articulos/seriec_162_esp.pdf (accessed May 2, 2014). Also see also Crettol and La Rosa (2006).

19. In the judicial district of Ayacucho alone 1,335 cases were closed because of lack of evidence.

20. While the TRC states clearly that missing and dead are different categories, both legally and socially, it refers to dead and missing as fatalities and concludes that the total number can be estimated at 69,280 (CVR 2003, 13–14).

21. See http://coravip.blogspot.com/, http://heedersoto.wordpress.com/documental/ (accessed May 2, 2013).

22. While we refer to Putis as a community it is in fact the make up of eight communities.

23. More information available at http://epafperu.org/en/paradero-esperanza/ (accessed March 2, 2013).

24. According to the Final Report of the TRC the rural population of the district of Chungui decreased by 51 percent based on the difference between the census of 1981 and 1993 (CVR 2003).

25. Important information regarding the clandestine graves at Los Cabitos came from an interview by journalist Ricardo Uceda with Jesus Sosa Kerosene, former Colina group agent and member of the Intelligence Service of the Army based in Los Cabitos in the early 1980s. In any case while much of his information has been corroborated it constitutes a single account (Uceda 2004).

26. In a handful of cases it may be the opposite, victims may get justice but not closure. Ernesto Castillo Paez, a student from Lima was kidnapped in 1990 by police personnel and never seen since then. While the Inter American Court of Human Rights passed judgment

against the Peruvian State for the kidnapping and disappearance of Castillo Paez, no search operations have been implemented and the remains have not been located. More information available at: http://www.corteidh.or.cr/docs/casos/articulos/seriec_34_esp.pdf (accessed May 2, 2013).

27. See also the account by Jo-Marie Burt available at: http://www.globality-gmu.net/archives/2429 (accessed May 2, 2013).

28. The Law on Reparations does not apply to so-called subversive groups or their families even if the State committed crimes against them.

SELECTED BIBLIOGRAPHY

Baraybar, José Pablo, and Rebecca Blackwell. 2014. "Where Are They? Missing, Forensics, and Memory." *Annals of Anthropological Practice* 38: 22–42.

Baraybar, José Pablo, Valerie Brasey, and Zadel Andrew. 2007. "The Need for a Centralised and Humanitarian-Based Approach to Missing Persons in Iraq: An Example from Kosovo." *The International Journal of Human Rights*, 11 (3): 265–74.

Barrantes, Rafael, and José Peña. 2006. "Narrativas sobre el conflicto armado interno en el Perú: la memoria en el proceso político después de la CVR." In *Transformaciones democráticas y memorias de la violencia en el Perú*, IDEHPUCP. Lima. Available at: http://idehpucp.pucp.edu.pe/images/publicaciones/tranformaciones_democraticas_y_memorias_violencia_peru.pdf (accessed April 2, 2015).

Beristain, Martín. 2010. *Diálogos sobre la reparación. Que reparar en los casos de violaciones de los Derechos Humanos*, 322-46. Costa Rica: Instituto Interamericano de Derechos Humanos. Available at: http://iidhwebserver.iidh.ed.cr/multic/UserFiles/Biblioteca/IIDH/2_2011/6483.pdf (accessed June 25, 2014).

Best Urday, Kristel. 2011. "La demanda de justicia y los reveses de la impunidad. Reflexiones en torno a la construcción de las memorias de los familiares a partir de la judicialización del caso Parcco Pomatambo (Perú)." *Aletheia*, 1 (2): 1–17. Available at: http://www.memoria.fahce.unlp.edu.ar/art_revistas/pr.4809/pr.4809.pdf (accessed June 25, 2014).

Burt, Jo-Marie. 2009. "El juicio a Fujimori, visto desde un contexto regional y mundial." *Revista Argumentos*, 2: n. p. Available at: http://revistaargumentos.iep.org.pe/articulos/el-juicio-a-fujimori-visto-desde-un-contexto-regional-y-mundial/ (accessed December 10, 2014).

Comisión de Derechos Humanos (COMISEDH). 2012. *Los muertos de Ayacucho: violencia y sitios de entierro clandestinos*. Lima: COMISEDH.

Comisión de la Verdad y Reconciliación (CVR). 2003. *Informe Final*. Lima: CVR. Available at: http://www.cverdad.org.pe/ifinal/pdf/TOMO percent20IX/2.3. percent20PLAN percent20NACIONAL percent20FORENSE.pdf (accessed October 23, 2014).

Crettol, Carlos. 2013. "La Justicia después de la CVR." *Revista Ideele* 234. Available at: http://revistaideele.com/ideele/content/la-justicia-despu percentC3 percentA9s-de-la-cvr (accessed June 20, 2013).

Crettol, Monique, and Anne-Marie La Rosa. 2006. "The Missing and Transitional Justice: The Right to Know and the Fight against Impunity." *International Review of the Red Cross* 88 (862): 355–62. Available at: http://www.icrc.org/eng/assets/files/other/irrc_862_crettol-la-rosa.pdf (accessed June 25, 2014).

Diario La Republica. 2009. "Alan García reconoce excesos en la lucha contra el terrorismo." *Diario La Republica* (March 2, 2014). Available at: http://www.larepublica.pe/02-03-2009/alan-garcia-reconoce-excesos-en-la-lucha-contra-el-terrorismo (accessed April 2, 2014).

———. 2014. "Absuelven a militares y policías que asesinaron a comuneros de Lucmahuayco." *Diario la República* (March 23, 2014). Available at: http://www.larepublica.pe/23-03-2014/absuelven-a-militares-y-policias-que-asesinaron-a-comuneros-de-lucmahuayco (accessed June 25, 2014).

EPAF. 2007. *Report submitted to the International Committee of the Red Cross* (ICRC). Lima: EPAF.

Ford Deza, Elaine. 2004. "El proceso de transición democrática en el Perú y el liderazgo de Toledo." *Enfoques* 2: 143-56. Available at: http://ebookbrowsee.net/16218-cached-pdf-d560424318 (accessed April 2, 2015).

Godoy, José Alejandro. 2012. "Interview with Ronald Gamarra." *Memoria* 11. Available at: http://idehpucp.pucp.edu.pe/wp-content/uploads/2012/09/Entrevista-a-Ronald-Gamarra.pdf (accessed October 11, 2014).

Gonzales Cueva E. 2013. "Que la verdad demuestre su poderío." *Ideele Revista* 233: n. p. Available at: http://revistaideele.com/ideele/content/que-la-verdad-demuestre-su-poder percentC3 percentADo (accessed April 2, 2015).

Jelin, Elizabeth. 2002. *Los trabajos de la Memoria*. Madrid: Siglo XXI.

Ministerio de Relaciones Exteriores (MRE). 2012. *Documento de trabajo sobre las medidas adoptadas por diferentes sectores en relación a la Resolución AG/RES (XLI-O/11): "Las personas desaparecidas y la asistencia a sus familiares*." Lima: Ministerio de Relaciones Exteriores.

Naciones Unidas (UN). 2003. *Oficina del Alto Comisionado de las Naciones Unidas para los Derechos Humanos. Preguntas Frecuentes sobre el Enfoque de Derechos Humanos en la Cooperación para el Desarrollo*. New York and Genebra: United Nations.

Ombudsman's Report. 2013. "Ten Years of Truth, Justice and Reparation: Progress, Setbacks and Challenges of an Unfinished Process." *Ombudsman's Report* 162. Available at: http://www.defensoria.gob.pe/modules/Downloads/informes/defensoriales/INFORME-DEFENSORIAL-162.pdf (accessed November 12, 2014).

Presidency of the Council of Ministers (PCM). 2001. *Decree N° 065-2001-PCM Presidency of the Council of Ministers*. Available at: http://www.cverdad.org.pe/lacomision/nlabor/decsup01.php (accessed November 12, 2014).

Quintanilla, Pablo. 2012. "¿Que es ser un caviar?" *Diario* 16 (April 23, 2012). Available at: http://diario16.pe/noticia/15620-a-quae-es-ser-un-caviar (accessed January 13, 2015).

Reátegui, Félix. 2012. *Desaparición forzada y derechos de las víctimas. La respuesta humanitaria a las demandas de verdad, justicia y reparación en el Perú*. Lima: Instituto de Democracia y Derechos Humanos de la Pontificia universidad Católica del Perú.

Rendon, Silvio. 2013. "La polémica sobre las cifras: Las sobreestimaciones de la CVR." *Revista Ideele* 233. Available at: http://revistaideele.com/ideele/content/la-pol percentC3 percentA9mica-sobre-las-cifras-las-sobreestimaciones-de-la-cvr (accessed April 2, 2015).

Trelles, Jorge. 2011. "Trelles: nosotros matamos menos." *Peru 21* (May 9, 2011). Available at: http://peru21.pe/noticia/759958/trelles-nosotros-matamos-menos-que-otros (accessed January 15, 2015).

Uceda, Ricardo. 2004. *Muerte en el Pentagonito, los cementerios clandestinos del ejercito Peruano*. Planeta Editores.

Ulfe, María Eugenia. 2013. *¿Y después de la violencia qué queda? Víctimas, ciudadanos y reparaciones en el contexto post-CVR en el Perú*. Buenos Aires: CLACSO. Available at: http://biblioteca.clacso.edu.ar/clacso/becas/20130628122643/Ydespuesdelaviolencia.pdf (accessed January 2, 2015).

Vasquez Huaman, Enrique. 2012. *El Perú de los pobres no visibles para el Estado: La inclusión social pendiente a julio del 2012. Documento de discusión Dd/12/04*. Lima: Centro de Investigación de la Universidad del Pacífico.

Willakuy, Hatun. 2008. *Abbreviated Version of the Final Report of the Truth and Reconciliation Commission*. Lima: Truth and Reconciliation Commission.

World Bank. 2011. *Peru on the threshold of a new era*. Lima: World Bank.

INTERVIEWS

Interview in Quechua with Placida Huaccachi Cayampi, Colcabamba, February 24, 2011.

Interview with Hector Garcia Callampi, President of the Community of Putaccasa, December 2012.

Interview in Quechua with Rolando Bautista Lopez, Municipal Agent, Putaccasa, November 2013.

Interview with Nolberto Aponte Mendoza, President of the Association of Victims of Huamanquiquia, Huamanquiquia, March 2013.
Interviews with Guillermo Bravo del Pino in May 2013 and March 2014.

Part V

Uruguay

Chapter Seven

Uruguay and the Reconceptualization of Transitional Justice

Debbie Sharnak

As part of the United Nations's (UN) efforts to address issues of transitional justice (TJ), the body appointed Pablo de Greiff as the first Special Rapporteur on the promotion of truth, justice, reparation, and guarantees of non-recurrence in 2012 (Special Rapporteur 2013). De Greiff received the lofty task of working in places where there have been gross violations of human rights, to monitor and report on these situations, and to promote and ensure accountability for crimes committed (Becker 2013; OHCHR 2013). Just over a year into his tenure, in October 2013, he traveled to Montevideo, Uruguay to carry out this mandate. Uruguay continues to grapple with the legacies of its authoritarian rule, which lasted from 1973–1985. The government, therefore, invited de Greiff to meet with key stakeholders, non-governmental groups, and governmental actors to discuss the ways that transitional justice remains a persistent issue in the nation (Lessa and Le Goff 2013a). De Greiff's trip resulted in a report lauding the country for its continued efforts to serve justice and promote rule of law but also urging further action, particularly on accountability for cases of torture, which have received considerably less attention than those of citizens who were disappeared during the dictatorship (El Pais 2013; UN 2014).

De Greiff's conclusions remain important for the nation and his urgings for future action are not entirely surprising, especially in light of the twin blows to TJ efforts in early 2013. The transfer for a prominent human rights judge from her criminal jurisdiction and the Supreme Court's decision to, in effect, relegalize the nation's official amnesty law by stating that the statute of limitations has passed for many of the cases that were awaiting trial created an uproar in the country.

Uruguay's transitional period began in 1984, when the nation held democratic elections in the country for the first time in fourteen years. The results were released in November 1984 and a new government took office in March 1985. In the direct aftermath of the country's military rule, the transitional government under the direction of Julio María Sanguinetti failed to employ transitional justice mechanisms—there were no trials, no official truth commission, and no memorialization efforts.[1] Despite many on the Left, like Frente Amplio leader Liber Seregni, who originally believed in 1985 that "there can be no doubt, there is a commitment [by the government] . . . to do justice," this did not occur (Brecha 1985b). In fact, the new civilian government went far in the opposite direction, passing the Ley de Caducidad de la Pretensión Punitiva del Estado (Law of Expiry), in December 1986, which provided amnesty for all those involved in crimes during the nation's military rule.[2] A stunned activist community, who had been behind the push to pressure the government to transition to democratic rule and end the nation's human rights abuses, mobilized to put the issue of amnesty on a ballot in 1989 with hopes of overturning the law. Their efforts, however, ended in failure as the population actually voted to uphold the law with a 56 percent majority, reaffirming a culture of impunity. The support for the amnesty law and the protection of officers from prosecution felt, as one Uruguayan who had campaigned for the repeal explained, like "the ultimate defeat" (Michelini Interview 2012). Another campaigner described the "disillusionment and disappointment" that followed the defeat, noting that "people were very hurt, very broken" (Bustamante Interview 2014).

From a transitional justice perspective, for many Uruguayans, the referendum results "sealed the issue of past human rights violations legally and politically" for several decades (Burt, Lessa, and Fried Amilivia 2013, 8). For years, a silence came to envelope Uruguayan society regarding the crimes committed during the dictatorship (Sharnak and Goldberg 2013). Many scholars who subsequently examined the period similarly discounted Uruguay as largely a failure of the transitional justice movement that swept through much of the Southern Cone during the period. While the definition of transitional justice has evolved, as this chapter will show, one current (and very basic) definition of transitional justice is that it is a set of responses to systematic or widespread violations of human rights that seeks recognition for victims and to promote possibilities for peace, reconciliation, and democracy through a set of holistic, accountability-based mechanisms such as reparations, truth-telling, memorialization, and prosecution. Among other claims, transitional justice argues that in the aftermath of authoritarianism, atrocity or civil war, its process can help build a stronger democracy and human rights culture, recognize victims, and promote civic trust.[3] Even with this most skeletal definition of the concept, for many years after the referendum defeat, scholars who addressed the situation in Uruguay at all often pointed to the 1989 vote as clear evidence of a repudiation of claims for accountability and a failure of transitional justice efforts.

What de Greiff's visit makes clear, however, is that despite shutting down accountability efforts for several decades, Uruguayans are reopening the issue of transitional justice in the twenty-first century. Over the past ten years, the country resumed efforts to employ transitional justice measures through a state-sponsored truth commission, some trials, and an official public apology. Similarly, literature in the field of transitional justice, which had largely ignored Uruguay as a central case study, has begun to refocus its efforts on the nation in journals ranging from the *International Journal of Transitional Justice* to the *Journal on Latin America.* In academia, the practitioner field, and on the ground in the country, Uruguay holds renewed appeal in the field of transitional justice. This increase in scholarship on Uruguay's process of transitional justice reevaluates the political changes that allowed for the nation's recent efforts to grapple with the past and rightly inserts Uruguay into the conversations on the state of the transitional justice field. While these initiatives are important and interesting, this chapter seeks to move beyond evaluations of Uruguay's recent efforts at transitional justice to account for the ways that the field of transitional justice more broadly has been evolving in new directions to allow for Uruguay to be part of these conversations, not just because it has resumed its efforts, but also because the field has begun to critically reexamine the basic concept of transitional justice.

This chapter therefore examines how Uruguay's continued struggle with accountability efforts, and its reevaluation within the field, questions some of the central assumptions of transitional justice, primarily regarding the perceived length of a transition, the effects of different generation's advocacy efforts, the uneven adoption of the concept of transitional justice between the global North and South, and different claims of justice in the aftermath of traumatic experiences. Uruguay's transitional justice process seems to fall short when evaluated within a traditional conception of transitional justice that assumes accountability can occur within a short time frame. When evaluated with a longer view, Uruguay's attempts to deal with its past shed light on the possibility that persistent human rights advocacy, including renewed pressure from the second generation of survivors' children, can have great effect. Recent filings in courts to start another set of trials place into view a longer time frame for reckoning with the past, where any one achievement or failure cannot alone be used to evaluate a nation's human rights trajectory. Rather, they can offer opportunities to open space for discussion and further grappling with traumatic periods as discussions for justice evolve over time (Stern 2010).

This chapter explores these issues by first examining how Uruguay initially appeared to fit within the regional frame as a model of transitional justice that emerged in the 1980s and largely defined transitional justice as a transition from authoritarian rule. Second, this essay will trace the historiographical evolution of transitional justice and investigate how transitional justice developed into a distinct field in the late 1990s and early 2000s. During this period, Uruguay failed to utilize the newly established set of transitional justice mechanisms, which meant that Uruguay's experience countered the model that was being established since there was a lack of state-sponsored accountability. As a result, scholars ceased to invoke Uruguay in their explorations of transitional justice models. In this second phase, Uruguay did not fit the developing model of transitional justice, which was aimed at building a stronger human rights culture. Lastly, the essay highlights the continual changes in the field of transitional justice, which is now in what I believe is its third phase of historiographical revision, wherein scholars and practitioners are questioning many of the central assumptions of the field, including how to define the length of a "transition." This change, along with Uruguay's recent attempts to reckon with its authoritarian legacy, requires that Uruguay be reexamined in a transitional justice frame that reflects the changing contours of the entire field.

In historian Paige Arthur's conceptual history of transitional justice, she argues that the field of transitional justice largely emerged in the late 1980s out of discussions about issues facing Latin American countries where multiple repressive regimes had recently fallen. During the ensuing transitions from authoritarianism to democratic rule, human rights activists, lawyers, legal scholars, policymakers, journalists, donors, and comparative political experts began to discuss a new set of human rights concerns, including competing moral imperatives, such as how to reconcile legitimate claims for justice and claims for stability and social peace. The 1988 Aspen Institute Conference was one of the first in a series of conferences during the late 1980s and early 1990s which brought together these diverse actors in an effort to "compare experiences of the pursuit of justice initiatives in varying transitional contexts."[4]

Funded by the Ford Foundation and sponsored by the Justice and Society Program within the Institute, this initial discussion took place in Maryland, where the participants focused on the broad topic of how to address all the "moral, political, and jurisprudential issues" that arise when considering whether to punish human rights violators (Henkin 1989). They tackled questions such as what was the responsibility to the victims, violators, and societies at large, and further grappled with understanding how the domestic constituencies and international audiences could play a part in addressing legacies of abuse (Henkin 1989). Uruguay remained a key case study, particularly as the recent amnesty law and the upcoming referendum loomed large in the discussions. José Zalaquett, a Chilean, presented a paper for the conference which noted the complicated relationship between the amnesty law and the desire for truth, noting that "Uruguayans would have probably accepted more readily amnesty laws if they had been accompanied by a disclosure of truth about the use of torture and about the fate of the disappeared" (Zalaquett 1989, 64).

Uruguayans, however, were also invited to offer their own input and experience at these initial discussions, and they often presented alternative approaches.[5] At the first few conferences that examined the concept of transitional justice, Uruguay had two representatives, Luis Pérez Aguirre, the head of *el Servicio Paz y Justicia* (SERPAJ)-Uruguay, and Rafael Michelini, a politician from the Frente Amplio party and the son of assassinated senator Zelmar Michelini. In addition, Lawrence Weschler had spent considerable time in the country reporting on the transition and then wrote a formative book on the topic, *A Miracle, A Universe: Settling Accounts with Torturers* (Weschler 1998). He was also present at many of the foundational meetings, grappling with what transitions meant and how his experience in Uruguay could contribute to discussions about transitional justice.

These conversations further developed in Salzburg, Austria a few years later, where the "Project on Justice in Times of Transition" went a step further than Ford's initial conference. Rather than focusing on all the broad issues involved in transitions, it keyed in on the topics of *acknowledgement*—"whether to 'remember' or 'forget' abuses" and *accountability*"—whether or not to prosecute the perpetrators" (Charter 77 Foundation 1992). Participants discussed the ways that "being freed from the prison of dictatorship does not necessarily mean that a society is suddenly ready to bury its past" (Boraine, Levy, and Scheffer 1994, 67). Weschler laid out Uruguay's struggle over the amnesty law through both the court system and attempts to overturn the law through referendum. As opposed to Zalaquett's willingness to accept the political constraints that produced the amnesty but push toward truth, Weschler was more critical of the nation's approach to the amnesty law. Weschler poignantly brought up this perspective when he recalled a conversation he had with Uruguayan president Julio Mario Sanguinetti who quoted the historian Ernest Renan, saying, "nations are built on great rememberings *and* great forgettings" (Boraine, Levy, and Scheffer 1994, 58). Weschler criticized this view in light of the fact that the small country was "broken" by their lack of ability to access the truth while having to, in many cases, live in the same towns and pass their torturers on a daily basis.

Rafael Michelini, who was in the early 1990s a Deputy in the Chamber of Representatives for Uruguay for the Frente Amplio, also weighed in. While he acknowledged that the threat of a military resurgence did exist in 1986, he believed that "Uruguay should have taken the risk and defeated the amnesty" (Charter 77 Foundation 1992). He believed that if the people had overturned the law, popular will would have overcome the military's opposition without the country falling back into authoritarian rule. Instead, he argued that in the defeat of the referendum, rule of law had not been reestablished since "many in the military may think they could take over again without fear of accountability." According to Michelini, official forgetting did not promote reconciliation, like the government claimed, but rather, divided civil society and failed to reform the structures that had allowed for a takeover in the first place (Ibid.).

Aguirre, whose contributions to these international conferences is less well-documented in conference reports, left behind a series of articles describing his view on this topic in the Uruguayan leftist paper, *Brecha.* In these, he also argued against impunity and toward confronting the truth. For example, Aguirre claimed that impunity was a "gear of repression" by explaining that "whoever seeks peace based on forgetting is doomed to failure. Likewise, it will fail if it is founded on violence. Peace will always be the fruit of justice."[6] His organization, SERPAJ, also played a major role in promoting truth and justice as a necessary part of the country's transition. They launched a human rights campaign in 1986 which specifically argued for "justice for peace, because those who violated human rights are a threat to peace."[7] Then later in the decade, SERPAJ also led the efforts for a community-organized truth commission report, *Nunca Más*, after the government failed to produce a state-sponsored measure like in neighboring Argentina. While those deeply involved in Uruguay's transition who participated in these global discussions proved critical of Uruguay's approach to justice issues, the key tension between forgetting and accountability was continually addressed at conferences in various global contexts and Uruguay's approach proved instructive and important to these debates.

These early works and deliberations over conceptions of transitional justice are noteworthy for two main reasons: first, they discussed transitions, and the cases they studied, as occurring in the very narrow sense of when a society shifts from authoritarianism to democratic rule.[8] Second, these discussions on justice centered on how to reconcile the competing claims for some form of accountability with the desire for stability.[9] Even though the peace versus justice debate is still prominent in transitional justice literature, clear arguments for justice as being an integral part of peace were not yet fully articulated at this stage of the field's development.[10] Instead, scholars and practitioners discussed how the two could be integral components in these types of transitions. These blurry lines, and the debates which followed in the emerging field, are what I argue is the first phase of transitional justice historiography.[11]

It is important to recognize the conceptual fuzziness of these initial discussions about transitional justice, where Uruguayans were key participants and where scholars analyzed Uruguay as one of the primary examples for the origins of the field. These scholars were just beginning to debate if and what constituted justice in this first stage of transitional justice literature and there was no clearly defined set of mechanisms that countries undergoing transitions were expected or recommended to utilize. While Argentina was often held up as a global model, scholars also utilized Uruguay as an example during their initial conversations. For instance, in the "Justice in Times of Transition" project, attendees discussed Uruguay as a case of a nation that had made the "decision to forget" during its transitional phase. Even though they acknowledged that amnesty laws could "deeply divide civil society and pervert rule of law," the scholars and human rights practitioners assessed the effects of the amnesty, the reasons behind it, and the way it shaped the current institutions of both the civilian government and of the military (Charter 77 Foundation 1992). Neil Kritz also included Uruguay in his foundational book on transitional justice in the early 1990s as a case study for exploring the debates about amnesty laws and community-organized truth telling efforts.[12] The reason Uruguay remained so central was because, as Arthur makes clear, the field developed out of narrow discussions analyzing the nature of transitions from authoritarian rule to democracy, particularly in Latin America. Despite its shortcomings in working toward accountability, Uruguay fit this description and thus scholars used the nation's experience as a case study for investigation.

In this first phase of the historiography, transitional justice was not conceptually strong enough to make claims about strengthening human rights culture and democracy. Uruguay remained a central part of the conversation because it represented an example of the specific type of transition that discussions about transitional justice emerged out of. Therefore, the fact that Uruguayans voted "no" on overturning the amnesty law that would have allowed prosecutions in 1989 was still offered as an alternative transitional pathway; it did not necessarily contrast with claims of the movement at the time, which were tenuous at best. Uruguay went through a transition, even though it was weaker than many of its regional counterparts—the pacted, or negotiated, transition limited the range of options to deal with the past. Since the military regime had not collapsed, they were able to negotiate a transition and were thus able to retain some power in the new regime, which weakened possibilities for justice (Sikkink 2011, 32). Despite the fact that Uruguay would not utilize any of the mechanisms that came to define the field in the 1990s, for scholars of transitional justice, Uruguay merited analysis in this first phase because it underwent a transition from authoritarianism to democracy.

In the next decades, however, transitional justice literature developed in a direction that excluded Uruguay as a useful example because the field began to define the use of justice mechanisms as the centrally defining feature of transitional justice. From the 1990s through the mid-2000s, transitional justice grew into a professionalized field. During the second historiographical phase, Ruti Teitel published the foundational book, *Transitional Justice*, in which she asserted the importance of justice in times of transitions, including but not limited to analyzing the contextual nature of these transitions, the law's role, and political circumstance (Teital 2000). Teitel elaborated on this early work by explaining that by the early 2000s transitional justice had become "normalized in contemporary orthodoxy" in transitional societies.[13]

Likewise, Harvard Law School professor Martha Minow (1998) helped strengthen emerging claims in the field, arguing that prosecutions alone were not an adequate solution, but rather, that justice needed to address victims' concerns as well.[14] Her solution was to institute a combination of mechanisms that mediated somewhere between full vengeance and total forgiveness, including truth commissions, some prosecutions, and reparations, three of the mechanisms that became the foundation for the field of transitional justice.[15] The professionalization of the field also elaborated on these initial strategies as scholars of the field, as well as practitioners, began to include additional mechanisms such as security sector reforms, memorialization, and disarmament, demobilization and reintegration into the transitional justice toolbox (Jelin 2007; Loden 2007; Theidon 2007). Uruguayan voices, which were so integral to the first phase of discussions, tended to recede in the second phase of the literature on transitional justice due to the country's failure to employ justice mechanisms. Fundamental works in the field, instead, proffered a new set of arguments about the necessity for a combination of mechanisms to work toward accountability—none of which Uruguay employed in close to the first two decades of transition back to democratic rule.

As a result, throughout the late 1990s the field expanded to include more mechanisms, or "tools" as sites for analysis, as well as the type of transitions where they could be utilized. Whereas previously, the primary cases for understanding transitional justice had been Latin American transitions from authoritarian governments to democratic rule, now all over the globe, transitions from mass atrocity, civil war, and genocide also were contexts to understand and apply a transitional justice framework. In 2001, a group of practitioners went on to found the International Center for Transitional Justice (ICTJ), institutionalizing the field of transitional justice and minting a field of experts and practitioners who worked to develop a set of handbooks for the UN, generated scholarship for the field, and established units that focused on individual mechanisms to advance the field further and offer advice on how to implement transitional justice around the world.

During this stage of the transitional justice historiography, Uruguay was generally considered a failure on account of the fact that it no longer fit the conceptual model of transitional justice used by practitioners.[16] Transitional justice became more than just a transition that grappled with questions of justice and accountability, but rather a transition that utilized certain mechanisms. Accordingly, Uruguay's blanket amnesty and overall failure to reckon with its past excluded the nation from being considered to have been through a process of transitional justice. As Minow explained, Uruguay's amnesty precluded it from the "transitional justice" model because the nation's amnesty was total; it did not implement an amnesty, like in South Africa, that, at the very least, came along with some sort of acknowledgment of remorse and truth testimony (Minow 1998, 56).

During this second historiographical phase, Uruguay's official commitment to amnesty in the 1989 vote explained why they were excluded from the new transitional justice model. During this period, many Uruguayans activists also remained quiet domestically about the issue of reopening trials. SERPAJ (1991; 1993), for example, focused more of their activities on security, education, and equality.[17] Even the group, Madres y Familiares de los Desaparecidos, whose entire mission was shaped around issues of the disappeared, focused less on accountability. Their slogan changed from "truth, justice, and never again," during the 1980s, to "truth, memory, and never again" after the referendum's failure diminished possibility for justice. As Gabriel Bucheli explain, members abandoned the group in droves after the crushing blow, and only four remained (Bucheli 2005, 72). Instead, activity that the Madres did continue to focus on included denunciations in the international system. Similarly during this period, a group of human rights lawyers in the country appealed to the Inter-American Commission on Human Rights (IACHR) and the United Nations Human Rights Commission (UNHRC) to determine whether the amnesty law violated the International Covenant on Civil and Political Rights. Both bodies found the law incompatible with obligations that the state had under international law; however, domestically, Uruguay was under no obligation to follow the rulings. Instead, the government preferred to ignore the decisions and continue a culture of silence and impunity surrounding violations during the country's military rule (Lessa 2013, 142). As a result, the Uruguayan state did not utilize any of the transitional justice mechanisms that were emerging as core to the field; Uruguayan officials were turning the page with no accountability, no official truth commission, no reparations, and no prosecutions. Only the original conception of transitional justice, as a transition with conceptually unclear lines, included Uruguay as an apt example. If the claims that transitional justice measures could build a stronger human rights culture were at this point true, Uruguay simply did not employ a transitional justice framework. Transitional justice had failed in Uruguay to even get off the ground; it had been repudiated at every turn.

Only in the third phase of transitional justice historiography, which is occurring right now, does Uruguay again return as a primary case for analysis. At present, many of the central assumptions of transitional justice are being questioned, including the length of transitions, the effectiveness and impact of transitional justice measures, and as Lars Waldorf criticizes, the overreach of the transitional justice field as a whole to expand into different fields such as development and peace-building (Duggan 2010; McAdams

2011; Waldorf 2011). Ariela Peralta, a lawyer who works at Uruguay's Institución Nacional de Derechos Humanos y Defensoría del Pueblo (INDDHH), also explained that she believed the concept had been stretched too thin and moved away from many of the core concepts (Peralta Interview 2014). Even Kathryn Sikkink, who documented the spread of global normative shifts and achievements in the last few decades, outlined the way the expansion of the doctrine appears to be slowing down and receiving some backlash (Sikkink 2011, 262).

Reconceptualizing some of the central assumptions of the field is critical to this third phase of the historiography; and it also allows Uruguay's relevance to resurface, most poignantly under the question of the perceived length of a transition. Harvey Weinstein, a former editor-in-chief of the *International Journal of Transitional Justice,* asked whether it was not hubris to believe that transitional justice mechanisms could help society emerge from unspeakable atrocities and achieve reconciliation only a few years after peace or a transition.[18] Uruguay's experience with transitional justice processes, i.e., whether transitional justice contributed to a stronger democratic and human rights culture, seems to fall short of that mark when evaluated within the second historiographical conception. However, when examined within a longer time frame, as the third historiographical phase seems to be moving toward, Uruguay proves illustrative of broader trends.[19]

Uruguay's pacted transition precluded the possibility of any immediate transitional justice mechanisms: there were no lustration, TRCs, or trials in the initial phase. However, in 2000, the state instituted an official truth commission, the Peace Commission (which released its final report in 2003), and in 2010, the Uruguayan Supreme Courts found that the Amnesty Law was unconstitutional—and there is now the possibility of trials beginning again.[20] These measures have come under much debate and scrutiny but the fact that they occurred at all was the result of the persistence by human rights groups and a change in the domestic and international political climates.[21] In addition, this new set of accountability mechanisms place into view a longer time frame for reckoning with the past and grappling with accountability issues where any one achievement or failure should not alone be used to evaluate a nation's trajectory, but rather be seen as offering opportunities toward new possibilities that can open new spaces for discussion and further grappling with traumatic periods (Stern 2010).

These advancements, however, must be viewed in light of setbacks as well. Judge Mariana Mota, who had long fought for holding military leaders accountable for crimes committed by the military dictatorship, was transferred in February 2013 from her criminal post to a civilian jurisdiction without any explanation, just as trials were slated to begin (Lessa and Le-Goff 2013b). Days later, the Uruguayan Supreme Court ruled that the dictatorship's crimes could not be considered crimes against humanity and that the statute of limitations had expired for trying these complaints. The ruling effectively meant that most gross human rights violations committed under the dictatorship will go unpunished unless another successful complaint is able to make it through the court system (Sharnak and Goldberg 2013).

These setbacks fall into a larger pattern in Uruguay, where no path toward accountability has proven easy in the thirty years since the military government ended. However, the argument about cumulative achievement against the odds builds off of Steve Stern's analytic framework for historical accountability. In the case of Chile, Stern examines how individual moments in the struggle for memory and human rights coexisted with the sense that each of these moments, when analyzed in isolation, may fail to advance justice in a meaningful way. In this manner, Stern identified how a longer view became necessary in analyzing the Chilean struggle over Pinochet's legacy. With the perspective of time, these moments of failure or shortcomings became cracks to open up larger discussions and resistance to impunity. They provided spaces for public reckonings and laid the groundwork for establishing a more robust legal culture and determination to build societies steeped in human rights.[22]

Uruguay appears to fit this model, which the recent attention that scholars are giving to the country in transitional justice literature supports. Jo Marie Burt, Francesca Lessa, and Gabriela Fried Amilivia (2013) recently published an article that examines how local civil society actors have struggled to keep the issue alive throughout the past three decades, which produced significant breakthroughs through persistence and innovative strategies. Meanwhile, Elin Skaar (2013) locates the ability for prosecutions to move forward, in spite of the Amnesty Law and two failed referendums in 1989 and 2009, with the increasing receptivity of human-rights-friendly executives and liberal-minded judges.

While scholars around the globe are also engaging in this conversation about impunity in the country, many Uruguayans do not utilize the term "transitional justice" with the same enthusiasm as researchers from the United States and Europe. Gabriela Fried and Francesca Lessa, two scholars who work in the U.S. and the U.K. respectively, edited a collection of essays, *Luchas contra la impunidad: Uruguay 1985–2011.* Most of the chapters were written by Uruguayans. However, the only authors to employ the term transitional justice were scholars from the global North, despite the fact that the topic fit squarely within the terrain of transitional justice (Fried and Lessa 2011). What this points to is that despite the fact that there is a resurgence in describing Uruguay's battle with impunity as transitional justice in the North, many Uruguayans are still reluctant to describe their nation's process with truth and memory in such terms. Even Gerardo Caetano, who is one of only a handful of Uruguayan researchers who directly analyzed transitional justice in Uruguay through studying archives of the repression, wrote more about

Uruguay's shortcomings with regard to transitional justice processes rather than its achievements in 2011. He noted that Uruguay's poor record on preserving their archives makes transitional justice practices particularly difficult (Caetano 2011). Therefore, there appears to be a continued gap between international scholars who utilize Uruguay as a case study in transitional justice literature during the third historiographical phase, while Uruguayans themselves are debating the concepts but are still reluctant to describe their impunity battles as transitional justice.

From these recent attempts to reopen conversations about the past and utilize accountability mechanisms, as well as the subsequent scholarly attention, two conclusions about the field begin to emerge. First, transitional justice processes often take decades to occur. There is not always an immediate possibility for engaging transitional justice mechanisms. In the 1980s in Uruguay, several factors contributed to Uruguay's intransigence toward a fuller effort of justice claims. For example, political conditions inhibited the political will needed for what came to be called transitional justice. Many of the most vocal human rights activists from the earlier part of the decade, such as Enrique Tarigo, took positions in the new government and advocated against accountability, which undercut a unified civil society movement. While other community actors continued to work against the efforts of the democratically elected government, the government had high levels of legitimacy and effectively used the fear of a possible military coup as justification for their lack of trials and accountability (Brahm 2007, 299). In addition, human rights claims differed among groups and survivors, with only some including the goals of transitional justice.[23] This work fundamentally raises questions for the field of transitional justice, particularly in asking about different concerns for survivors of authoritarian rule and whether justice is initially an important consideration for everyone during the immediate period of transitions.[24]

Weschler has acknowledged that with the passage of time, he has "all sorts of retrospective misgivings about our general righteousness, or certainty" during the transitional years. Explaining his involvement in these early conversations, he noted that "some things precisely required the passage of time to sort themselves out." Weschler compared those first years as similar to "defusing a bomb," which required time, before "all sorts of things became possible" (Weschler Interview 2014). The country's recent resumption of pursuing transitional justice mechanisms, and Weschler's current reevaluation of his role in these critical discussions only seems to further this point.

Thus, Uruguay is one of the cases emerging from around the globe which questions central assumptions of transitional justice as it enters its third historiographical phase.[25] However, as de Greiff noted during his trip to Montevideo in October 2013, Uruguay also spotlights some of the problems with justice being delayed too long since transitional justice aims to allow victims to benefit from the clarification of facts. Unfortunately, this elucidation might be lost if victims pass away before this occurs, or before perpetrators give their testimony. De Greiff noted that many victims in Uruguay are at an advanced age and urged the country to move forward quickly in their accountability measures (OHCHR 2013). Journalist Elizabeth Kolbert echoes this point in an article on recent Nazi trials where many defendants are passing away before they can be brought to justice. These last minute attempts to pursue cases is struggling against the fact that in many circumstances, "way too much time" had already passed. Kolbert poses the question: "What does it say about the law's capacity for self-correction that the correction came only when it no longer really matters?" She also quoted Dr. Martin Luther King Jr. who extolled the long arc of justice but also noted, that "in this unfolding conundrum of life and history there is such a thing as being too late" (Kolbert 2015) Uruguay is currently confronting this exact dilemma between the expectations of transitional justice extending to a longer timeframe, but butting up against the possibility of being too late.

Second, and perhaps most interesting, is an important insight emerging from Steve Stern and Scott Straus's volume on human rights, which claims that the very idea that justice restores balance or has the ability to strengthen human rights cultures is a historically constructed notion by scholars that exists on a fluid and shifting terrain (Stern and Straus 2014, 18). There is little empirical data, so far, which can explain the impact of transitional justice tools and the causal relationship between justice and stability. These foundational transitional justice claims are still being debated by activists, practitioners, and scholars (van der Merwe, Baxter, and Chapman 2009).[26] Indeed, analyzing Uruguay's trajectory affirms the fluidity of the transitional justice field, which has continued to shift and evolve in the short time frame in which it has existed. The term has also been adopted unevenly by scholars in the global north and Uruguayans themselves, suggesting the variability within the field in different areas of the world. Ultimately, if transitional justice is itself a fluid term with varying meaning, it becomes even more important for the history of Uruguay to examine the changing discourses of human rights in the country and the diverse interpretations of justice during the 1980s. Gaining greater insight into both of these ideas during the country's transitional phase will contribute to a greater understanding of the current state and direction of historical accountability in the nation as a whole. The debates in Uruguay expose the limitations of transitional justice's foundational myths, but reconstructing the history will only help further rebuild a clearer picture of the past—and the current battles over it.

NOTES

1. The Uruguayan government did create the Comisión Investigadora sobre Situación de Personas Desaparecidas in 1985. However, it had extremely limited powers and resources, which meant that the report did not conclusively find that the military government had a policy of human rights violations. Many believed that trials would follow from the report, which did not occur after the amnesty law was passed (Brecha 1985a, 2–3; Hayner 2010). The Service for Peace and Justice (SERPAJ) wrote a community-organized truth commission which was published in 1989 and titled *Nunca Más*. It was modeled after Argentina's truth commission. However it lacked the same state acknowledgment of their part in the crimes committed, or the power of state resources to gather information (Servicio Paz y Justicia 1992).

2. Amnesty is increasingly included as a transitional justice mechanism, particularly as part of a "minimalist approach" to transitional justice. However, this inclusion is typically predicated on either a conditional amnesty (for example, the revelation of truth or remorse like in South Africa) or amnesty combined with other measures, such as truth commissions and some trials, or at the very least, not applied in a blanket manner, like it was in Uruguay (Roniger 1999, 140–42; Olsen, Payne, and Reiter 2010).

3. A longer and more in-depth definition that explains the various claims of transitional justice can be found at "What Is Transitional Justice?" *International Center for Transitional Justice*. Available at: http://ictj.org/en/tj/ (accessed February 10, 2010). I would also argue that it is important to make a distinction about transitional justice claims. Most current scholars of transitional justice make the case for its use in transitions not because it creates a stronger human rights culture, but rather because it is the best chance for democratic stability and building a human rights culture. There is an important difference between creating, and the chance to create.

4. The University of South Carolina also hosted a conference, "The Challenge of Transitions," in March 1987, although records from that conference have been much more difficult to recover. "Foro sobre transición democrática," *Brecha* (April 10, 1987): 8, Archivo de Diarios; (Chilean Review 1987, 3; Whitehead 1996, 172; Arthur 2009, 326–27).

5. Uruguay undoubtedly underwent a transition from authoritarianism to democratic rule; however, there were distinctly nondemocratic aspects of the transitions. For example, Wilson Ferreira Aldunate, the most outspoken voice of the opposition in the Blanco Party, was not allowed to stand for election in 1984. After spending most of the dictatorship in exile, he returned to Uruguay in June 1984 to attempt to run for the presidency, where he was promptly thrown in jail until five days after the presidential election (Roniger 1999, 29).

6. Luis Pérez Aguirre, "La Impunidad Asesina a la Democracia por la Espalda," *La Brecha* (February 21, 1986). Archivo de Diarios.

7. Internal Memo, Talking Points for the Radio, n.d., Folder "Campaign-July," SPERAJ Archives, Montevideo, Uruguay.

8. Arthur explains the various types of transitions that could have been used due to the "varied instances of political change throughout the world since World War II which resist categorization in a neat typology. Many terms might have been used: 'revolutions,' 'transfers of power,' 'regime change,' or 'restorations,' 'independence,' 'modernization,' 'political development,' or perhaps 'transitions' of one sort or another. These terms encapsulate change from capitalism to socialism, military dictatorship to civilian rule, authoritarianism to democracy, communism to liberal democracy, communism to a market economy, and more." Arthur explains, however, that the transition to democracy stood out largely because democracy was a desirable goal for many people; there was the delegitimation of modernization theory; the transformation of transitions came from socioeconomic transformation to legal-institutional reform; and there was a global decline of the radical left (Arthur 2009, 337).

9. Some of the foundational works in these early years that began to make a case for some justice include Orentlicher (1991), Méndez (1997), and Zalaquett (1991).

10. This debate is exemplified in some of the early pieces by José Zalaquett, a Chilean lawyer, and Juan Méndez, an Argentinian lawyer, see Zalaquett (1985; 1992) and Méndez (1992; 1997).

11. This is not to say that different concepts of transitional justice had no historical precedent. Two of the better books on the historical precedents involve Jon Elster's work on trials and purges during ancient Athens and Gary Bass's history of war crime tribunals that began over 200 years ago. However as a unique set of practices and conceptual structure, I agree with the many scholars who date the conception of transitional justice as a coherent ideology to the 1980s. (Bass 2000; Elster 2004).

12. Interestingly though, Kritz largely focused on international perceptions of transitional justice, publishing excerpts from America's Watch reports, Weschler's book, a U.S.-based law professor, Robert Goldman, and only at the end published part of the SERPAJ's *Nunca Más* report (Kritz 1995, 383–430).

13. It is notable that Teitel (2003) was also careful to point out the contradictions and limitations of TJ.

14. In just a sentence or two, it is impossible to give adequate credit to Minow's nuanced and thoughtful argument. Minow's work is careful to acknowledge that no form of accountability can ever give closure or allow "complete" forgiveness to the horrors people experienced. However, in the wake of the massive violence of the twentieth century, Minow advocates against "forgetting" and toward some truth and justice beyond trials as a response, which places her in the movement for a more comprehensive view of transitional justice. Indeed, her work proved foundational for the field (Minow 1998).

15. While this chapter only accounts for a few of these foundational works due to space constraints, there were a number of "field foundational" works that should not be forgotten including (Roht-Arriaza 1995; McAdams 1997; Minow 1998; Teitel 2000).

16. This trend of excluding Uruguay from the TJ model is reflected in literature on the field. For example, in the preeminent journal on transitional justice, the *International Journal of Transitional Justice,* Uruguay was only the focus of one article in 2013 during the first eight years of the journal's inception. Nineteen other articles mention Uruguay at least once, although in all these articles, it is just in passing, without any taking real a real analytical lens to the nation's context. Even that number is incredibly small. There have been twenty-two issues published in the first eight years of the journal with over 216 articles. In contrast, Argentina is cited in sixty-one articles, with thirteen of them focusing on the nation.

17. Author Interview with Pancho Bustamante (September 11, 2014), Montevideo, Uruguay.

18. Weinstein (2011, 2) even compares the ongoing transitional process in Spain and the United States after the Civil War and Reconstruction to this process. Having worked in the research unit at ICTJ from 2007–2009, one of the central questions we also asked ourselves during internal debates was what new processes of transitional justice meant for the field and the idea of what constituted a "transition." The Khmer Rouge's tribunal in Cambodia, taking place over thirty years after the cessation of the genocide, was a central example of this shift. Was this just an individual accountability mechanism or should it be part of the process of understanding just how long transitions actually took?

19. Collins (2010) is central toward this movement of reconsidering transitional justice, although instead of shifting the explanation of transitional justice itself, she looks at post-transitional accountability trajectories, which differs from many scholars who are reevaluating the central concept of TJ itself. In her work, Collins does look at Uruguay.

20. While activists continue to fight to reopen trials, both events proved to be a major setback. Any trials that occurred before this point, including the trials of Juan Maria Bordaberry and General Gregoio Álvarez, were predicated on decrees of executive exception of the amnesty law (Skaar 2013, 494).

21. One great symposium which questioned many of the fundamental assumptions with TJ, but from a memory perspective, occurred at NYU in 2011 (NYIFTH 2011).

22. The global trends and normative shifts toward accountability have helped open up space now as well (NYIFTH 2011; Sikkink 2011).

23. There is new research being done to explore the different demands of victims that cannot be lumped into one homogenous bunch (Vinck and Pham 2014).

24. This topic has been explored in one survey that begs for more studies on the topic and deeper analyses (ICTJ 2005).

25. Cambodia's historical accountability efforts are another fantastic example, albeit in a very different manner.

26. This edited volume begins to address the gap in literature on this topic, suggesting different approaches the field can take to begin to study TJ's impact. In addition, Leigh Payne has been working on comparative qualitative data sets to evaluate arguments within the field (Olsen, Payne, and Reiter 2009).

SELECTED BIBLIOGRAPHY

Arthur, Paige. 2009. "How 'Transitions' Reshaped Human Rights: A Conceptual History of Transitional Justice." *Human Rights Quarterly* 31 (2): 321–67.

Bass, Gary Jonathan. 2000. *Stay the Hand of Vengeance: The Politics of War Crimes Tribunals*. Princeton Studies in International History and Politics. Princeton, N.J: Princeton University Press.

Becker, Jo. 2013. *Campaigning for Justice: Human Rights Advocacy in Practice*. Palo Alto, Stanford University Press.

Boraine, Alex, Janet Levy, and Ronel Scheffer, eds. 1994. *Dealing with the Past: Truth and Reconciliation in South Africa*. Cape Town: IDASA.

Brahm, Eric. 2007. "Transitional Justice, Civil Society, and the Development of the Rule of Law in Post-Conflict Societies." *International Journal of Not-For-Profit Law* 9 (4). Available at: http://www.icnl.org/research/journal/vol9iss4/special_2.htm (accessed May 4, 2014).

Brecha. 1985a. "Desaparecidos: Durante la Dictadura militar en Uruguay, se cometió genocidio." *Brecha* (October 25, 1985): 2–3. Archivo de Diarios, Palacio Legislativo, Montevideo, Uruguay.

———. 1985b. "Seregni: Tenga la seguridad de que se hará justicia." *Brecha* (October 18, 1985): 5. Archivo de Diarios, Palacio Legislativo, Montevideo, Uruguay.

Bucheli, Gabriel. 2005. *Vivos Los Llevaron: Historia de La Lucha de Madres Y Familiares de Uruguayos Detenidos Desaparecidos.* Montevideo: Ediciones Trilce.

Burt, Jo-Marie, Francesca Lessa, and Gabriela Fried Amilivia. 2013. "Civil Society and the Resurgent Struggle against Impunity in Uruguay (1986–2012)." *International Journal of Transitional Justice* 7 (1) : 1–22.

Caetano, Gerardo. 2011. "Los Archivos Represivos En Los Procesos de 'Justicia Transicional': Una Cuestión de Derechos." *Perfiles Latinoamericanos* 37: 9–32.

Charter 77 Foundation. 1992. *Project on Justice in Times of Transition (Report of the Project's Inaugural Meeting)*. Salzburg (March 7–10, 1992).

Chilean Review. 1987. "Chile's Transition Discussed in South Carolina." *Chilean Review* 1 (3): n. p.

Collins, Cath. 2010. *Post-Transitional Justice: Human Rights Trials in Chile and El Salvador*. University Park, PA: Pennsylvania State University Press.

Duggan, Colleen. 2010. "Editorial Note." *International Journal of Transitional Justice* 4 (3): 315–28.

El Pais. 2013. "Relator de ONU advierte a Uruguay sobre decisión de Suprema Corte." *El Pais,* (October 4, 2013). Available at: http://www.elpais.com.uy/informacion/onu-advierte-uruguay-derechos-humanos.html (accessed November 5, 2013).

Elster, Jon. 2004. *Closing the Books: Transitional Justice in Historical Perspective*. New York: Cambridge University Press.

Fried, Gabriela and Francesca Lessa. 2011. *Luchas contra la impunidad: Uruguay, 1985-2011.* Montevideo: Ediciones Trilce.

Hayner, Priscilla. 2010. *Unspeakable Truths: Transitional Justice and the Challenge of Truth Commissions*. New York: Routledge.

Henkin, Alice. 1989. "Conference Report." In *State Crimes: Punishment or Pardon*. Maryland: The Aspen Institute.

ICTJ. 2005. "Forgotten Voices: A Population Based Survey on Attitudes on Peace and Justice in Northern Uganda." International Center for Transitional Justice and University of California-Berkeley, Human Rights Center.

———. 2011. "What Is Transitional Justice?" *International Center for Transitional Justice.* Available at http://ictj.org/en/tj/ (accessed 10 February 2010).

Jelin, Elizabeth. 2007. "Public Memorialization in Perspective: Truth, Justice and Memory of Past Repression in the Southern Cone of South America." *International Journal of Transitional Justice* 1 (1): 138–56.

Kolbert, Elizabeth. 2015. "The Last Trial." *New Yorker* (February 16, 2015): 24-30.

Kritz, Neil, ed. 1995. *Transitional Justice: How Emerging Democracies Reckon with Former Regimes.* Washington DC: United States Institute of Peace Press.

Lessa, Francesca. 2013. *Memory and Transitional Justice in Argentina and Uruguay: Against Impunity*. New York: Palgrave Macmillan.

Lessa, Francesca, and Pablo-Louis Le Goff. 2013a. "Skewed Priorities in Uruguay." *Al Jazeera* (November 18, 2013). Available at: http://www.aljazeera.com/indepth/opinion/2013/11/skewed-priorities-uruguay-20131118133045296340.html (accessed May 1, 2014).

———. 2013b. "Uruguay's Culture of Impunity Continues to Rear its Head," *Al Jazeera* (February 22, 2013). Available at: http://www.aljazeera.com/indepth/opinion/2013/02/201321910565944 0890.html (accessed May 1, 2014).

Loden, Alexander. 2007. "Civil Society and Security Sector Reform in Post-Conflict Liberia: Painting a Moving Train without Brushes." *International Journal of Transitional Justice* 1 (2): 297–307.

McAdams, A. James. 1997. *Transitional Justice and the Rule of Law in New Democracies.* Notre Dame, IN: University of Notre Dame Press.

———. 2011. "Transitional Justice: The Issue That Won't Go Away." *International Journal of Transitional Justice* 5 (2): 304–12.

Méndez, Juan E. 1997. "Accountability for Past Abuses." *Human Rights Quarterly* 19 (2): 255–82.

Minow, Martha. 1998. *Between Vengeance and Forgiveness: Facing History after Genocide and Mass Violence*. Boston: Beacon Press.

New York Institute for the Humanities (NYIFTH). 2011. "Second Thoughts on the Memory Industry." New York Institute for the Humanities (May 7, 2011). Available at: http://nyihumanities.org/event/second-thoughts-on-the-memory-industry-a-symposium (accessed May 2, 2014).

OHCHR. 2013. "Observaciones preliminares del Relator Especial para la promoción de la verdad, la justicia, la reparación, y las garantías de no repetición al final de su visita oficial a la República Oriental del Uruguay." United Nations Office of the High Commissioner for Human Rights (October 4, 2013). Available at: http://www.ohchr.org/SP/NewsEvents/Pages/DisplayNews.aspx?NewsID=13849andLangID=S (accessed May 1, 2014).

Olsen, Tricia, Leigh Payne, and Andrew Reiter. 2010. "The Justice Balance: When Transitional Justice Improves Human Rights and Democracy." *Human Rights Quarterly* 32 (4): 980–1007.

———. 2009. *Transitional Justice in Balance: Comparing Processes, Weighing Efficacy.* Washington DC: United States Institute of Peace.

Orentlicher, Diane F. 1991. "Settling Accounts: The Duty to Prosecute Human Rights Violations of a Prior Regime." *Yale Law Journal* 100 (8): 2537–615.

Roht-Arriaza, Naomi. 1995. *Impunity and Human Rights in International Law and Practice*. New York: Oxford University Press.

Roniger, Luis. 1999. *The Legacy of Human Rights Violations in the Southern Cone: Argentina, Chile, and Uruguay*. New York: Oxford University Press.

SERPAJ. 1991. *Derechos Civiles de la Población Montevideana y Actuación Policial en Barrios Periféricos*. Montevideo: SERPAJ.

———. 1993. *Derechos Humanos en Uruguay: Informe 1993*. Montevideo: SERPAJ.

Servicio Paz y Justicia. 1992. *Uruguay, Nunca Más: Human Rights Violations, 1972–1985.* Trans. Elizabeth Hampsten. Philadelphia: Temple University Press.

Sharnak, Debbie, and Abby Goldberg. 2013. "Uruguay's Struggle for Historical Accountability." *Upside Down World* (July 25, 2013). Available at: http://upsidedownworld.org/main/uruguay-archives-48/4390--uruguays-struggle-for-historical-accountability (accessed May 2, 2014).

Sikkink, Kathryn. 2011. *The Justice Cascade: How Human Rights Prosecutions Are Changing World Politics*. New York: W. W. Norton.

Skaar, Elin. 2013. "Wavering Courts: From Impunity to Accountability in Uruguay." *Journal of Latin American Studies* 45: 483–512.

Special Rapporteur OHCHR. 2013. United Nations Office for the High Commissioner of Human Rights. Available at http://www.ohchr.org/EN/Issues/TruthJusticeReparation/Pages/Index.aspx (accessed November 19, 2013).

Stern, Steve J. 2010. *Reckoning with Pinochet: The Memory Question in Democratic Chile, 1989–2006*. Durham: Duke University Press.

Stern, Steve J., and Scott Straus, eds. 2014. *The Human Rights Paradox: Universality and Its Discontents*. Critical Human Rights. Madison: University of Wisconsin Press.

Teitel, Ruti G. 2000. *Transitional Justice*. New York: Oxford University Press.

———. 2003. "Transitional Justice Genealogy." *Harvard Human Rights Journal* 16: 69–94.

Theidon, Kimberly. 2007. "Transitional Subjects: The Disarmament, Demobilization and Reintegration of Former Combatants in Colombia." *International Journal of Transitional Justice* 1 (1): 66–90.

United Nations (UN). 2014. "Informe del Relator Especial sobre la promoción de la verdad, la justicia, la reparación, y las garantías de no repetición, Pablo de Greiff, relativo a su misión al Uruguay." A/HRC/27/56/Add.2 (July 24, 2014). United Nations. General Assembly.

United Nations Office for the High Commissioner of Human Rights (OHCHR). 2013. "Biography of Special Rapporteur." Available at: http://www.ohchr.org/EN/Issues/TruthJusticeReparation/Pages/PablodeGreiff.aspx (accessed November 19, 2013).

Van der Merwe, Hugo, Baxter, Victoria, and Audrey R Chapman. 2009. *Assessing the Impact of Transitional Justice: Challenges for Empirical Research*. Washington DC: United States Institute of Peace Press.

Vinck, Patrick, and Pham Puong. 2014. "Consulting Survivors." In *The Human Rights Paradox: Universality and Its Discontents*, eds. Steve J Stern and Straus, 107–24. Madison, WI: University of Wisconsin Press.

Waldorf, Lars. 2011. "Rethinking Transitional Justice: Should It Address Socio-Economic Wrongs?" presented at the Sawyer Seminar (April 22, 2011). Madison, WI.

Weinstein, Harvey M. 2011. "Editorial Note: The Myth of Closure, the Illusion of Reconciliation: Final Thoughts on Five Years as Co-Editor-in-Chief." *International Journal of Transitional Justice* 5 (1): 1–10.

Weschler, Lawrence. 1998. *A Miracle, A Universe: Settling Accounts with Torturers*. Chicago: University of Chicago Press.

Whitehead, Laurence. 1996. *The International Dimensions of Democratization*. New York: Oxford University Press.

Zalaquett, Jose. 1992. "Balancing Ethical Imperatives and Political Constraints: The Dilemma of New Democracies Confronting Past Human Rights Violations." *Hastings Law Journal* 43 (6): 1425–38.

———. 1991. *Derechos Humanos y Limitaciones Políticas En Las Transiciones Democráticas Del Cono Sur*. Santiago: Colección Estudios Cieplan.

———. 1985. "From Dictatorship to Democracy." *The New Republic* (December 16, 1985).

INTERVIEWS

Bustamante, Pancho. Author Interview (September 11, 2014).

Michelini, Felipe. Author Interview (June 14, 2012).

Peralta, Ariela. Author Interview (April 29, 2014).

Weschler, Lawrence. Author Interview (October 9, 2014).

ARCHIVES

Archivo de Diarios, Palacio Legislativo, Montevideo, Uruguay.
SERPAJ Archives, Montevideo, Uruguay.

Part VI

Latin America

Chapter Eight

Concluding Reflections

Roberto Gargarella

This book explores many fundamental issues related to transitional justice in the Americas.[1] The revival in International Human Rights Law that it examines coincides with a new activism by international judicial actors and institutions, and a renewal in the legal doctrine (Nino 1993; Elster 2004; Uprimny et al. 2006; Almqvist and Espósito 2012; Clark and Palmer 2012). Among the factors that triggered these changes that I want to highlight in these comments is the human rights crisis, which has affected the world in the last decades. For instance, during the 1970s, different countries in the Americas experienced the presence of dictatorial or quasi-dictatorial governments, and internal wars. Similarly, many other countries in Eastern Europe suffered ethnic cleansing and massive murders made in the name of nationalist ideologies at the end of the twentieth century. For these and other reasons, domestic and international law began to dramatically change.

The challenges that this new situation presents with regard to the law were enormous: how to face grievances of such significance? How could the law respond to these brutalities in a reasonable and efficient way? How should it deal with the demands of victims and their acquaintances who were so brutally insulted, eliminated, disappeared? What should be done to honor the demands of the offended, and at the same time preserve the stability of democracy? How to do this when, in many instances, large parts of the population and/or the main social institutions (typically, the whole coercive forces) were fully involved in the production of those atrocities? Was it even thinkable to deal with such challenges in ways that were both morally sound and politically feasible?

MASSIVE ATROCITIES AND CONSTITUTIONAL REFORMS

The dimension of the challenges ahead makes it virtually impossible for the law to adequately deal with the massive violation of human rights. Clearly, problems that are not only legal, but also political, social and economic, require solutions that are not only legal. Unfortunately, very frequently, massive atrocities were followed by merely legal responses, with the natural consequence that the law became unable to deliver what had been promised, much less satisfy the obvious over-expectations that were generated. As the editors of this volume put it in their introduction, "too much is expected from transitional justice, leading to deception among the population it promised to support—the survivors, families of victims and human rights activists" (Schneider and Esparza 2015, this volume, xxi).

Now, it is interesting to focus on the nature of those legal responses. In many occasions, and given the seriousness of the challenges imposed by widespread human rights violations, the legal response reached the highest levels, calling for the promotion of constitutional reforms. These reforms were directed at "incorporating" international human rights law into the domestic law. Regrettably, however, these changes were not accompanied by other constitutional modifications affecting the organization of state powers (Gargarella 2014). In other words, people adopted a legal strategy for confronting these new human rights violations that kept the old power structure untouched (what I call the "engine room of the constitution").[2]

As those reforms were restricted to the rights section of the Constitution, profound reforms to all sections of the Constitution remained wanting. The power structure was not "adjusted" accordingly. For example, the recognition of new participatory rights requires a less vertical organization of powers (rather than the reaffirmation of hyper-Presidentialist systems); an expansion in the list of human rights requires additional reforms directed at favoring their enforcement and facilitating the community's access to those rights; etc. The absence of more profound reforms tends to put the renewed declaration of rights at risk. As a consequence, human rights policies often fell prey to judicial bureaucracies, with the risk of having matters that were essentially political, depoliticized. On other occasions, dominant political forces manipulated human rights policies in pursuit of their own interests. This book offers numerous examples of the latter. We learn, for instance, that President Uribe, in Colombia, "hijacked the transitional justice rhetoric, proclaimed a Colombian 'transition,' justified a demobilization initiative and covered impunity" (Díaz 2008; Schneider and Esparza 2015). We also recognize that in other countries, like Argentina (which according to some represents a "model" to be followed in this area), Presidents Néstor and Cristina Kirchner used the punishment of past human rights violators as a way of masking policies that in many cases violated the human rights of present generations—typically, indigenous communities (see Figari Layús 2015, in this volume).

This situation—the growing contradiction between constitutions that are every day more generous, and a constitutional practice that seems to be every day more unjust—must be highlighted, and be the object of closer theoretical attention: it is actually this contradiction that has provoked reactions, resistance and protests within civil society in general, and particularly among the victims of massive violations of rights, their acquaintances and NGOs.

THE VOICES AND DEMANDS OF THE VICTIMS

One of the main focuses of this book is showing the importance and influence of popular mobilizations in the reopening of human rights trials and investigations, and their contribution to the task of bolstering a collective exercise of political memory. At the same time, and precisely as a result of the way in which it cares about the viewpoints of the victims, the book helps us recognize some of the inadequacies and shortcomings of the transitional justice paradigm. Notably, the book challenges the "triumphalist" transitional justice discourse and literature: transitional justice is celebrated as "victim-focused," yet the book shows how often the victims' expectations have been frustrated and their demands denied (for instance, Baraybar, Tejero, and Santos refer to the high rates of acquittal that characterized transitional justice in the region).

The point is, I believe, particularly important: the "triumphalist" discourse concerning transitional justice seems palpable, while the failings of the same paradigm are manifest. For those reasons, it is enormously important that new studies on the subject bring a more realistic analysis to what actually happened in the region, in these areas. In particular, renewed approaches should make a special effort at taking the viewpoints and experiences of the victims seriously—as this book does—replacing, at least for a while, the "view from above" with a "view from below," and abandoning, at least for some time, the exclusive perspective of "heroic" judges, high commissioners, lawyers and politicians.

Now, the fact that the voices of victims and their acquaintances need to become relevant in the process of building collective justice; or the fact that these frequently ignored voices deserve special public and political attention and protection, after the unimaginable sufferings that were imposed upon them, does not mean that they should exclusively define the content of transitional justice. In other words, the need to take those voices seriously does not mean that they should become the only or the decisive ones to be heard in the justice process. And I want to be emphatic about this point because certain currents within contemporary Criminal Law—typically, so-called penal populism—have articulated very implausible and conservative responses to past crimes in the name of crude and unsophisticated readings of the demands of the main victims of those crimes (Roberts and Stalans 2003; Pratt 2007). It is neither true nor morally or legally acceptable what penal populists suggest; namely, that the only response to grave crimes consists of more and harsher punishments.

Similarly, while critics may accuse international political authorities or international courts of expropriating and deciding over problems that belong to the entire society, the same argument may be raised when particular local groups, like victims and their families, try to dominate post-conflict processes in a similarly one-sided manner. Again: problems that are fundamentally collective should be understood, examined, deliberated and decided collectively.

THE GOALS OF TRANSITIONAL JUSTICE: JUSTICE, PUNISHMENT, TRUTH

What role can the law possibly play in transitional justice processes? Two main alternative responses immediately occur. One of them emphasizes the value of justice, while the other underlines the value of truth.[3] Of course, the values of justice and truth are not necessarily in tension or contradiction with each other. The search for truth mainly implies looking for individual and collective responsibilities (who did what; who gave the orders to commit these or those abuses; who followed those orders) and also the gathering of detailed information concerning the victims of those atrocities (what happened to each of these victims; where the missed bodies are; etc.). The search for justice mainly implies addressing impunity—so far, the most common result after the occurrence of massive atrocities. Thus defined, the goals of truth and justice seem perfectly consistent one with the other. Unfortunately, these two values have become in tension, as a result of the particular way in which "justice" has been defined in these cases. In effect, very commonly, the search for justice has become transformed into attempts to impose punishment to (all) those accused of human rights violations, which—I shall maintain—tends to put the value of truth at risk.

One fundamental problem created by collapsing the concept of justice into that of punishment is the following: the search for punishment activates a judicial process usually directed at distributing years of prison among the perpetrators of massive atrocities. Facing this threat, those who are accused of grave atrocities tend to deny charges and hide the information they have: it would be simply irrational for them to admit that they committed the worst atrocities and consequently receive the most severe judicial condemnation. As a result, in many occasions, human rights violators feel collectively motivated not to disclose any information concerning past atrocities, so as to avoid punishment—in some occasions they actually signed a *pacto de sangre* for ensuring that result.[4] In sum, the politics of punishment encourage human rights violators to prevent the disclosure of truth. As some Criminal Law researchers maintained, there seems to exist a strong tension between the structure of criminal procedure and the "truth-seeking" intention that is frequently shared by those who promoted the trials (Pastor 2004; 2005; 2009).[5] Precisely for these reasons, communities that want to privilege the search of truth tend to look for alternatives to punishment.

Researcher Claudia Hilb, for instance, compared the case of South Africa—a country that decided to privilege the value of truth over the value of justice—with Argentina, a country that followed the opposite option. Her conclusions are similar to the ones we present here. For Hilb, "in one case, we talk about Trials and Justice, while in the other case, we talk about Truth and Reconciliation. Probably, Argentina's response implied paying a cost in terms of Truth, while in the South African case the cost was paid in terms of Justice" (Hilb 2013, 7). Interestingly, and in order to provide additional support to her argument (about the existing tension between punishment and truth) Hilb refers to the case of "Captain Scilingo," in Argentina: Scilingo was the only and single member of the Army Forces who confessed to the horrible crimes in which he participated during the country's dictatorship.[6] Scilingo was then tried in Spain, and condemned to 640 years in prison for crimes against humanity. His immediate response was a retraction of his testimony: Scilingo denied the truth of his words, even though in the end the change in his posture had no effect on his sentence (Hilb 2013, 10).

Concerning retribution, the fact is that there are also different ways for reproaching someone for the offenses he committed—ways that do not necessarily imply engaging the State in the "deliberate imposition of pain" (as Hart defined the idea of punishment, 1968). Thus defined, punishment refers to a practice that is particularly difficult to justify: in what sense could the State's imposition of pain be a proper response to those who previously imposed pain? What is the difference between this imposition of pain and vengeance? Why should the State engage in the practice of "an eye for an eye"? The use of the coercive State apparatus for "the deliberate imposition of pain" seems much less acceptable given the variety of responses available for grave crimes.[7]

OVERCOMING POVERTY AND DEPENDENCY

Many of us would agree that it is import to seek justice, truth and/or punishment after massive human rights violations. Importantly, punishment is not the only mechanism to address past injustices. Studying the case of Argentina, Catalina Smulovitz reveals the variety of legal and non-judicial strategies explored during times when criminal sanctions were limited through amnesty laws (monetary reparations; appealing to international tribunals; public apologies and commemorations; social ostracism; preserving historical memory; and establishing "truth trials," to name but a few).[8] While some people regard these mechanisms as sufficient, critics have maintained that all of these so-called transitional justice mechanisms remain an inadequate response to mass violence and have failed to achieve ambitious goals such as justice or a stable peace. Radical injustice and massive human rights violations, these critics hold, are rooted in profound social, economic, and political conflicts—structural problems that largely transcend the legal sphere. These critics claim that we can only overcome them if we address the underlying causes of massive injustices.

In this book, Steve Dobransky makes this association by referring to Central America's problem with coping with poverty and economic dependency, mainly from the United States. In his view, transitional justice failed to tackle the root causes that led to war and violence in the first place. In particular, he claims that the transitional justice paradigm failed to offer a solution to the problem of poverty and economic dependency on foreign companies. In his words, "transitional justice failed to capture the most important elements of 'justice' and the root causes of violence—mass poverty and inequality."

A diagnosis like Dobransky's is most probably right in at least one crucial respect: massive human rights violations seem to be clearly correlated to unchanged power structures. However, the conclusions that some may derive from those premises, concerning the failings of the law, may be inadequate. Perhaps the problem we face is not that the law has not done enough to overcome the causes of injustice, but rather that we are expecting the law to overcome problems that the law—given its nature, its resources, its force—is simply unable to overcome. In other words, problems that largely transcend the legal sphere like economic, social, or political issues may require solutions that likewise are beyond the legal sphere—economic, social, or political solutions.

The fight against inequality and injustice is thus necessary and urgent everywhere, and perhaps particularly in Latin America—but is also an enterprise that requires civic commitments, social mobilizations, and political actions that go far beyond what the law can give us, and far beyond what we could reasonably expect from it. What we can expect and demand from the law, such as trials and investigations, is nonetheless extremely important and may come hand in hand with other deeper social and economic reforms. Legal instruments may even be a first important step—a relevant stimulus—to achieve other, more fundamental and radical goals. In fact, one may reasonably claim that at least in some Latin American countries like Uruguay,

Chile, or Argentina, the fights for taking perpetrators to court were either the result of or coincided with political activism and social mobilization, or triggered demands for social justice.

A BRIEF CONCLUSION

It is impossible to close this analysis without a short and general conclusion about the success or failure of the transitional justice paradigm in Latin America. The fact is—and this book helps me raise this point—that different and contradictory developments occurred in different countries at different times. Let us take Argentina as an example, the case I know the most. The history of post-authoritarian Argentina was characterized by a sequence of forward and backward movements.

In brief, after massive human rights violations and a self-amnesty law at the end of the dictatorship, a period of intense and lasting popular activism began, in which the victims and their relatives played a major part. Meanwhile we had fair trials, exemplar judicial sentences, partial and fuller amnesties, "truth trials" (trying to overcome the impunity imposed by the new amnesty laws), and judicial decisions validating the amnesties. Subsequently, human rights' institutions and NGOs challenged the validity of the amnesties, and both the judiciary and Congress invalidated the new amnesty laws. This in turn paved the way for the judiciary to start a new round of sentences and for the government to coopt the human rights cause.

In sum, many important and also contradictory developments occurred throughout these years. Perhaps Argentina's case is unique, but which country would not be special? The point here is that even taking just one single case, the final assessment cannot but be complex, balanced, and nuanced rather than simple, categorical, and unqualified. If it is difficult to draw a balance for a single country like Argentina, we need to be even more careful when discussing an entire region.

Now, I do not want to take these complexities as an excuse for avoiding raising some critical points, which the book actually helps us to raise: the existence of significant tensions between the (self-congratulatory, "triumphalist") transitional justice discourse and Latin America's historic experience; the way in which the victims' viewpoints have frequently been ignored, their demands frustrated, and their struggles coopted; the problems created by a law that has been in many cases unable to fulfill the expectations that it generated; the regularity with which impunity won over the overconfident discourse of justice; the persistence of profound structures of injustice, which make the quest for transitional justice utopian or naive. Findings of this kind define the critical profile of this book, and also characterize one of its main contributions: the book provides us reasons to put in question what is becoming the "common sense" thinking within the dominant discourse on the topic. In so doing, this work stimulates our critical thinking, rather than reinforcing a merely celebratory approach to issues of transitional justice.

NOTES

1. Let me define the term as "the set of judicial and non-judicial measures that have been implemented by different countries in order to redress the legacies of massive human rights abuses," including "criminal prosecutions, truth commissions, reparations programs, and various kinds of institutional reforms." See https://www.ictj.org/about/transitional-justice.

2. Since the 1990s, in countries such as Argentina and Bolivia, human rights treaties were explicitly awarded the status of constitutional law. In other cases, such as those of Costa Rica or El Salvador, these treaties were endowed with supra-legal status (Rossi and Filippini 2010). Some new Constitutions, like those of Peru or Colombia, included interpretive clauses in their texts, incorporating specific references to International Law. The Brazilian fundamental legal order refers to the existence of non-enumerated rights, amongst which are those related to principles and treaties to which Brazil is party. Guatemala made reference to International Human Rights Law by establishing guidelines for the country's foreign policy. The Chilean reform assigned special duties in the area of Human Rights with which all state organs must comply (Dulitzky 1998).

3. For a discussion concerning the problems of not properly defining the fundamental values at stake (like justice or democracy) in these matters, see the work of Steve Dobransky in this volume.

4. The same logic explains why, before leaving their positions in power, human rights violators tend to destroy or burn down all information that could reveal the crimes they committed.

5. In Pastor (2009), the Argentine professor lists a series of reasons supporting the argument that it is a mistake to choose "the broken criminal procedure to guarantee the right of victims referred to as the right to truth" (id., starting at 50). The list includes references to teleological, epistemological, methodological, technical, political and historical reasons.

6. Scilingo confessed his tremendous crimes before journalist Horacio Verbitsky, who published the testimonies of Scilingo in Verbitsky 1995.

7. With regard to the alternatives to punishment, for the moment I will merely make reference to the vast amount of specialized literature on the subject, while citing the compared historical experience, which is also rich. See, for example, Braithwaite (1998; 2000); Cuneen and Hoyle (2010). The comparative experience, in fact, allows us to see that other countries have chosen forms of response other than punishment to address massive rights violations. South Africa is the most-cited example in this sense, because of its primary preoccupation with seeking, before penal punishment, the truth of what occurred.

8. Smulovitz (2009).

REFERENCES

Almqvist, J. and Espósito, C. 2012. *The Role of Courts in Transitional Justice,* New York: Routledge.

Baraybar, J. et al. 2015. "How Transitional Is Justice? Peru Post Conflict Revisited" in Schneider and Esparza, *Transitional Justice and Legacies of State Violence in Latin America: A Janus Face Paradigm?*, Lanham, MD: Lexington Books.

Braithwaite, J. 1998. "Restorative Justice." In M. Tonry, ed., *The Handbook of Crime and Punishment,* Oxford: Oxford University Press, 323–44.

———. 2000. "Restorative Justice and Social Justice", 63 *Sask. L. Rev.* 185.

Christie, N. 1977. "Conflicts as Property," *The British Journal of Sociology,* vol. 17, n. 1, 1–15.

———. 1981. *Limits to Pain*, Oxford: Martin Robertson and Co. Ltd.

Clark, P., and N. Palmer. 2012. "Introduction: Challenging Transitional Justice," in N. Palmer, P. Clark and D. Granville, eds., *Critical Perspectives in Transitional Justice*, Cambridge: Intersentia, 1–16.

Correa Sutil, J. 1993. "The Judiciary and the Political System in Chile: The Dilemmas of Judicial Independence During the Transition to Democracy," en Irwin Stotzky, ed., *Transition to Democracy in Latin America: The Role of the Judiciary*, Westview Press.

Cuneen, C. and Hoyle, C. 2010. *Debating Restorative Justice,* London: Hart Publishing.

Díaz, C. 2008. "Challenging Impunity from Below: The Contested Ownership of Transitional Justice in Colombia," in McEvoy, Kieran and Gregor, *Transitional Justice from Below,* Portland: Hart.

Dobransky, S. 2015. "Free Trade and the De-Mining of Transitional Justice," in Schneider and Esparza, *Transitional Justice and Legacies of State Violence in Latin America: A Janus Face Paradigm?*, Lanham, MD: Lexington Books.

dos Santos Macdowell, C. 2015. "Transitional Justice from the Margins:Legal Mobilization and Political Memory in Brazil," in Schenider and Esparza, *Transitional Justice and Legacies of State Violence in Latin America: A Janus Face Paradigm?*, Lanham, MD: Lexington Books.

Duff, A. 2008. "Authority and Responsibility en International Criminal Law," to appear in S. Besson and J. Tasioulas, eds., *Philosophy of International Law*, Oxford: Oxford University Press.

Elster, J. 2004. *Closing the Books. Transitional Justice in Historical Perspective,* Cambridge: Cambridge University Press.

Figari Layús, R. 2015. "Challenging the Transitional Justice Paradigm: Human Rights Trials in Argentina," in Schneider and Esparza, *Transitional Justice and Legacies of State Violence in Latin America: A Janus Face Paradigm?*, Lanham, MD: Lexington Books.

Filippini, L. 2007. "El derecho internacional de los derechos humanos no es un préstamo," *Revista Jurídica de la Universidad de Palermo,* vol. 8, n. 1, 191-213.

Garibian, S. 2009. Le crime contre l'humanité au regard des principes fondateurs de l'Etat moderne. Naissance et consécration d'un concept, Paris: Schulthess.

Gargarella, R. 2014. *Latin American Constitutionalism, 1810-2010,* Oxford: Oxford University Press.

Hart, H. 1968. "Prolegomenon to the Principles of Punishment," in H. Hart, *Punishment and Responsibility,* Oxford: Oxford University Press.

Hilb, C. 2013. "Cómo fundar una comunidad después del crimen?" *Discusiones: Comunidad, perdón y justicia* , n. 12 (2013), pp. 31–58.

Kelsen, H. 1967. *Pure Theory of Law,* California: University of California Press.

Luban, D. 2004. "A Theory of Crimes Against Humanity," *Yale Journal of International Law,* 29, 85.

Maurino, G. 2008. "A la búsqueda de un pasado," en R. Gargarella ed., *Teoría y Crítica del Derecho Constitucional*, Lexis Nexis, Buenos Aires.

Nino, C. 1993. *Radical Evil on Trial,* New Haven: Yale University Press.

Pastor, D. 2004. *Tensiones: Derechos Fundamentales, Persecución Penal Sin Límites*

———. 2005. *El Poder Penal Internacional.*

———. 2009. *Encrucijadas del Derecho Penal Internacional y del Derecho Internacional de los Derechos Humanos.*

Pratt, J. 2007. *Penal Populism: Key Ideas in Criminology,* London: Taylor and Francis.

Puppo, A. 2015. "El monismo internacionalista kelseniano: entre nobles sueños y dudosas asunciones teóricas", Manuscript, ITAM, Mexico.

Roberts, J., L. Stalans et al. 2003. *Penal Populism and Public Opinion. Lessons from Five Countries,* Oxford: Oxford University Press.

Rossi, J. and L. Filippini. 2010. en P. Arcidiácono et al. *Derechos sociales: justicia, política y economía en América Latina*, Bogotá: Siglo del Hombre-Universidad de Los Andes.

Schneider, N. and M. Esparza. 2015. "Whose 'Transition'? Whose Voices? Latin American Responses to 'Transitional Justice,'" in Schneider and Esparza, *Transitional Justice and*

Legacies of State Violence in Latin America: A Janus Face Paradigm?, Lanham, MD: Lexington Books.

Sierra, L. 2012. "Supermajority Legislative Requirements and the Constitutional Court in Chile," Working Paper, SELA, Mexico.

Sikkink, K. 2011. *The Justice Cascade. How Human Rights Prosecutions are Changing World Politics.* New York: Norton.

Smulovitz, C. 2009. "I Can't Get No Satisfaction: Accountability and Justice for Past Human Rights Violations in Argentina." Paper presented in the context of the project "Comparing the Effectiveness of the Accountability Mechanisms in Eastern Europe and Latin America" organized by the Colegio de México and the University of the United Nations in association with Oxford University 2009.

Tejero, L. 2015. "We, the Victims: Violence, transitional justice and political subjectivities in the Peruvian context of post-conflict recovery," in Schneider and Esparza, *Transitional Justice and Legacies of State Violence in Latin America: A Janus Face Paradigm?*, Lanham, MD: Lexington Books.

Uprimny, R., Saffon, M., Botero, C. Restrepo, E. 2006. *Justicia transicional sin transición?*, Bogotá: De Justicia.

Verbitsky, H. 1995. *El Vuelo,* Buenos Aires: Planeta.

Useful Online Resources

REDE LATINO-AMERICANA DE JUSTIÇA DE TRANSIÇÃO (RLAJT—THE LATIN AMERICAN TRANSITIONAL JUSTICE NETWORK)

Available at: http://www.rlajt.com (accessed May 5, 2015).

The Rede Latino-Americana de Justiça de Transição (RLAJT) or Latin American Transitional Justice Network was established in 2011 by the Brazilian Amnesty Commission (a subsection of the Ministry of Justice), the Brazilian Foreign Ministry, and the United Nations Development Program (UNDP), in cooperation with the International Center for Transitional Justice (ICTJ). While still in its constitutive phase, the institution's stated key objective is to facilitate and promote the communication and expertise in the field of transitional justice and spread knowledge about the Latin American experience. This new network may play an increasing role in the field of transitional justice studies and be of particular importance for future research on the paradigm's resonance and development in the region.

The network's webpage provides a series of resources on transitional justice in Latin America including publications, video and audio material, and weblinks to important Latin American institutions such as truth commissions. In the future the RJLAT webpage is going to host the organization's yearly reports.

The host institution of the Latin American Transitional Justice Network (RLAJT) changes every two to three years. Presently, it is hosted by the National University of Brasília (Universidade Nacional de Brasília, UNB). As of May 2015, RLAJT included the following members: The Center for Legal and Social Studies (Centro de Estudios Legales y Sociales, Argentina), the Amnesty Commission (Comissão de Anistia, Brazil), the Law Department of the University of Rosario (Facultad de Derecho de la Universidad del Rosario, Colombia), the Study Group of the Internationalization of Law and Transitional Justice (Grupo de Estudos sobre Internacionalização do Direito e Justiça de Transição, Brazil), the Institute of Democracy and Human Rights of the Pontifical Catholic University of Perú (Instituto de Democracia y Derechos Humanos de la Pontificia Universidad Católica del Perú, Peru), the Institute of Human Rights of the Centroamerican University (Instituto de Derechos Humanos de la Universidad Centroamericana, El Salvador), Open Memory (Memoria Abierta, Argentina), the Nucleus of Preserving Political Memory (Núcleo de Preservação da Memória Política, Brazil), and the Human Rights Observatory of the University of Diego Portales (Observatorio Derechos Humanos de la Universidad Diego Portales, Chile).

THE UNIVERSITY OF WISCONSIN'S TRANSITIONAL JUSTICE DATA BASE PROJECT

Available at: https://sites.google.com/site/transitionaljusticedatabase/ (accessed February 5, 2014).

Funded by various research institutions and run by the political scientists Leigh A. Payne, Tricia D. Olsen, and Andrew G. Reiter, the Transitional Justice Database Project has compiled a bibliography (starting in 1970), which as of February 2014 contained 2,497 entries of scholarly work related to the subject of transitional justice. While not always updated, the webpage contains useful indicative bibliographies on post-authoritarian countries in Latin America.

THE CENTER FOR JUSTICE AND INTERNATIONAL LAW (CEJIL)

Available at: http://cejil.org (accessed at May 2, 2015).

According to its official mission statement, CEJIL seeks to "contribute to the full enjoyment of human rights in the Americas through the effective use of the tools of the Inter-American System and international human rights law. " CEJIL demands states' responses to grave human rights violations, the reduction of inequality and exclusion, and the guarantee of rule of law in the Americas. It has been monitoring the implementation of the decisions of the Inter-American Commission and Court.

Besides information on criminal prosecutions, the CEJIL webpage offers publications, multimedia sources, and links to numerous human rights organizations including the Human Rights Committee (HRC) and the Committee Against Torture (CAT).

THE INTER-AMERICAN COURT OF HUMAN RIGHTS

Available at: http://www.corteidh.or.cr (accessed at May 2, 2015).

Created in 1980, the Inter-American Institute of Human Rights of the Organization of American States (OAS) was established as "an international independent entity of academic nature, dedicated to teaching, research and the promotion of human rights, with a multidisciplinary focus and emphasis on America's problems." Headquartered in San José, Costa Rica, its official mission is to support to the Inter-American system of international protection of human rights.

The webpage provides information on criminal prosecutions and an on-line library catalogue operated by a keyword function.

THE INTERNATIONAL CENTER FOR TRANSITIONAL JUSTICE (ICTJ)

Available at: https://www.ictj.org (accessed May 3, 2015).

ICTJ is an international non-profit organization specializing in the field of transitional justice. It has been the prime institution promoting the transitional justice paradigm worldwide. According to its mission statement, ICTJ provides technical assistance to (1) governments, the justice sector, the UN and other international bodies; (2) advises victims' associations and human rights organizations; and (3) researches, analyzes, and reports on transitional justice developments worldwide.

The webpage offers a wealth of scholarly publications, reports, and multimedia resources. Many publications are co-funded by the United Nations, governments or philanthropic organizations, mainly based in the United States. Even if the resources need to be read with a critical eye, the webpage offers useful material on the rise of the paradigm, the development of the transitional justice field, and individual country cases.

THE UNITED STATES INSTITUTE OF PEACE (USIP)

Available at: http://www.usip.org/ (accessed May 3, 2015).

The United States Institute of Peace is an independent, nonpartisan institution established and funded by the Congress of the United States to increase the nation's capacity to manage international conflict without violence. Besides links to publications, the U.S. government funded Webpage provides helpful information on truth commission's worldwide including Latin American commissions.

THE HISTORICAL MEMORY PROJECT (HMP)

Available at: www. historicalmemoryproject.com (accessed May 3, 2015).

Housed at the City University of New York (CUNY), the HMP actively recovers historical memory and records of state violence with a particular focus on Latin America. Its mission is to "cultivate historical memory of the forcibly disappeared, the tortured, the massacred, the victims of sexual violence, and those whose human rights were violated by planned and coordinated actions," to raise awareness of mass atrocities and state violence, and to denounce "state crimes, wars, and genocide in Latin America" by collecting and providing access to primary sources, including human rights courts files, forensic evidence, expert witnesses, oral testimonies, war photography, and journalistic accounts. The HMP website offers a series of primary sources on state violence including a rich collection of photo material, court files containing forensic and ballistic reports, newspaper articles, letters, testimonies, and audiovisual materials.

Index

Abrams, Jason, 11
Abrão, Paulo, 45–46, 52, 57, 66
accountability, 30; actors, 41; civil, 39, 56; criminal, 56–57; individual, 60–65
AECID. *See* Spanish Agency for International Development Cooperation
Africa, xix; Rwanda, xiv; truth commissions and, xxivn11; Uganda, xxivn12. *See also* South Africa
Agência Brasileira de Cooperação do Ministério das Relações Exteriores (Brazilian Agency of Cooperation of the Foreign Relations Ministry), 68n3
agency, 41
agrarian reform, 51
Águila, Gabriela, 14n3
Aguirre, Luis Pérez, 139, 140
Alfonsín, Raúl, 7
Alianza Anticomunista Argentina (Argentine Anti-Communist Alliance) (Triple A), 4
Almeida, Crimeia Schmidt de, 61
alpacas, 116
Álvarez, Gregorio, 149n20
American Convention on Human Rights, 59
amnesty, 45; laws, 5–6, 7, 9, 14n4; self-amnesty, 61, 65, 163; in Uruguay, 142–143, 148n2
Amnesty Commission (*Comissão de Anistia*) (CA), 29–30, 44, 46, 48, 64; accountability measures and, 30; compensation payments and, 29, 31; publications by, 45; reparation commissions and, 43
Amnesty Law (1979), 25, 26, 28, 45, 52, 65, 144, 145; confirmation of, 31; critiques of, 44; impunity and, 32; interpretation of, 42; legal action and, 56; limits of, 64; social mobilization and, 46
"The Amnesty Law as an Impediment to Justice in Brazil (*A Lei de Anistia como Obstáculo à Justiça no Brasil*)", 64
ANFASEP. *See* Asociación Nacional de Familiares de Secuestrados, Detenidos y Desaparecidos
anti-mining groups, 85
Araguaia Guerrilla case, 39; CNV and, 49; IACHR and, 34n19, 46, 59, 60, 64, 65; legal action and, 56, 57; transnationalization of, 59
arbitrary arrests, 5, 48
ARENA, 24
Argentina, xxii, 61, 112, 158, 161, 163; Buenos Aires, 6, 7; global justice norm and, 41; as global role model, xi, 140; human rights treaties in, 164n2; internal security in, 5; Junta trials in, xx, 5; La Plata, 7, 9; legal action and, 42; reparations in, 123; truth commissions and, xix; Tucumán, 5, 14n2

Argentinean Association of the Madres de la Plaza de Mayo, xi
Argentine Anti-Communist Alliance (*Alianza Anticomunista Argentina*), 4
Argentinian human rights trials, xiii, 3–4; conclusion to, 12–13; desirability of, 12; development of, 6–8; investigation stage of, 6; justification of, 10–12; repression and, 4–6; transitional justice rhetoric and, 8–10
Armed Forces, 24, 48, 68n5, 109, 125
Arraes, Miguel, 60
Arthur, Paige, 10, 138, 140, 148n8
Asociación Nacional de Familiares de Secuestrados, Detenidos y Desaparecidos (ANFASEP), 96
Aspen Institute Conference, 138
Atencio, Rebecca J., 43, 44
Ayacucho, Peru, 121, 124

Baraybar, José P., xiii, xvi, xxi, xxiii
Bass, Gary, 149n11
Belo Horizonte, Brazil, 57
Black women, 39
Blanco Party, 148n5
BNM. *See Brasil: Nunca Mais*
Boesenacker, Aaron P., xix, xxi
Bolivia, xxivn12, 164n2
boomerang effect, 59
Booth, W. James, 66
Bordaberry, Juan Maria, 149n20
Brasil: Nunca Mais (Brazil: Never Again) (BNM), 27, 47, 57
Bravo del Pino, Guillermo, 118
Brazil, xxi, 19–20, 37–40; abuse of transitional justice in, 31–33; civil-society groups in, xvii; Communist Party of, 49; conclusion to, 66–67; democracy in, 25; exceptional political moment and, xxii; legal mobilization by nonstate actors in, 43–50; legal mobilization for memory, truth, and justice in, 50–52; new legal actions in, 60–65; post-transitional justice studies and, 40–43; redemocratization in, 57–60; social construction of transitional justice in, 26–28; State as protagonist in, 29–30; transitional justice definition in, 20–23; transition in, 23–26; transnational and local legal actions against State in, 52–57; transnational legal mobilization in, 57–60
Brazilian Agency of Cooperation of the Foreign Relations Ministry (*Agência Brasileira de Cooperação do Ministério das Relações Exteriores*), 68n3
Brazilian Amnesty Committee (*Comitê Brasileiro pela Anistia*), 56
Brazilian Bar Association, 65
Brazilian Commissions, 27
Brazilian Constitution (1988), 25, 26, 28, 32, 57
Brazilian Labor Party (PT), 28
Brazilian Lawyers Association (OAB), 25
Brazil: Never Again (*Brasil: Nunca Mais*), 27, 47, 57
Brecha (newspaper), 140
Broad, Robin, 78
Brooks, Rosa Ehrenreich, xiv
Brown University, 68n4
Bucheli, Gabriel, 143
Buenos Aires, Argentina, 6, 7
Burt, Jo-Marie, 41, 145
Butler, Judith, 99

CA. *See* Amnesty Commission
Cabañas region, El Salvador, 76
Caetano, Gerardo, 146
CAFTA. *See* Central American Free Trade Agreement
Cambodia, 149n18
Canada, xiv, 82
Cardoso, Fernando Henrique, 29, 44, 45, 59, 68n2
Castillo Paez, Ernesto, 128n26
Catholic Church, 27
Catholic University of Porto Alegre, 68n4
causality, 39
Cavalcanti Filho, José Paulo, 48
Cavanagh, John, 78
CBA. *See Comitê Brasileiro pela Anistia*
CEJIL. *See* Center for Justice and International Law
CELS. *See* Center for Legal and Social Studies

CEMDP. *See* Special Commission on Political Deaths and Disappearances of Persons
Census for Peace, 115
Center for Justice and International Law (CEJIL), 60, 64
Center for Legal and Social Studies (*Centro de Estudios Legales y Sociales*) (CELS), 10, 14n15
Center for Social Studies (CES), 68n4
Center of Operations for Internal Defense (*Centro de Operações de Defesa Interna*) (DOI-CODI), 60
Central American Free Trade Agreement (CAFTA), 76, 81–83
Centro de Estudios Legales y Sociales (Center for Legal and Social Studies), 10, 14n15
Centro de Operações de Defesa Interna (Center of Operations for Internal Defense), 60
Centro Poblado Menor, 125
CES. *See* Center for Social Studies
CFMDP. *See Comissão de Familiares de Mortos e Desaparecidos Políticos*
"The Challenge of Transitions" (conference), 148n4
Chile, 99, 111, 112, 123, 145; domestic trials in, xx; legal action and, 42; post-transitional justice and, 41
Chuschi, Ayacucho, 111
citizenship, 126; in Peru, 121–122; unequal, xxiii
civil accountability, 39, 56
civil liability, 42
civil rights, 21
civil society, xxivn9, 96; actors, 38, 41, 49; groups, xvii, xxi
Civil War, 149n18
Clark, Phil, xv, xxi
CMAN. *See* Comisión Multisectorial de Alto Nivel
CNV. *See* National Truth Commission
Cold War, xii, xiv–xv
Colina group, 120, 128n16
collective action, 41
collective reparation, 101, 115–116
Collins, Cathy, xv, xx, 38, 149n19; accountability actors and, 41; post-transitional justice and, 41–42, 52
Collor de Melo, Fernando, 59
Colombia, xiii, 8, 13, 22, 158
Columbia University, 68n4
Comisión Investigadora sobre Situación de Personas Desaparecidas, 148n1
Comisión Multisectorial de Alto Nivel (CMAN), 95
Comissão de Anistia. *See* Amnesty Commission
Comissão de Familiares de Mortos e Desaparecidos Políticos (Commission of Families of the Disappeared and Killed for Political Reasons) (CFMDP), 50, 56
Comissão Especial obre Mortos e Desaparecidos Políticos (Special Commission on Political Deaths and Disappearances of Persons), 43, 46, 47–48, 59, 68n2
Comissão Nacional da Verdade. *See* National Truth Commission
Comitê Brasileiro pela Anistia (Brazilian Amnesty Committee) (CBA), 56
Commerce Group, 76–77, 80
Commission of Families of the Disappeared and Killed for Political Reasons (*Comissão de Familiares de Mortos e Desaparecidos Políticos*), 50, 56
Communist Party of Brazil, 49
Communist Party of Peru-Sendero Luminoso (PCP-SL), 109, 111, 118, 127n2
Complutense University of Madrid, 104n2
Comprehensive Reparation Plan Law, 95
CONADEP. *See* National Commission on the Disappearance of Persons
CONAVIP. *See* Coordinadora Nacional de Organizaciones de Afectados por la Violencia Política
Congress, 26, 29, 92
Constituent Assembly, 26
constitutional reforms, 158–159
contagion, 41
context sensitivity, xxi
Coordinadora Nacional de Organizaciones de Afectados por la Violencia Política (CONAVIP), 92, 100, 101, 104n4, 123

Costa Rica, 81, 164n2
Council of Reparations, 114
counter-hegemonic globalization, 51
CPI. *See* Parliamentary Commission of Inquiry
crimes against humanity, 25, 65, 120, 144, 161
criminal accountability, 56–57
Criminal Chambers, 120
criminal justice, shortcomings of, 120–121
criminal liability, 42

databases, xx
death flights, 5
death squads, 4
Decree Law No. 261, 14n2
de facto impunity, 14n4
Defense Ministry, 31
de Greiff, Pablo, 135, 137, 146
de jury impunity, 14n4
democracy, 33, 78, 85; in Brazil, 25; elections in Uruguay, 136
democratization, xxii, 21; redemocratization, 25, 57–60
Departamento de Ordem Política e Social (Department of Political and Social Order) (DOPS), 55
dependency, overcoming, 161–163
desaparecido. See forced disappearances
Diaz, Catalina, xiii
"Direct [Elections] Now", 26
Direito à Memória e à Verdade: Comissão Especial sobre Mortos e Desaparecidos Políticos (*The Right to Memory and Truth: Special Commission on Political Deaths and Disappearances of Persons*), 43
disillusion, xiii, xxiii, 93
DNA analysis, 120
Dobransky, Steve, xvi, xxi, xxii, 162
DOI-CODI. *See* Center of Operations for Internal Defense
domestic political processes, 38
domestic trials, xx, 12
Domingo Peron, Juan, 4
Dominican Republic, 81
DOPS. *See Departamento de Ordem Política e Social*
"Dossier of the Political Dead and Disappeared after 1964" (CPI), 28
Due Obedience laws (Obediencia Devida), 5, 7, 61

Eastern Europe, 22, 157
economic exploitation, xvi, xxi
Ejército Revolucionario del Pueblo (ERP), 5
electoral college, 25
El Salvador, xix, xxii, 75–77; CAFTA and, 81–83; human rights treaties in, 164n2; post-transitional justice and, 41, 85; sovereignty in, 81–83; transitional justice in, 77–80, 83–85
Elster, Jon, 22–23, 149n11
empirical evidence, xxi
empowerment movements, 79
engine room of the constitution, 158
EPAF. *See* Peruvian Team of Forensic Anthropology
equal citizenship, 121–122
Equipo Peruano de Antropología Forense (Peruvian Team of Forensic Anthropology), xxiii, 109, 110, 115, 124–125
ERP. *See* Ejército Revolucionario del Pueblo
Erundina, Luiza, 28
esclachos (naming and shaming practice), xx, 68n9
escraches (naming and shaming practice), xx
ethnic cleansing, 157
ethnographic studies, xxi
exception, 20, 24, 32
exceptional political moment, xxii
excesses, 95, 113, 127n6
external factors, of transitional justice policy, 40
extrajudicial executions, 48, 65, 110, 121, 123

Farabundo Martí Liberation Front (FMLN), 84
Federal Council of Brazil Lawyers, 34n21
Federal Public Attorney Office (*Ministério Público Federal*) (MPF), 42, 44, 60
feminist studies, 39

Fernández de Kirchner, Cristina, 6, 158
Ferreira Aldunate, Wilson, 148n5
Fiel Filho, Manoel, 69n11
Figari Layús, Rosario, xx, xxii
Figueiredo, João, 25
Final Report, of TRC, 91, 94, 96, 101, 102, 114, 121, 123
Fletcher, Laurel E., xvii, xx
FMLN. *See* Farabundo Martí Liberation Front
forced disappearances, xii, 5, 48, 55, 109; CNV and, 49; justice policies on, 122–123
Ford Foundation, 138
forensics, illustrative power of, 109
forgiveness, 77
Foucault, Michel, 93
France, 114
Frankfurt University, 68n4
free decision, 3, 13
free markets, 78
free trade, 78, 83, 84
Frente Amplio, 136, 139
Fried Amilivia, Gabriela, 41, 145
Fujimori, Alberto, 94, 97, 112, 120, 127n5, 128n16; historical narratives and, 113; TRC and, 94; trial against, xx
Fujimori, Keiko, 127n5
Fujimorismo, 127n5
Full Stop laws (Punto Final), 5, 7, 61
funas (naming and shaming practice), xx

Gacaca courts, xiv
García Pérez, Alan, 94, 114, 115
Gargarella, Roberto, xxiii
GDP. *See* gross domestic product
gender differences, 21
gender-specific investigations, xix
General Attorney Office, 64
Genro, Tarso, 29
German Technical Cooperation Agency (GTZ), 102
Germany, 22
globalization, 78; counter-hegemonic, 51
global justice norm, 41
gold mining, 81
Gómez Bendezú, Mirta, 121
government narratives, 114, 119
Granville, Danielle, xxi
grassroots movements, xii, 75, 76, 79–80
Grocescu, Raluca, xvi
gross domestic product (GDP), 122
Grupo Tortura Nunca Mais (Torture Never Again Group) (GTNM), 50, 56–57, 60
GTZ. *See* German Technical Cooperation Agency
Guatemala, xix, xxivn13, 81, 164n2
Guzman, Abimael, 127n6

hard evidence, 21
Harvard Law School, 142
Hazan, Pierre, xiv, xvi, xvii, xx
health care, 101–102
hegemonic thinking, 39
Herzog, Clarice, 55–56
Herzog, Vladimir, 55, 64, 69n11
high-aggregate quantitative studies, xx
Hilb, Claudia, 161
historical narratives, 113–114
Honduras, 81
hooks, bell, 39
Huaccachi Cayampi, Placida, 116
Huamanquiquia, Peru, 116, 118
Huancavelica, Peru, 121
Huánuco, Peru, 121
hubris, of transitional justice, xvi
humanitarian umbrella, 123
human rights treaties, 164n2
Human Rights Watch, 60

IACHR. *See* Inter-American Court of Human Rights
ICSID. *See* International Centre for Settlement of Investment Disputes
ICTJ. *See* International Center or Transitional Justice
ideological appropriation, xiii
illustrative power, of forensics, 109
IML. *See* Institute of Legal Medicine
impugnación, xx
impunity, 9, 13, 14n4, 140, 146, 160; Amnesty Law and, 32; laws, 9; for public agents, 25
INDDHH. *See* Institución Nacional de Derechos Humanos y Defensoría del Pueblo
indigenous groups, 67
individual accountability, 60–65

individual reparation, 101
Institución Nacional de Derechos Humanos y Defensoría del Pueblo (INDDHH), 143
Institute of Legal Defence—Ideele, 121
Institute of Legal Medicine (IML), 110
instrumentalization of fear, 96
Inter-American Court of Human Rights (IACHR), 47, 52, 128n18, 143; Araguaia Guerrilla case and, 34n19, 46, 59, 60, 64, 65; self-amnesty and, 61, 65
Interamerican Human Rights System, 24
internal factors, of transitional justice policy, 40
internal security, in Argentina, 5
International Center or Transitional Justice (ICTJ), xv, xix, xxiii, 105n9, 142; CA and, 45; Reparation Plan Law and, 95; Uruguay and, xviii
International Centre for Settlement of Investment Disputes (ICSID), 82
International Covenant on Civil and Political Rights, 143
International Human Rights Law, 157
International Journal of Transitional Justice, 137, 144, 149n16
international organizations, 38
"International Seminar on Transitional Justice", 68n4
invisibility, 43–44
invitation to remember, 124

Janus-faced paradigm, 66; transitional justice as, xii–xiv
Japan, 94
Jobson, Marjorie, xvii
joint interest, xxivn9
Journal on Latin America, 137
juicios de la verdad (truth-finding trials), xx, 162, 163
Junín, Peru, 121
Junta trials, xx, 5
justice, 160–161; global norm of, 41; legal mobilization for, 50–52; negotiated, xix; retributive, xiii; right to, 20, 57
Justice and Society Program, 138
justice cascade, 12, 37
"Justice in Times of Transition" project, 140
justice vs. peace dilemma, 14n16

Karunananthan, Meera, 78
Khmer Rouge, 149n18
Khulumani support group, xvii
kidnapping, 14n4, 61, 128n26
King, Martin Luther, Jr., 146
King's College, 68n4
Kirchner, Néstor, xiii, 6, 14n5, 158
Kolbert, Elizabeth, 146
Kritz, Neil, 140

Laban, Alexander Hinton, xix
Laplante, Lisa, 102
La Plata, Argentina, 7, 9
Latin American Council of Social Sciences, 68n4
Law 8,159 (1991), 59
Law 9.140, 29, 31
Law 21264, 14n3
Law of Expiry (*Ley de Caducidad de la Pretensión Punitiva del Estado*), 136
legal action, xxii, 34n21, 52–57; Amnesty Law and, 56; Araguaia Guerrilla case and, 56, 57; Argentina and, 42; CEMDP and, 45; Chile and, 42; civil accountability and, 39; individual accountability and, 60–65; nonstate actors and, 42; post-transitional justice and, 38, 41
legalism, 20, 21; limitations of, xvi
legal mobilization, xxii, 38, 39, 66; for memory, truth, and justice, 50–52; by nonstate actors, 40, 43–50; transnational, 57–60
legal opportunity structure, 67n1
Legal Paradigm, 11
legal studies, xvi
"*A Lei de Anistia como Obstáculo à Justiça no Brasil* (The Amnesty Law as an Impediment to Justice in Brazil)", 64
Lessa, Francesca, 41, 145
Levante Popular da Juventude (Youth Popular Uprising), 46, 52, 68n9
Ley de Caducidad de la Pretensión Punitiva del Estado (Law of Expiry), 136
LGBT population, 21, 67
Lima, Peru, 91

"Limits and Possibilities for Legal Responsibility of Agents who Violated Human Rights during the State of Exception in Brazil (*Limites e Possibilidades para a Responsabilização Jurídica dos Agentes Violadores de Direitos Humanos durante o Estado de Exceção no Brasil*)", 64
litígio estratégico (strategic litigation), 51, 60
Llewellyn, Robin Oisín, 78
locality, xvii–xix
López Rega, José, 4
Lorde, Audre, 39
Los Cabitos military base, 123, 126
Lucanamarca, Peru, 127n6
Luchas contra la impunidad: Uruguay 1985–2011 (Fried Amilivia and Lessa), 145
Lucmahuayco, Peru, 121
Lula da Silva, Luiz Inácio, 45, 59, 64
lustration processes, xx
Lutz, Ellen, 37

Madres y Familiares de los Desaparecidos, 143
Mãos Amarradas (Tied Up Hands), 55
margins, 39
McCann, Michael, 50, 66
McEvoy, Kieran, xvi, xvii, 21, 23, 41
McGregor, Lorna, xvii, 23, 41
memory, 49, 93, 124; legal mobilization for, 50–52; Peru and, 113–114; politics of, 32, 45, 46; reconciliation by, 48; right to, 20, 24, 44, 57
Menem, Carlos, 5, 7
Merry, Sally Engle, 104n5
Merwe, Hugo van der, xix, 21
MESA. *See* National Roundtable Against Metallic Mining
Metalclad, 82
Mexico, 82
Michelini, Rafael, 139, 140
Michelini, Zelmar, 139
Middle East, 22
Military Courts, 57
MIMDES. *See* Ministry of Women and Social Development
mining, 76–77, 78–80, 82, 83–85; anti-mining groups, 85; of gold, 81
Ministério Público Federal (Federal Public Attorney Office), 42, 44, 60
Ministry of Defense, 64, 120–121
Ministry of Justice, 43
Ministry of Social Welfare, 4
Ministry of Women and Social Development (MIMDES), 115
Minow, Martha, 142, 149n14
A Miracle, A Universe: Settling Accounts with Torturers (Weschler), 139
Mitterrand, François, 114
MNCs. *See* multinational corporations
Moore, Jen, 78
Moraes, Mário Sérgio de, 69n11
Morales de Cortiñas, Nora, xi
Mortos e Desaparecidos Políticos: Reparação ou Impunidade? (*Political Deaths and Disappearances: Reparation or Impunity?*) (Teles, J.), 59
Mota, Mariana, 144
Movement of Landless Rural Workers, 51
MPF. *See* Federal Public Attorney Office
MRTA. *See* Tupac Amaru Revolutionary Movement
Mukal, Lika, 104n3
multinational corporations (MNCs), 78

NAFTA. *See* North American Free Trade Agreement
naming and shaming practices, xx, 68n9
National Amnesty Convention, 26
National Bank, 118
National Commission on the Disappearance of Persons (CONADEP), xxivn12, 9
National Constituent Assembly, 57
National Criminal Court (*Sala Penal Nacional*), 120, 121
National Human Rights Plan, 64
National Policy on Public Archives, 59
National Roundtable Against Metallic Mining (MESA), 79
National Truth Commission (*Comissão Nacional da Verdade*) (CNV), 24, 35n29, 43, 46, 64, 67; Araguaia Guerrilla case and, 49; final report of, 47–49

Nazareth de Uchu, Peru, 118
Nazism, 22, 146
negotiated justice, xix
Neves, Tancredo, 26
NGOs. *See* nongovernmental organizations
Nicaragua, 81
nongovernmental organizations (NGOs), xiii, 10, 38, 39, 47, 97, 98; mining companies and, 79; strategic litigation and, 51
nonstate actors: legal action and, 42; legal mobilization by, 40, 43–50
North American Free Trade Agreement (NAFTA), 82
Nuremberg Trials, 19, 77, 93

OAB. *See* Brazilian Lawyers Association
OAS. *See* Organization of American States
Obediencia Devida (Due Obedience laws), 5, 7, 61
Office of the Ombudsman, 114, 118, 120, 128n13
Office of Transition Initiatives (OTI), 105n19
official narratives, 114
El Olimpo, 6
Olsen, Tricia D., xix, xx, xxi
Oomen, B., xiv
Operation Independence, 5
Oreja de Perro, Peru, 125
Organization of American States (OAS), 24, 31, 34n19, 48
Oronccoy, Peru, 125
OTI. *See* Office of Transition Initiatives
Oxford University, 68n4

Pablo de Olavide University, 68n4
pacification, 25
Pacific Rim Mining Corporation, 76–77
Palmer, Nicola, xv, xxi
Paniagua, Valentin, 94
PAR. *See* Program for Support to Repopulation and Development to Emergency Areas
Paradero Esperanza, 125
para-police groups, 4
pardons, 7
Parliamentary Commission of Inquiry (CPI), 28
Pastor, D., 164n5
Payne, Leigh A., xix, xx
PCP-SL. *See* Communist Party of Peru-Sendero Luminoso
Peace Commission, 144
peasants, 67, 112, 120
penal populism, 159–160
Peña Romero, Jesus, xiii, xxi, xxiii
Peralta, Ariela, 143
Perón, Isabel, 4, 5, 14n2
Peru, xiii, xxii, xxiii, 91–93, 109–111; conclusion to, 103–104, 126; conflict in, 111–112; criminal justice shortcomings in, 120–121; equal citizenship in, 121–122; Fujimori, A., and, xx; historical narratives and, 113–114; justice policies on forced disappearances in, 122–123; memory and, 113–114; reparations in, 114–119, 123; social inequality in, 121–122; transitional justice failures in, 100–103; transitional justice field in, 94–96; transitional justice mechanisms in, 112–113; victims' needs in, 124–125; victims' organizations in, 96–100
Perus Cemetery, 28, 60
Peruvian Team of Forensic Anthropology (*Equipo Peruano de Antropología Forense*) (EPAF), xxiii, 109, 110, 115, 124–125
Pham, Phuong N., xvii
phases, of transitional justice paradigms, 37, 47
Pinochet, Augusto, 145
Plan of Integral Reparations (*Plan Integral de Reparaciones*) (PIR), 117
police: para-police groups, 4; violence by, 33
Political Amnesty and Transitional Justice Journal (*Revista Anistia Política e Justiça de Transição*), 30, 45
Political Deaths and Disappearances: Reparation or Impunity? (*Mortos e Desaparecidos Políticos: Reparação ou Impunidade?*) (Teles, J.), 59
political decisions, 7
political opportunity structure, 67n1
political rights, 21
political transitions, 19

popular advocacy, 51
post-transitional justice, xv, 38, 52, 66, 75; Brazil and, 40–43; El Salvador and, 41, 85
poverty, xxi, xxii, xxiii, 83; overcoming, 161–163; structural, 110
preference, human rights trials and, 3, 10, 13
private wealth, 85
privatization, 78
Program for Support to Repopulation and Development to Emergency Areas (PAR), 115
Project on Justice in Times of Transition, 139
Prosecutor's Office, 120
protest, xx; social, 5
PT. *See* Brazilian Labor Party
public agents, impunity for, 25
public documents, 59
public shaming events, 32
punishment, 160–161
Punto Final (Full Stop laws), 5, 7, 61
Putaccasa, Peru, 116
Putis, Peru, 120, 125

qualitative research, 40
quantitative research, 40; high-aggregate, xx
Quinalha, Renan, xvi, xxii

Ratner, Steven, 11
Recife, Brazil, 57
reconciliation, 9, 25, 31; by memory, 48
Reconstruction, 149n18
redemocratization, 25, 57–60
redress, xx, 77
Registry of Victims (*Registro Unico de Victimas*) (RUV), 110, 114, 118, 119
Regulation of Law of Reparations, 118
Reiter, Andrew G., xix, xxi
Renan, Ernest, 139
Reparation Council, 102
Reparation Plan, 101, 102
Reparation Programme, 92
reparations, 44, 46; collective, 101, 115–116; individual, 101; payments, 29, 100; in Peru, 114–119, 123; politics of, 46; right to, 20
Reparations Council, 95
repeated surveys, xx
retributive justice, xiii
revenge, 27
Revista Anistia Política e Justiça de Transição (*Political Amnesty and Transitional Justice Journal*), 30, 45
rights talk, xii
right to know, 123
The Right to Memory and Truth: Special Commission on Political Deaths and Disappearances of Persons (*Direito à Memória e à Verdade: Comissão Especial sobre Mortos e Desaparecidos Políticos*), 43
Rio de Janeiro, Brazil, 50, 57
Rio Grande do Sul, 55
Risse, Thomas, xii
Rivera, Carlos, 121
Rodríguez-Garavito, César A., 50
Rojas, Percy, xiii, xxi, xxiii
Romeu, Inês Etienne, 55
Ropp, Stephen C., xii
Rousseff, Dilma, 43, 48, 59, 68n5, 68n8
Rowen, Jamie, xx
rule of law, xiv, xvii, 11, 24, 26, 32
RUV. *See* Registry of Victims
Rwanda, xiv

Sacsamarca, Peru, 116
Sala Penal Nacional (National Criminal Court), 120, 121
Sanguinetti, Julio María, 136, 139
San Sebastian, El Salvador, 76, 80
Santos, Cecília, xvii, xxi, xxii
São Paulo, Brazil, 28, 50, 55
Sarney, José, 26
Schabas, William, xxivn11
Scilingo (Captain), 161
Secretariat on Human Rights (*Secretaria de Direitos Humanos*) (SDH), 43, 44, 64
Seils, Paul, xvi
self-amnesty, 61, 65, 163
Sendero Luminoso (Shining Path), 94, 100, 111, 113, 125
Seregni, Liber, 136
Servicio Paz y Justicia (SERPAJ), 139, 140, 143, 148n1

sexual abuse, 14n4, 97
sexuality, 21
shaming: naming and shaming practices, xx, 68n9; public events of, 32
Sharnak, Debbie, xv, xviii, xxiii
Shaw, Rosalind, xvii, xx
Shining Path (Sendero Luminoso), 94, 100, 111, 113, 125
Sikkink, Kathryn, xii, xix, xx, 37, 41, 143; domestic trials and, 12; justice cascade and, 12
Sistema Integral de Salud (SIS), 119, 128n14
Skaar, Elin, 145
"slow, gradual and safe" redemocratization, 25
Smulovitz, Catalina, 162
Snyder, Jack, xiii
Soares, Elizabeth, 55
Soares, Manoel, 55
social construction, of transitional justice, 26–28
social inequality, xvi, xxi, xxii, 121–122
social mobilization, 38, 46
social movements, 23, 25, 50–51; Amnesty Law and, 46; in Brazil, 26, 28; Constituent Assembly and, 26; stubbornness of, 28
social protests, 5
social society, xxivn9
sociology of absences, 39
Sousa Santos, Boaventura de, 39, 50
South Africa, 13, 142, 148n2; Khulumani support group in, xvii; post-apartheid, 22; TRC and, 8
sovereignty, 81–83
Spain, 149n18, 161
Spanish Agency for International Development Cooperation (AECID), 102
Special Commission on Political Deaths and Disappearances of Persons (*Comissão Especial obre Mortos e Desaparecidos Políticos*) (CEMDP), 43, 44, 46, 47–48, 59, 68n2
Special Coordination Unit of the Public Prosecutor, 10
standardization, 21, 22; of options, 11
state repression, xvi
State University of Rio de Janeiro, 68n4
Stern, Steve, 145, 147
strategic litigation (*litígio estratégico*), 51, 60
Straus, Scott, 147
structural poverty, 110
structural violence, xvi; root causes of, xxi, xxiii, 76, 110
subaltern cosmopolitan legality, 50
subjection, 99
subversive organizations, 111, 117, 119, 129n28
Superior State Court of São Paulo, 61
Supreme Court, 31, 32
Supreme Decree 51-2011-PCM, 100

Tarigo, Enrique, 146
task forces, 5
technology of government, 93
Teitel, Ruti, xiv, xv, 19, 33n2, 93, 141
Tejero, Laura, xiii, xvi, xxiii
Teles, Edson, xxii, 55, 66
Teles, Janaína de Almeida, 59, 64
Teles, Maria Amélia, 61
terrorism, 94, 95, 97
theft, 14n4; of victims' pain, 103
Theidon, Kimberly, 102
Third Supra-Provincial Court of Lima, 120
Tied Up Hands (*Mãos Amarradas*), 55
Toledo, Alejandro, 113, 114
Torelly, Marcelo, 45–46, 52, 57, 66, 68n3
Torres-Valverde, Diana Anahi, 78
torture, 5, 33, 55, 68n6, 135; BNM and, 57; CNV and, 48; of Herzog, V., 55–56; by Triple A, 4
Torture Never Again Group (*Grupo Tortura Nunca Mais*), 50, 56–57, 60
transition, 20, 28; in Brazil, 23–26
Transitional Government, 112
Transitional Justice (Teitel), 141
Transitional Justice (working group), 25
Transitional Justice Database, xxivn1
transitional justice entrepreneurs, 97, 99, 105n11
transitional justice from above, 23, 42, 45
transitional justice from below, 41
transitional justice paradigm, xi–xii, xx–xxii, 10–12, 37; as Janus-faced, xii–xv, xix, xxi; main criticisms of,

xv–xvii; environment and, 76; free trade and, 80, 83; root causes of violence and, 78, 110; poverty and, 162
transitional justice prescription, 75
transitional phase, 27
transnational human rights advocates, 38
transnational legal activism, 51
transnational legal mobilization, 57–60
TRC. *See* Truth and Reconciliation Commission
Treat, Jonathan, 78
Trejo, Lita, 80
Triple A. *See Alianza Anticomunista Argentina*
triumphalist discourse, 159, 163
truth, 49, 160–161; legal mobilization for, 50–52; politics of, 46; right to, 20, 24, 44, 57, 95
Truth and Reconciliation Commission (TRC), 92, 93, 95, 98–99, 101, 103; Final Report of, 91, 94, 96, 101, 102, 114, 121, 123; Fujimori, A., and, 94; Peru and, 110, 111, 112, 113, 114, 119, 120, 126; South Africa and, 8
truth commissions, xix, xxivn11, xxivn12, 10
truth-finding trials (*juicios de la verdad*), xx, 162, 163
Tucumán, Argentina, 5, 14n2
Tupac Amaru Revolutionary Movement (MRTA), 109

Uganda, xxivn12
Ulfe, Maria Eugenia, 99
UN. *See* United Nations
UNCITRAL. *See* United Nations Commission on International Trade Law
UNDP. *See* United Nations Development Program
unequal citizenship, xxiii
UNHRC. *See* United Nations Human Rights Commission
United Nations (UN), xiv, 45, 48, 135, 142
United Nations Commission on International Trade Law (UNCITRAL), 82
United Nations Development Program (UNDP), 68n3, 93
United Nations Human Rights Commission (UNHRC), 143
United States, xiv–xv, 50, 78, 81, 82–83, 84, 149n18
United States Agency for International Development (USAID), 105n19
universality, 21
University of Carlos III, 68n4
University of Coimbra, 68n4
University of São Paulo, 59
University of South Carolina, 148n4
University of Wisconsin, xxivn1
Uribe, Álvaro, 158
Uruguay, xxii, xxiii, 41, 135–148; amnesty in, 142–143, 148n2; democratic elections in, 136; ICTJ and, xviii
USAID. *See* United States Agency for International Development
Ustra, Carlos Alberto Brilhante, 60, 61

vernacularization, 92, 104n5
victimhood, 96, 99, 104n2, 105n16
victims' rights, 23
victims' voices and demands, 159–160
Víctor Fajardo, Peru, 116, 118
Vinck, Patrick, xvii
Vinjamuri, Leslie, xiii, xix, xxi
visibility, 43–44

Waldorf, Lars, xiv, xvii, xx, 143
Walling, Carrie Booth, xix–xx
water contamination, 79, 80, 83
wealth, private, 85
Weichert, Marlon, 60
Weinstein, Harvey M., xvii, xx, 144, 149n18
Weschler, Lawrence, 139, 146
widows and widowers, 117
women, 39, 96, 97
World Bank, 80, 81, 82, 84
World War II, 19, 77, 148n8

Ycaza, Carla de, xxivn11
Youth Popular Uprising (*Levante Popular da Juventude*), 46, 52, 68n9
Yugoslavia, 22

Zalaquett, José, 139

About the Contributors

José Pablo Baraybar is the executive director and founding member of the Peruvian *Forensic Anthropology Team* (EPAF). He graduated in archaeology from the University of San Marcos (UNMSM) in Lima, Peru, and holds two master degrees; one in bioarchaeology, and one in physical and forensic anthropology from the University of London and Granada in Spain, respectively. His interests include forensics, memory, and transitional justice. He has more than twenty years of experience in the field of forensics and human rights from countries all over the world.

Steve Dobransky is an adjunct professor at Lake Erie College and a PhD candidate at Kent State University. He holds an MA from Ohio University in international relations. Dobransky's work appeared in academic journals including *American Diplomacy*, *International Journal on World Peace*, and *Journal for the Study of Peace and Conflict*. Besides academia, he is an active member of the InterReligious Task Force on Central America (IRTF) in Cleveland, Ohio, on human rights and social justice issues in Latin America.

Marcia Esparza is associate professor in the Department of Criminal Justice at John Jay College, New York, and the founder and codirector of the Historical Memory Project (HMP). She is the author of *Silenced Communities: Legacies of and Resistance to Militarization in Santo Tomas Chichicastenango, Guatemala (1997–2004)* (New York: Berghahn, 2015). Esparza co-edited *State Violence and Genocide in Latin American: The Cold War Years* (Routledge, 2009) with Henry R. Huttenbach and Daniel Feierstein, and has published in leading academic journals like the *Journal of Genocide Research*. For her research on the aftermath of war in Chile and Guatemala, she received prestigious fellowships from the Ford Foundation (2010–2011) and the National Endowment for the Humanities (2011–2012).

Rosario Figari Layús is a researcher at the Institute for Interdisciplinary Research on Conflict and Violence (IKG), Bielefeld University and a PhD Candidate at the University of Marburg, Germany. She holds a master's degree in social sciences from Humboldt University of Berlin and a degree in sociology from the University of Buenos Aires. Her current research focuses on the role and impact of juridical processes of human rights violations in Argentina. Figari Layús is the author of *The Role of Transitional Justice in the Midst of Ongoing Armed Conflicts: The Case of Colombia* (Potsdam University Press, 2010).

Roberto Gargarella is a professor of constitutional theory and political philosophy at the Law School of the Universidad de Buenos Aires and the Universidad Di Tella and a researcher for CONICET in Buenos Aires and the Christian Michelsen Institute in Norway. He has also been a visiting fellow at universities worldwide including Columbia, New York University, and Harvard. Gargarella has published extensively on issues of legal and political philosophy, as well as on U.S. and Latin American constitutionalism. His publications include *Latin American Constitutionalism (1810–2010): The Engine Room of the Constitution* (Oxford: Oxford University Press, 2013), and *The Legal Foundations of Inequality: Constitutionalism in the Americas 1776–1860* (New York: Cambridge University Press, 2010).

Renan Quinalha is a PhD candidate in law at the University of São Paulo (USP). He is a member of the directorate of the Study Group of the Internationalization of Law and Transitional Justice (Grupo de Estudos sobre Internacionalização do Direito e Justiça de Transição, Idejust) and has served as an assistant to the local truth Commission of the state of São Paulo. He is the author of *Justiça de Transição: contornos do conceito* (São Paulo: Dobra Editorial, 2013).

Jesus Peña graduated in philosophy from the Catholic University in Lima, Peru (PUCP), and has worked for the EPAF since 2008 where he is responsible for project development. He has also participated in the organization of advocacy and awareness campaigns on missing persons, and published on transitional justice with the Institute of Democracy and Human Rights of the Pontifical Catholic University of Peru (IDEHPUCP).

Percy Rojas graduated with a degree in history from the National University of San Marcos (UNMSM) in Lima, Peru, and joined the EPAF in 2009. In charge of the memory work program, he collects testimonies from victims of the internal armed conflict (1980–2000) in Spanish and Quechua. Those testimonies are disseminated in different formats to raise awareness on the issue of disappeared persons.

Cecília MacDowell Santos is an associate professor of sociology at the University of San Francisco and a Researcher of the Center for Social Studies, University of Coimbra. She received her PhD in sociology from the University of California, Berkeley. Santos has published widely on issues of human and women's rights, violence, memory, and justice, as well as transnational legal mobilization and the State in Brazil and in Portugal. She co-edited with E. Teles and J. A. Teles, *Desarquivando a Ditadura: Memória e Justiça no Brasil* (São Paulo: Hucitec, 2009, two volumes); and with B. S. Santos, P. Abrão, and M. Torelly, *Repressão e Memória Política no Contexto Íbero-Brasileiro: Estudos sobre Brasil, Guatemala, Moçambique, Peru e Portugal* (Brasília: Ministry of Justice, 2010).

Nina Schneider is a visiting scholar at the National University of Brasília (UNB) and an associate fellow of the *Zukunftskolleg* at the University of Konstanz, Germany. She holds a PhD in history from the University of Essex, UK, and is the author of *Brazilian Propaganda: Legitimizing an Authoritarian Regime* (Gainesville: University Press of Florida, 2014) and "Waiting for (an) 'Apology': Has Post-Authoritarian Brazil Apologized for State Repression?" *Journal of Human Rights*, vol. 13, no. 1 (2014).

Debbie Sharnak is a PhD candidate at the University of Wisconsin-Madison in history, studying human rights, international relations, and transnational networks. Her current project examines human rights and transitional justice in Uruguay. She was a Fulbright Scholar in Uruguay for 2014. Sharnak has been published in *Diplomacy & Statecraft, Foreign Policy, NACLA, Upside Down World,* and *Latin Correspondent.* She has also worked at various NGOs including the New Media Advocacy Project, the International Center for Transitional Justice, and Amnesty International.

Edson Teles is professor of philosophy at the Federal University of São Paulo (UNIFESP), victim of the military regime and activist in the Commission of Relatives of Political Dead and Disappeared. His parents and aunt were imprisoned and tortured, while he and his sister (four and five years old at the time) were held captive in the same repression center and forced to bear witness of the violence against their own parents. Teles has published widely on the question of memory and justice in Brazil including C. M. Santos, E. Teles, and J. A. Teles, (eds) *Desarquivando a ditadura: Memória e justiça no Brasil* (São Paulo: Hucitec, 2009, two volumes), and E. Teles and V. Safatle (eds) *O que resta da ditadura: A exceção brasileira*. São Paulo: Boitempo, 2010.

Laura Tejero Tabernero is a PhD candidate in social anthropology at the Complutense University of Madrid. Her current research focuses on the politics of victimhood in Peru after the Truth and Reconciliation Commission. She holds a master's degree in anthropology and holds expertise in the management of Non-Governmental Organizations (NGOs). Tejero has been working as a consultant for non-governmental organizations and conducted both quantitative and qualitative research for universities and public institutions. In 2013, she was a Marie Curie Research Fellow at the International Conflict Research Institute at the University of Ulster. Tejero currently works for the Campaigns and Communications Directorate of the International Secretariat of Amnesty International.

www.ingramcontent.com/pod-product-compliance
Lightning Source LLC
LaVergne TN
LVHW101447200926
848483LV00001B/76